GOD'S
BLUE BOOK 1
Teachings to Lift You Up

Rita Ring
Carefully discerned by
Fr. Edward J. Carter S.J.

Shepherds of Christ Publications

Shepherds of Christ Publications
Shepherds of Christ Ministries
P. O. Box 627 China, IN 47250
(Toll Free): 1-888-211-3041   **U.S.A.**
Int'l: (812) 273-8405 ***Fax:*** 812-273-3182
Web: www.sofc.org   ***email:*** info@sofc.org

Tel: (513) 932-4451
Toll free: (888) 211-3041
Fax: (513) 932-6791
Email: info@sofc.org
http://www.SofC.org

Shepherds of Christ Publishing recognizes and accepts that the final authority regarding private revelation rests with the Holy See of Rome, to whose judgment we willingly submit.

This book is published by Shepherds of Christ Publications, a subsidiary of Shepherds of Christ Ministries, a tax exempt, religious public charitable corporation organized to foster devotion to the Two Hearts, the Sacred Heart of Jesus and the Immaculate Heart of Mary.

Prayer for Union With Jesus

Come to me, Lord, and possess my soul. Come into my heart and permeate my soul. Help me to sit in silence with You and let You work in my heart.

I am Yours to possess. I am Yours to use. I want to be selfless and only exist in You. Help me to spoon out all that is me and be an empty vessel ready to be filled by You. Help me to die to myself and live only for You. Use me as You will. Let me never draw my attention back to myself. I only want to operate as You do, dwelling within me.

I am Yours, Lord. I want to have my life in You. I want to do the will of the Father. Give me the strength to put aside the world and let You operate my very being. Help me to act as You desire. Strengthen me against the distractions of the devil to take me from Your work.

When I worry, I have taken my focus off of You and placed it on myself. Help me not to give in to the promptings of others to change what in my heart You are making very clear to me. I worship You, I adore You and I love You. Come and dwell in me now.

January 17, 1994

About the cover:

This is God's Blue Book. I knew the color would be blue. I saw it in my mind's eye. It is God's blue book, for our living light. Blue for Mary, never dark. It is light and our Hearts are lifted in peace to Him. He lifts us up like balloons into a light blue sky. He even provides the sky. We become selfless and unattached and we ascend into the sky, free of weight on our heels. We sail the skies as if in a hot air balloon and He watches us on our way. Our destination color is blue. We go to a light blue book for our answers. We sail His sky in our hot air balloon, light and unattached, floating free. We just go where His wind takes us, never knowing where or why. We are free and happy because He is at the helm. Alleluia.

Put a balloon, red and orange, on the front, as in the fire of His love. We are thus powered through His blue sky.

11/17/93

Jesus speaks: This is the picture I want in My messages. When you read these messages, look at My picture and know I love you. These messages are My words of love for each of you.

Open Anywhere   Love, Jesus

I give my heart to Jesus and Mary with you in love.

Our new address is:
　　Shepherds of Christ
　　P. O. Box 627
　　China, IN 47250

Love
Rita

In My Heart

by C. Ring
Chords by Joseph Lee

In my heart, is a love I ne - ver felt ___ be-fore, ___ and

In my heart, is a love I ne - ver found ___ be-fore. ___ I

looked, and searched, and walked the whole wide world, and

in Your Heart, I found my life, my re-_fuge. ___ Be-cause ___

in Your Heart, ___ I al-ways found ___ just what I need - ed, and

in Your Heart, ___ I al-ways found just what I want-___ed. And

You, my God, my on - ly love, ___ are in my heart ___ to ___

Dedication

To my family, Bob, Carol, Sharon, Cathy and Joe.

Acknowledgements

For his gracious assistance in discerning this text and for helping me on my spiritual journey, I extend my heartfelt appreciation to Father Edward J. Carter, S.J., Professor of Theology, Xavier University, Cincinnati, Ohio.

A great many people have given unselfishly of their time and talents to make this book possible but a certain few stand out for their special contributions. They have been there from early on and continue to be there whenever help is needed: Ellen Sartori for typing these messages and for giving of herself for those seemingly endless hours of service to Jesus; and my uncle Andrew Weber, who has been so strongly supportive.

Table of Contents

To The Reader

Jesus wants to share His love with you. He comes in these letters to tell you how you can be in intimate union with Him.

All of us possess everything we need to have an intimate union with Him. He has been giving me messages since October of 1991. For at least a year I sat in front of the tabernacle and begged him to talk to me. I wanted words. I prayed to the Holy Spirit and begged and begged Him to baptize me. After a long and seemingly endless search, trying to hear God, He told me to "feed the hungry." For six weeks this was all I heard. I thought maybe I wasn't feeding my children well or eating well enough myself. What a long wait for three words! At long last one day, as I was writing to Jesus, I received a letter back. He told me, "I am Jesus, Son of the Living God." I did not want to write this but it kept coming—and so did many other messages. I knew nothing of anyone getting messages. I wrote them, reluctantly, and hid my notebooks. The letters kept coming, many during the night. I would be awakened, then given long letters which I felt compelled to get up and write down. I read these letters privately and my life began to change. I felt a new life within me.

He taught me of His fervent love and how truly present He was. He taught me how precious I was to Him. Over and over again He would call me His precious child and tell me how He loved me, how He clothed me with dignity and honor. He told me over and over how He was right by my side always. He is teaching me to give up all fear and to trust in Him. He is teaching me to let go of myself and let Him run my life. I am trying every day to do His will.

He is also telling you in your heart all you need to know. He has all the answers for you there in your heart. You must be silent and go to Him so you can hear His words for you.

Sit in front of the tabernacle and be with Him. Do not pray prayers. Sit and be open and just be with Him. Read these letters there. These are Jesus' love letters to you. Sit in front of the tabernacle and let Him talk to you. Sit silent awhile. Read these letters part of the time. Open any page and He will talk to you. Do not read this like a book, cover to cover. Just open to a page and read that page. That is the way He speaks to you.

Introduction

Note: *Read before the Tabernacle.*

Jesus: How, child, do I, Jesus, tell you I love you? You hold on to silly things when God is in your midst and is ardently loving you. I am Jesus Christ, the Son of God. I am writing to each precious child this day. I am on fire for love of you. I remain in the Eucharist to be with you with My ardent love. I did not want to leave My beloved ones at the Last Supper. I love you so, My dear and ardently loved children. I remain with you this day in the Blessed Sacrament, the same Jesus Who died a brutal death on the Cross.

Do you know I am truly present there? Do you know that God waits every day for you in the tabernacle? Do you comprehend even a minute amount of My love? You will never know of how I love you on earth.

I, Jesus, truly the Son of God, came to earth a man and suffered a brutal death for love of you. I love you so much! I remain with you this day. I long for your love. I want you to come and be with Me in front of the tabernacle. I wait, I yearn for you to come and whisper your love to Me. I am a person and I love you this day, with such an ardent on-fire love! No human could ever compare a speck to My love for you.

I wait, little ones, in the tabernacle. I wait for you to come and receive Me in Communion. I want you to want Me so much you cannot wait to come and receive Me. I want to be the love, the center of your life!

I am Jesus. I am the Son of God. I am writing to you this day. I want to possess your very soul and live in you. I have all you need, sweet ones. Oh, you are so blind! I long for your union with Me. I wrote the book of love. I instituted it, yet you go to the world for your love and do not even come to Me! Oh, I love you, little ones. Little ones, beloved of the Father, loved by the Holy Spirit, mothered by My very own mother! What more can I say? The rest is up to you!

I give you your will with such love and I want your love freely given. I am God. What do you think you could ever need that I do not give you? I am the Savior of this world. I am Jesus, the Son of God. I am waiting for you. I am longing for you. I am yearning for you. I am God. I have all you ever will need!

Surrender this life to Me. Pray My Prayer for Union with Me. I want to possess your soul and operate from your very being. I am Jesus. I am the Son of God. I am the Sacred Heart of Jesus. I am Who am. I died and rose on the third day.

Harken to My call, harken to My pleading. Spend your days in love with Me. Nothing matters unless it is rooted in Me and rooted in My love. I am the Son of God. I am the Sacred Heart of Jesus. I love you with the tenderest love. I am waiting this day for just you, My beloved one. Come to Me for I am the tenderest of all hearts. I am the Sacred Heart of Jesus.

God's Blue Book, Volume 2, April 13, 1994

Teachings to Lift You Up

Cling to Me

Jesus: My dear child, if you stay close to Me, then I live in you and you live in Me. I am He Who created you and I love you with such an intensity that you will never know. My words are your truth. You must abide in My heart in all things. There is no room for doubt. My ways are steadfast, direct, and without error.

You must stay rooted in Me to ward off the power of the evil one. His grip is paralyzing and crippling. His power is stronger every day.

When you live in Me, I am in your heart and he has no power over Me. I am your God. I am your true lover. I want to protect you. I want to guard you from this force. Stay rooted firmly in Me and he will have no power.

I am He Who comforts you. My hand is upon you. Hold tight to Me, My child. My eyes are fixed right on you. You are My most precious child. I love you as no other can. My arms are about you. My tenderness surrounds you. My love is in your heart. You go not alone. I walk with you.

I share every aspect of your life with you. Cling to Me, feel My presence. It is warm and secure within your chest. There is no room for fear, for I cast out fear and bring you comfort and joy.

5/13/93

Surrender

Jesus: Oh My child, I am with you. Drink in My presence. Know I never leave you. Even though everything seems mixed up, I am there.

I am here with you. You will know what to do. My hand is forever upon you, protecting you and keeping you from harm. I will never leave you. I am He Who comforts you. Breathe in My peace, My direction, My will, My way. Surrender it all up to Me and let yourself feel the freedom of surrender. Your life is guided by Me. You only have to operate.

I am puttering you about. You go as a little doll that is wound up. Does this little doll get anxious. Does it get tired? It just stops when the power is off. It isn't mad. It doesn't worry about food and who will wind it up. Nobody else matters. He just goes and does his thing when he is wound up. Otherwise he is motionless and sits and waits. Sit and wait on the Lord and I will grant your heart's request. You are powered by Me. There is no need for anxiety. I am He Who comforts you, runs you, loves you. You needn't worry. Just be for Me. Be My hands, My heart, My love. Be totally selfless and full of direction by Me. Do you feel used little child? I want to use you to do My work. I want to use you to walk for Me and talk for Me and smile for Me and be there for others for Me. Die of yourself and live in My love. I will use you, yes, I will. You will know when you grab back your control. You will stumble and fall and feel afraid. You will need to let go and surrender because you will want to get back control. Trust Me. I am here—no need to fret and fear and be anxious. I am always with you and you needn't worry ever, because I will never leave you orphaned and alone. I am always by your side. My hand is upon you. You are My precious daughter, My brother, My child. I am here, let go of it all. Surrender to My power. Feel it as it lifts you up like a balloon over the troubled earth. You don't care. You know it will all work out. Look at all you worried all your life—for what? Did it go away? No, you only suffered for your lack of trust. Trust Me and let it go. I am the God of Jacob and Joseph and all your ancestors. Doesn't it seem silly to think of them wasting their life worrying? It didn't add a moment to their life. Listen to My work and just do it, let go, live and be happy. My joy is there. You have been lifted up and now you see and feel this glory of the Lord. Alleluia. Alleluia. Alleluia.

My peace I give to you My child, not as man can give but as only I can give. Your heart is at unrest, but I have been with you and have seen you through. Hold tight to Me and grab hard onto My hand. Let go. You need not worry. You are engulfed in a sea of fear. With Me, there is no fear. I am peace and I give it now to you. Breathe in peace and Jesus, and out fear. Enjoy the fruits of this moment with your little ones. I am He Who comforts you. You will not be orphaned. My plan is always working with you. Hold My hand. Trust in Me. There are trials to test your love and strength. Offer them up for your sins and others.

You have partaken in a beautiful journey with the Lord. It may seem as if you have followed your tail around, but I have been with you through all of it and guided you. Your life unfolds a mystery and I have the key and know where you are going. You are following My path. It may seem a lit-

Morning Offering (for Shepherds of Christ Members)

My dear Father, I offer You this day all my prayers, works, joys and sufferings, my every breath, my every heartbeat, my every thought, all my actions, in union with Jesus in the Holy Sacrifice of the Mass throughout the world, in the Holy Spirit. I pray the Holy Spirit is with me every second today, enlightening me to do the Will of the Father and filling me with the fire of God's love.

I ask Jesus and Mary to be one in me in all that I do and I unite with all the angels and saints and souls in purgatory to pray continually to the Father for these intercessions, in this prayer, for this day.

For myself, I pray for grace-abundant grace, to know and love God more and more and to follow the Will of the Father. I pray to the Holy Spirit to transform me in the heart of Mary to be more and more like Jesus. I pray that I can forever dwell in the Hearts of Jesus and Mary. I pray for conversion of all those I hold dear who need conversion. I pray for each member of my family that they will be filled with Your abundant grace to grow in their knowledge and love of God.

I pray for all my friends that they will receive abundant grace to carry out the great plan of the Father, that they will grow forever closer to Jesus' Heart through Mary's heart, that we will all be led by the Holy Spirit to do His work, that we will, together, carry out the plan of the Father as He intends us to, to spread the love of the Sacred Heart of Jesus and Mary's heart to this world.

Jesus, I pray for myself so the Holy Spirit descends upon me and opens my heart to Your love so I will grow more and more deeply in union with You. I pray that I do not worry what other people think but try always to please the Father and do His Will. I pray that I may help lead many to Your burning love.

I pray for the following people in particular that they will be filled with the Spirit and grow deeply in their union with You, that they will receive abundant graces to know, love and serve You more. (Include special friends by name...)

I pray for priests the world over, for the success of the Priestly Newsletter, the Chapters and for the finances needed for the Newsletter. I pray for the circulation of the Blue Book messages, rosary meditations and tapes. I pray for all those involved in the publication of these messages.

I pray that You will shower Your abundant graces onto the priests reading the Newsletter the people reading and hearing the Blue Book messages and Rosary Meditations and all of Fr. Carter's publications.

We pray for the intentions we hold deep within our hearts, for our families and friends, for those requesting our prayers. We pray for children the world over and for the souls in purgatory. We ask God to shower His abundant grace on us and the members of our Shepherds of Christ Chapter so that we may grow more and more in our knowledge and love of God.

We consecrate ourselves to the Hearts of Jesus and Mary. We pray for Father Carter, for Father Smith, for Rita Ring, and for John Weickert, for all leaders and helpers in the Shepherds of Christ Movement, for Shepherds of Christ Ministries, and Our Lady of Light Ministry. We pray for all those who are working in these ministries.

We bind ourselves and our children and our friends to the Immaculate Heart of Mary. We place the precious blood of Jesus on ourselves, and all we touch, so that we will be protected from the evil one. We pray to St. Michael to cast the devil into hell.

We love You, God, we love You, we love You. We beg that we may receive the grace to love You more and more deeply. We adore You, we praise You, our beloved Father, Son, and Holy Spirit.

Imprimatur: Most Reverend Daniel E. Pilarczyk,
Archbishop Archdiocese of Cincinnati

Daily Prayers

Pray to be joined in one heart.

Holy Spirit Prayer. "Come, Holy Spirit, almighty Sanctifier, God of love, who filled the Virgin Mary with grace, who wonderfully changed the hearts of the apostles, who endowed all Your martyrs with miraculous courage, come and sanctify us. Enlighten our minds, strengthen our wills, purify our consciences, rectify our judgment, set our hearts on fire, and preserve us from the misfortunes of resisting Your inspirations. Amen."

Prayer to St. Michael and our Guardian Angels: "St. Michael the Archangel, defend us in battle. Be our safeguard against the wickedness and snares of the devil. May God rebuke him, we humbly pray, and do thou, O prince of the heavenly hosts, by the power of God, cast into hell Satan and all the other evil spirits who prowl about the world seeking the ruin of souls. Amen."

"Angel of God, my guardian dear, to whom God's love commits me here, ever this day be at my side, to light and guard, to rule and guide. Amen."

Act of consecration to the Sacred Heart of Jesus and the Immaculate Heart of Mary. "Lord Jesus, Chief Shepherd of the flock, I consecrate myself to Your most Sacred Heart. From Your pierced Heart the Church was born, the Church You have called me, as a member of Shepherds of Christ Associates, to serve in a most special way. You reveal Your Heart as a symbol of Your love in all its aspects, including Your most special love for me, whom You have chosen as Your companion in this most important work. Help me to always love You in return. Help me to give myself entirely to You. Help me always to pour out my life in love of God and neighbor! Heart of Jesus, I place my trust in You!

"Dear Blessed Virgin Mary, I consecrate myself to your maternal and Immaculate Heart, this Heart which is symbol of your life of love. You are the Mother of my Savior. You are also my Mother. You love me with a most special love as a member of Shepherds of Christ Associates, a movement created by your Son as a powerful instrument for the renewal of the Church and the world. In a return of love, I give myself entirely to your motherly love and protection. You followed Jesus perfectly. You are His first and perfect disciple. Teach me to imitate you in the putting on of Christ. Be my motherly intercessor so that, through your Immaculate Heart, I may be guided to an ever closer union with the pierced Heart of Jesus, Chief Shepherd of the flock."

tle crooked at times but it is directed and straight. Enjoy each moment. Now I go with you every second. You are not alone. I am here with you right now.

I am here always. My rod and staff is upon you. You have handled your trials well. Stay close to Me and feel My presence. All is well. The devil wants you to look at dark corners. Look into the light, into the sunlight of My heart. I am here with you My child. I love you!

Know this—you are chosen by Me to do My work, to stay close, to walk your journey close to Me, to carry your cross. It is the only way to Me. My way is not easy. It has bumps and pitfalls, but you know My plan is at work, even in the pits. You are My precious child. I love you. As you are tired, weary, place your yoke upon My shoulders and I will give you rest. Breathe in the richness of God. I am your shepherd. I know Mine and Mine know Me. Read this to My little children. I love them so. They are so dear and precious to Me.   6/17/93 Early Evening

I Am A Jealous God

Jesus: I am your God and you shall have no gods before Me, not money or power or man. You must make Me the center of your life. Whenever you are filled with anxiety you have made something else your God. You must hold fast to My presence by your side and know I am there and nothing can harm you. Though the earth be shaken and the sun not give its light, I will hold your hand and you will be My child. You needn't worry. Let go of it all, My child. The very hairs of your head are numbered. I am by your side in this cross. Sit back and enjoy this air, the freedom and silence. You need to be with Me. I am a jealous God. I do not want you to block My way to you with sorry thoughts of remorse. I am here and I am loving you at every turn. I am the God of all your Fathers. I am all power. You must only trust Me. Put all your doubt aside and know that I am present to you, My little one. I am God. Quit putting so much importance on what your friends have said to you. The devil uses them to get to you. You are very distracted and hurt. Snap out of it. I am Jesus and I am your God. They are not. They do not matter, My child. I am running the show. I could stop this whole world at this moment if I so desired. I am licking your wounds with My divine healing. You will not suffer this pain any more this day. This is a day created by Me to show you My love. Have the day and enjoy its fruits. Focus on My great love for you. I care for you as no other can. I miss your attentiveness to Me when you are distracted and bowed down.

I am a jealous God. I want your all. I want you doing My work. You are not spreading My love when you are engulfed in a sea of despair. A day lost without My love being spread through you is a day lost for all those around you. Forget them. They make you feel guilty and bad. They are being operated by Satan's snares. He is so cunning. You, My child, can't go there. You are loved dearly by Me. I am hurt by your pain. Ask for My grace to wash away all memory of this scourging, but to remember only how deeply I am affected by neglect in Communion from those who do not love Me.

You know how people hurt you, but you don't feel the pain. You know the evilness in cruel remarks, but you don't feel the pain, for My love is a balming ointment for you in the day of battle. I have felt all the pains. Meditate on My passion. I have suffered.

You need to let light flow through you. You need to cooperate with My grace to erase those feelings from your heart and trust in Me, My beautiful child. Trust that I am the God Who truly loves you. Unto death I have suffered for you. Meditate on this. I love you, little one. I love you.

8/23/93

Come To My Tabernacle

Jesus: My precious child, I long to be with you. I am here. You must find a way to be with Me every day in front of the tabernacle. If others distract you, you must find a way.

Satan is trying to stop My time with you. I am your true love and I long to spend time with you each day. Hold tight to My face. I am here little one. Don't ever doubt that again. My words are simple. They are truth. No one knows My intense love for them. I long for these moments with you. I am indeed here. If you have to come and be with Me during the day, I want these moments with you in front of the tabernacle. I am truly sitting here with you, Body and Soul.

I am Jesus, Son of the living God. Never doubt Me again. I have made myself known to you, My child. You offend Me so with your doubt and your busyness on other matters. You spend time fuming and fretting and feeling sorry for yourself when I am waiting here to be with you and talk to you. I don't care about other matters. I am very jealous. I want this time every day. You feel so bad inside when you are not alone with Me in church. That is where your comfort comes from. You are so upset inside when you do not spend it here. Don't you know these things? Being home is not the same. I am truly present in the tabernacle. You needn't run anywhere. You have a key to the church. I love you. I don't want to remind you that this is where it all is. I want you to love Me so much you don't even think you can function without time alone with Me in church. Come to Me every day. You do not go a day without food. You can't go a day without time absolutely alone with Me. If you do, it will be a disaster. Have you not felt the gnawing in your heart when you didn't do it yesterday? You crave this time alone and your tears are from not being alone with Him Whom you truly love.

I am Jesus Christ, Son of the one true God. I have chosen you to write these messages which are meant for all and you are busy—doing what, My child? Did you not cry and feel bad most of yesterday? This is your proof. You knew you wanted to be with Me here so badly you almost drove back out. You have to be alone with Me. In front of the tabernacle is best. I am the living God and I am in the tabernacle. You must be here or you will be so lost inside. Spend time with Me, My child. Nothing else matters. I am the one, true God and you shall not have other gods before Me. I command this because this is how you were created and this makes you most happy. Come to Me all you who labor and I will give you rest. I will give you peace, not as this world gives you peace, but My peace, which only I can give.

The gift I give to you, My child, is My Son. Would you refuse My gift? He waits for you every day and where do you go—to the grocery?— to do your wash? What do you do, child?

I am waiting for you. Would you keep Me waiting and turn your back? Is one hour too much for the Son of God? I give you 24 hours. One hour is so little to ask. This is where your peace lies. All else is fruitless.

Not one day should be spent without one hour of private prayer with Me, preferably in the church in front of the tabernacle. Come to Me My little babies. I want to comfort you. I want to care for you. You are all mixed up with your priorities. I grow tired that you don't listen and tell others of My great and glorious love for all My children. This is your main goal. Pray with Me and spread My intense love for all My children. Yes, and I will give you all you need, child. Quit thinking you have to do other things. You have to be with Me and I will make it all work out. I want all to know of My intense love for My children. I died that you might live, not in this world, but in the world to come. I am the way, the truth and the light. All else is useless if it is not rooted in Me and for My work. Time is very short, little one. Listen to My words. You have wasted enough time. Don't delay. All must know of My love for them. It is in Me that they are made whole. Nothing else matters, My child.

8/28/93

I Died In Peace

Jesus: You are hurried. Relax and soak in My peace. Only My peace will quiet you. Your days are full of changes. You are adapting well, but always come back to My peace. Breathe in Jesus, out anxiety and fear. In Jesus, out anxiety. Quiet your mind and focus just on My face. See My sorrowful face, see Me with thorns. Bring yourself back to the Passion. It is because of you and your sins I suffered and died for all My children. How great is My love for you that I would die for love of you. Think of this—that you have a friend Who died for you. Oh, how I love, how I long to be with you to tell you of My infinite love for you. Your human minds cannot even comprehend My Divine love! In your deepest meditation you couldn't come close to all the love I have for you. But you must keep trying to know and feel this love. This is your salvation. This is what sets you free in a world of hate. You can always be drawn back to My love and know it is waiting for you always. It never stops. It is infinite. This is what comforts your troubled soul. When they scorn you and mock you, think of Me loving you. I am the all-perfect love. Always come back to Me. Don't let the world get to you. I am here, with peace, love, joy, rapture, being connected to your heart so divinely. I love you so much! I wish you would totally feel this love the way I want you to.

The only way you can experience Me more is to let go of the world more. In this bustling world, My peace reigns. It is in the quiet of your heart. It is within you and you can stay connected at every moment. You never have to lose this peace no matter what goes on around you. You can be a pillar of peace because I am peace. I am joy. I died in peace and dignity. My peace was not shattered even to death. You can experience this peace if you stay in Me. It is My gift I give you. Remember I was at peace at My death. You are being strengthened in your trials. You are growing in My peace. You are learning not to shatter to anything, that if you stay rooted in Me I never leave you and you remain at peace though the earth be shaking. For I am He Who lives in you. You can have this same consistency, but you must stay so connected to Me every minute, every second. Breathe in Jesus, out fear. Look at My face. It is there for you. Look and see Me, I am your rock. You will not falter or fall on your face. Your heart is rooted in My peace and My love. It is consistent, it is everlasting, it is intense and it is My gift to My children who remain fixed in Me. I love you.   8/31/93

Oh!, The Gift of the Mass

Jesus: My dear child, I am the way, the truth and the light. He who abides in Me will have the light of life. The gift I give is My Body and Blood. Come and sup with Me and you will have life eternal. For My Blood is drink indeed, and My Body I give to you that you might live. This is all you need. Drink My Blood, eat My Body and you will have life eternal.

Oh, the gift of the Mass! What a gift you are given! Do you treasure this gift, My little ones? Do you know what transpires here or are you half dazed and not present? Be present, for this is the most magnificent event that there is! Dote on every word. Feel the intensity in your heart. Be present in body and soul. Beg to attend as you should to savor all the Mass has to give you! Every word is magnificent. I am here. I am the sacrifice. I shed My Blood that you, oh My precious ones, might live with Me forever in heaven. Praise Me. Thank Me. Know how truly blessed you are. You are so lucky to be here this day with Me. Nothing else you do even comes close to the importance of My Mass. Savor every moment. Participate with your hearts on fire.

You are the chosen that you are here. Come and be close to Me now. Prepare yourself for My marvelous event, just for you. Thank Me. Give Me honor. I am God and I am here for you. I am truly in this place, Body and Soul, humanity and divinity. God is here with you truly, little one. Should not My children flock to be present to Me, to see God, to receive God in their hearts? I am food, indeed. You need no other food. I give you food for life and I am here for you because of My intense love for you. Doesn't it make you want to shout for joy and sing praises to the God Who loves you? Come to Me with your hearts on fire, not all bowed down. If a king were here you would come with enthusiasm. I, My children, am God, yet you stay away and those who come are half asleep. I am greater than any earthly king. I am God and My kingdom is not of this world!

I want to be praised and honored and thanked and adored, but I am ignored and left out of their lives. Oh, how this hurts Me to the point of tears. They do not even speak to Me. This is agonizing. I am He Who made you and I sent My Son to dwell with you and you are busy eating cakes. Why are you My little blind children? You do not give the honor I deserve. All else is useless. If your lives are not rooted in Me, you are wandering this valley in darkness. Come to Me! Come into the light! I am He Who created you and loves you.

I am God and I long to be with you in My Son. This message I give to My children that they know how I wait and wait for them. I love them with such intensity as only God can give. No man can love you as God loves you. You will never know the extent of My love on earth. Oh, come to Me, My children! My arms are open wide. My heart is on fire with love for you. You are My chosen ones. I wait and wait for you. I never move from your side. I am here at every minute. Day and night, My hand is on each of you, protecting you. My love is so intense for you! Come, come, let me fill you to the brim and you will know that I have such gifts to give you. I am your God and I love you.

I cannot make humans understand My divine love. Listen to Me. Be attentive to My calling you. I wait, little ones. Come and be with Me in church before the tabernacle. Come to Me.   9/3/93

On Spiritual Bankruptcy

Jesus: I come to you with My heart on fire with love of you. You came to Me and I filled you. I made ready a path for you and you were guided by the hand of God. My blessings are numerous. I give you water for your thirst, love for your heart and blessings for your soul. You are filled with the gifts of the Holy Spirit and My Father watches your every step lest you stumble and fall. My child, I am your tremendous lover. I wait and watch by your side. I feel your pain, your grief, your sorrow.

No man can ever be as attentive to your needs as I, Jesus, your beautiful spouse. I am hyper-vigilant, I am with you. Never do I move. You have felt alone and scared and thought I was not there, but I am indeed here in this cross. This is the way to Me. The way to Me is picking up your cross and praising the one, true God Who gives this to you. The yearning will be satisfied by My love, and what a union it is—to connect with Me after spiritual bankruptcy! You have been dried out and thrown on the heap and now I pick you up. I breathe life into your soul. I wrap you in My cloth. I kiss your wounds and I hold you in My arms. Do you believe, child, that I am truly here? Oh, ye of little faith, in your desperation, you cried out to the one Who loves you and I made you whole. I filled you with beautiful, sparkling grace. Love abounded in your soul and you did not wait for naught. You waited for the Lord and I quenched the thirst in the hard, baked desert. You are filled in your dryness and you know that only the Person Who is almighty has this power. Come to Me, all who labor and are heavily burdened. I make the crooked ways straight. I give strength to the bowed down. I refresh your starved soul.

Oh ye of little faith, come, come, My children. I am your God. Did you think I would desert you? No, child. I make your ways brimming with milk and honey. I light your path with beaming light and you are free, fed, nourished, loved. You are filled to the brim with the wholeness of Me.

Only I can love you as God loves you. You know when I lick your wounds and make you better. It is in spiritual starvation that you realize the prize. I am He Who picks you up and sets your feet on solid ground. Come to Me and be filled with such love, only the love which I can give. The crooked ways are made straight, enemies speak to each other and are filled. My love abounds in the hearts of the bowed down and they know the might which I feed them. I am He, your God. Child, I stand by you when your heart aches. I pick you up as a child with a wounded knee, I bind your little wounds up, I kiss your little scared heart and I send you on your way to play. I am the Good shepherd. I know Mine and Mine know Me. I walk in the valley of darkness, down your path with you and I spread My light in all the dark corners.

You never fall. You never walk alone. You are not hurt. I am God. Do you think I will forget you. I never slumber. I never sleep. I watch day and night. I am God at your side.   9/12/93 Medjugorje, Yugoslavia

I Am In Control

Jesus: My child, I am here in all this muck. Yes, you are tried and I spit you out. You know Who has the power. You know whence you are coming. All life is indeed rooted in Me and from Me comes all that is. Do you comprehend this, My child? Do you know that no life is there without Me? People think they have power. Oh, they believe they are in charge. There is no power except through Me. If I choose to forget you, you cease to be. Cling to this power. Cling to Me as you follow the celebrity or the king or the Pope. I am God. I am One, I am True, I am Omnipotent, I am all that is. You must stay fixed to Me like glue, child.

Child, no life exists without Me. Turn your lives to Me, precious little ones. Turn over every minute, every second of every day. You think you have control of your life. You silly, silly children—what control? I make the stars shine, the sun shed its light, the moon light up the night. I make the baby in the womb, the trees grow, the animals live—and you say, "Oh, Yes, I can do all things." Little one, you can do no things unless I give you the power. You cease to be without Me. Oh, how silly you indeed are, little ones, to fret and fume and look for your answers. What are you doing? Live, child! I give you your answers in My times. All works as I have planned.

You and your willfulness! You mess things up and then come to pray. What is in your heads? Let your hearts be directed by My spirit. Come to Me first, every second. Then you never run amok, you do the right thing always. Pray, fast, look for My answers. Spend your time alone with Me, not in deliberation in your heads. Oh, ye children, what, what do you do to yourselves? I am here by your side. I am present truly in the tabernacle and you go to each other and ask your questions. When will you submit yourselves to the will of the father? Why do you wander in blindness in this barren desert?

Come to Me and I will give you rest. I will give you all you need, little ones. You are so silly. Power—you have none, child. You are powerless. You are willful. You must stay fixed to Me and My ways. Oh, oh how do I make you understand when you won't listen to Me? I speak, you don't listen. I love you so. I want you not to suffer your own dilemmas, but you turn your backs and ask your questions of those no smarter than you. Your wisdom comes from Me, the one, true God.

Come, little ones, My will for you is not a secret. You have to break the code. It is here. I make it known to you. "In the silence comes His word to the poor and lowly ones in pain." I am all you need, little blind, scared children. You need not be any of these things. Come to Me, beloved little ones, and I will set your toes on the right road. You will not falter. You will run and not get weary. You will indeed fly on eagles' wings and I will be there telling you all you need to know.   9/16/93

You Are Important To Me

Jesus: My dear child, I am not mad at you. You feel such fear in your heart. That is Satan. Focus on Me and My love. I love you intently. All will work out. You have to always see Me as by your side. You are so afraid inside that you are not good enough. You are, My precious child. I love you with My Godly love. You I guard, you I watch, you I wait for and want to be with. Feel your preciousness and value. There is not a time I like you, then I don't. I am not like man. I love you unconditionally. In your bad days, in your darkness, I wait, I watch, I am hyper-vigilant. I never leave your side. Know My presence in all things. Be assured of My fabulous love for you. Whatever transpires, I did it out of love of you. I long to be close to you and see you in heaven. You are My favored child. I watch and wait. Do not doubt yourself, little one. I am pleased with you.

Satan would have a field day if he could work on you.

You must never doubt your specialness. You must always know that you are My love. I love you so. All I do is for love of you. Make a list of all the times you felt My marvelous love, when you knew only I could have helped you. Keep this list in front of your mind. When doubt arises, read the list to yourself. Study and memorize this. This will help cast all doubts aside. The more you read and reread these letters, the more true I will become to you.

I am Jesus, the one, true God. I was crucified for love of you and you are still doubting your worth. You are so important to Me. I would die for you. Oh, little children, wake up, see your specialness. Know I love you with the greatest love. Cast Satan and his hatred and doubts aside. Send him back to hell! Let My light shine in your hearts. Be open to Me as loving you at every second. Know I, God, wait to be with you. Never look at yourself with anything but so much value and love. Then your light will shine because you will be filled by all I can give you.

You are My special, special child. Tell all of My intense love for them. It never dies, it does not flicker, it is so bright, it fills the empty heart and makes it radiate with love. Then you can do My work. You cannot work for Me when you are bowed down. It is only when you are filled up that My light shines from you. I, yes, make the crooked ways straight. I am the spark to the cold heart. I am He Who holds you in My hands and warms your troubled soul. I love you, I love you. Realize this so you may love others. See yourself with My light glowing about you. This will make you realize how special you are. You must love yourself, and see your own beauty, to love others for Me. You are indeed beautiful, you are precious, you are My child. I love you, baby. Know this—you are loved by your Father, the greatest Father that ever was. Your Mother is the most loving Mother. I am Jesus. I am your spouse. I love as no man ever could. The Holy Spirit is on fire with the love He gives you.

You are a fireball if you see yourself as such. Now love for Me with this fire. Set your hearts about the job of radiating My embers to all My children. You will shine and all will know I am your God and they are loved by Me.

I love you, children. Listen to Me. This is where your strength lies in this cold, cold world.

I love you. It is food. It is fuel. It is I, on fire with love of you.

Precious you, I love you, I love you, I love you.   9/17/93

You Are the Light in the Darkness

Jesus: Little child, come and be filled. It is here, with Me, that you are nourished and set free. Your love is made whole here. I give you joy in your soul. I sanctify you and you are made holy by Me. Yes, child, you are holy—I make you so. Respect yourself and the gift you are to this world. I shine from your eyes and I smile with your lips. I hug My hugs with your arms. Do you not know how I need you, so holy and pure?

Don't let Satan plant his little ugly words in your heart. He tries to bring you down. Shut him up, little one. Listen to Me proclaim your dignity and honor. See yourself beautiful, loving, smiling, being, spontaneous. Satan has no power over you. My light shines from your temple to your toes.

Do not let others affect your moods at all. No one can alter the way you are filled with My light. Your light shines in the darkness if you do not let them affect you. You must stay very fixed to Me to do this. Look at them and pray for them. Pray for all you talk to. They need your prayers. They need My grace to wake them to My love. You are My preacher of love. My love is ever abounding. It is not for a few, or some. It extends to all My children. I love every little one. I want to reach all. I want to give each My unbounded love, as they reject Me Whom they do not see. You know what they do to you they do more to Me. Pray for My little ones your life touches. This is the most important thing you can do.

Your power radiates from within or it is squelched by the devil and does not radiate at all. I create an energy in you. Stay focused in Me. You are not affected by those around you. When I died on the cross, nothing they said or did affected the way I was. My light was fixed. It shone on them who nailed Me to the cross. It shone in the darkness and many were saved who watched Me. Let your light shine for all the world to see. It is I Who am your generator. Like the houses in Medjugorje, only the houses with generators lit up the night. Others were pitch black. When the generator kicked in, the lights shone so bright in the darkness. You shine more when you are surrounded by darkness if you stay fixed in Me. I shone brightly at My death. In such brutality My light shone as the brightest light. In the night you must shine. Many are living in darkness. You do not go there.

No one need to affect your behavior. You are rooted in Me. I generate a power in you. I am God and My power is very powerful. You must ward off Satan's weak pull. Others want to draw you into their darkness. Do not go there. Shine as the brightest star, shine in the night, shine as a beacon light. You saw darkness in Medjugorje. You know this concept.

When it is dark, a light shines so bright.

Many of your brothers are in darkness. You must stay fixed in Me that your light shine bright as the light on the dark night. I give you this message, My lights of the world. Many lights light up the darkness and it shows in the dark night as if there is no darkness at all. Be the light to the darkness. Shine bright with a generator that is supplied by Me. Do not let your brothers pull you in. You remain in Me and you will never thirst. You will run and not get weary. You will fly on eagles' wings and your days will be joyous in the troubled world. Alleluia. I am your power.   9/18/93

Love Unlocks the Hardened Heart

Jesus: My dear child, I am the bread of life. I give food to the hungry. My life I give that you might have life. Treasure My gift to you and be so attentive to this gift. I am the one, true God and I give My gift to you. You will not thirst. You will run and not get weary. You are coming to My glorious event. All will be beautiful for I am with you in your honor and praise. I love you so, little one.

You scarce can speak when you receive Me. That is because you are realizing My True Presence. I am there, little one. I died for you that you might live forever and the gift I give is My life. What friend would lay down His life for another? This, My dear, is love, love as I teach you to give to your brothers—not only loving those who are nice, but also those who are not nice. To those who hate and scorn and ignore you, My gift I give to you. It is My life that you may live.

Come unto Me, all who labor and are heavily burdened. I give you all you need. I make your ways straight and I set your foot on solid paths. I am the God of all your ancestors. You come to Me and I fill you as I did them. I give you water for your thirst and food for your soul. You are sheltered under My wing as a little bird. I take care of you and protect you from the scorching sun. I give you little worms and protect you. I give you water for your thirst. You live and grow. And who takes care of these little birds? I do. Did you wonder who was watching out for them? Well, wonder no more. Are you not more valuable. Do you not know how precious you are to Me? I am your love and I watch out for you every minute. I pick you up when you stumble and fall. I watch your every move.

Oh, little one, stop fuming and fretting. You are indeed wasting your life away and I need you to do My work. What is My work? It is staying fixed in Me. It is smiling My smiles. It is being gentle. It is being kind. It is being as I am in the world. It is not being like the world. The world is hard, and hardened in heart. Its people wander in hatred and wonder why they feel glum in their hearts. Wander in love and feel joy in your hearts, little ones.

Love makes the little scared child feel unafraid. Love comforts a hurting soul. Love given to all is My way. The world is out for itself. It wants you to step on your brother, get even with him, never give more than you get. Oh, you selfish world, what a terrible agony to carry in your heart— keeping track of all you were given so you cannot give any more to them.

Hard cheeked, stone-jawed, do you feel good? Little hardened hearts, give and you shall receive, seek and you shall find, knock and it shall be opened to you. It is in giving that you receive. Give your smiles, your time, your money. These are your brothers, little one. Do not refuse what is their due.

Walk and not get weary, run and fly, follow Me and your hearts are joyous. I fill you with good things. Your heart is filled to the brim with love. Come, little ones, open your eyes. There is more work done in love than in hatred. Love your enemies. Love those who are mean to you. You will receive more benefits than they. It hurts your hearts to be "even-Stephen". It is a needless task. Fill your soul with My love, little ones. I can do these things with you.

You will only act from love. Love is the key to unlock the hardened heart. Love the child I created and hate the evil the devil does through them. They are My beautiful children. They do evil works. Pray for them, little ones. They surely need your prayers and your love. I love them. Love for Me. I need you to love, little children. Love one another and be there for each other. Minister to the haters. They are still beautiful in My sight. I love them and you.   9/21/93

I Am First

Jesus: Empty churches, empty hearts, cruelty, hate for each other. Oh, why do they not listen? Oh, I am here. I give them all they need. They won't turn to Me. Where are they, My little dumb children? They have turned their hearts off and to evil works, hatred of their brothers, their self-promotion. All they do is operate from crippled hearts. Their hearts can be at peace. They can be joyous. They can have all they need but they do what they want. They are willful, they don't listen. They close themselves off. They hear Satan's promptings and they follow his way which is evil.

Oh, My children, I cry, I love you so. Where are you? Come to Me. My way is peace, My way is love, My way is joy, My way is the way. All other ways are so useless. They are not of Me. Why, children, don't you listen? I cry by night and cry by day. I send My mother. I talk to you. They close their hearts and choose their evil ways. Oh, please listen to Me, little ones. I cannot let this massacre go on much longer. There is so much hate, such vileness, such disobedience, such abuse. What do you want with all this sin? It casts a dark light in your soul and your hearts wither and die. Oh, children, please come to Me, spread My message of love. I need you to tell these little sick children about Me. You may be rejected but, if one soul listens to you, then it will be saved.

The world needs you to spread My light. I am in you and working in your heart. Your heart is full and plump and filled by Me. My love is so full in a heart that stays fixed to Me. You, My child, must do this work. Speak. Time is short.

Woe to those who teach My children such vileness and hurt My little ones. They will pay for their misdeeds. My love is abounding and encompassing. It reaches to the ends of the earth. Woe to those who spread filth. They will answer for corruption of My children.

I love My children. I want you to speak of My love. All of you lights, speak. Do not hold back. The time is at hand. Smile, be filled by Me. Generate My presence. You know I am in you, little ones. I have all the power. No one has power except through Me. My ways are the right ways. Your ways must be in Me. I will help you all in your earthly things, but make Me First. I am First. Talk to Me every day. I need to teach and comfort you. You need to be alone with Me. I am all there is. All else is useless if it is not rooted in Me. I cry and I wait for My children. You who know Me have the true treasure. Cherish this treasure. I am here with you, truly present, always by your side. You are never alone. You are fixed in Me and I know Mine and Mine know Me. We have the true joy. All other joy only lasts a moment and then it dies, sooner than it came. My joy never dies. It lasts for all eternity. I give you all you need, little ones. Come and be filled by Me. My light is on you, My power is within you. You don't do it. I do it through you. Make yourself My empty vessel. I fill you and work in you. I love My world through you. I want to use you to love My children. Give yourself to Me, little babies. I am here and I am waiting. Let Me save My world through you. Your tongue is My tongue. Speak and I will talk for you. Don't worry, many will listen and be saved because of your willingness to speak for Me. For those who turn away, they will suffer for turning from Me. In their arrogance they say nay and they pay with their lives, not this life but the life of My kingdom. This is no joke. Many are so far from Me. Help your brothers. If they reject you, they will suffer this loss forever. I am making My words available through you. You must remain open and let Me use you. I need you, I need you. Stay close to Me. Open your mouth—My love will pour out to your brothers. Pray for courage to do My will. I love you, little ones.

9/22/93

The Way of the Cross
Is the Way to My Heart

Jesus: Little child, you are so precious to Me. I hate to see you suffer. Offer it up to Me. Accept your cross and it will make you holy. I know you strive to be holy. Share in My Passion. Walk with Me, little one. The Way of the Cross is the way to My heart. It is a beautiful way. It brings you to Me. I wait with open arms to caress you, little beauty.

I love you. I am the prize for your suffering. Nothing is so valuable. Accept your cross that you may gain the golden reward, My love.

I am your Jesus. I never leave you. I share your sorrow and wipe the tears from your eyes. Lay you little head on My lap. The road is rocky but the reward is a reward, indeed. I am clothed in white and embrace you. I give you rest. I love you so much. Think of Me, sweet one. Don't think of your problems.

I love you.

9/26/93

Come, Be Alone With Me

Jesus: I am the Good Shepherd. I know Mine and Mine know Me. I know the inner workings of the heart and your desire to be alone with Me. Forget everybody else. Just let Me talk to you now. I am truly here, just you and Me. I am your precious Savior, even in distraction. Find My peace. Feel My warmth by your side. Let go of every problem, every distraction. See Me looking at you, My eyes gentle, My smile very slight, loving you in My gaze. All else is fuzzy around you. I am with you—you and Me alone. I am standing in front of you, My hands outstretched, dressed in white. You feel My peace surround you. Warmth. It is as if smoke surrounds us and we are encased in this screen of smoke, all by ourselves.

Feel My power radiating to you. You are engulfed in peace. The world could stop and you wouldn't know and you wouldn't care. I am all you need. Your heart stops beating except for My presence. We are so close. There is such peace there that you never want to leave or care about anything else. I am the Lord, your God. I am your all. I am with you and you are filled by Me. It is such a fullness. The light and warmth that surround us are nothing you could describe. Power—waves of power in the air almost like a magnet—nothing else matters. This is how it is in your life. All is insignificant except in Me. You can be with Me in a crowd. You can block out all things around you and feel My presence. This is what you must learn to do—be alone with Me in a crowd. I am all that matters. Anywhere you are, all people, places and things are insignificant if not seen in Me.

Through the day you must have these moments alone with Me. Come and sit with Me now. I am standing in front of you or I can be sitting with you, but think of us all alone, Me clothed in white, a smoke screen about us. My arms are open and I embrace you and you feel engulfed by My love. You are filled with such peace when you come to sit here alone with Me. See this picture. Feel the pull to Me in your heart—a flutter, a magnetism to be drawn to Me. I am all you need. Nothing else is important. I fill you so you will radiate My love to your brothers. I call you to this place with Me that you are filled to do My work. Come alone and be with Me. I wait with open arms at any time to be with you! It pleases Me so for you to stop and sit with Me, even in a crowd. At work, anywhere you are, come and sit with Me and I will give you My peace and love and your day will start anew. You are refreshed and sent on My mission with My love in your heart. I am the Good Shepherd. I know Mine and Mine know Me. I bid you come and sup with Me. I love you, little one. I am your Jesus. I love you.   10/2/93

Use Your Talents

Jesus: I am your Savior, Son of the Living God. I come to you that you might have life, not as the world gives you life, but My life which is life eternal. I carved you from My special carving and made you little less than an angel. I love you and cherish all the moments when you, My special child, come to sit with Me. I wait here and I hope you will choose to come, but I never force you. Your will is totally free and I give it to you because of My love and the will of the Father. I inform you in numerous ways. You do not have to guess and wonder. Come be with Me in this silence and all you need to know will be told to you. Your life is unfolding as a beautiful rose. Each petal falls and you plant My odors about as I so desire. I make your life full and sure as you trust in Me. No need for worrying, My little flower. My ways give you freedom if you listen to your heart. I am a personal God and you know Me as giving you fullness and life. You know there is some magnetism to Me and the way you crave to be part of Me. This is the work of the one, true God Who created you with a thirst that can only be quenched by Me. All roads that lead to Me give you fullness, worth, peace and joy, not as the world thinks, but as you yourself know true peace and joy. When I really touch you, you do not remain the same. I shed My Blood for you that you will have the life only I can give. What friend in this world would die for you? You, My child, were worth My dying for. I came that you will have life eternal and the gift I give is My Precious Blood for your sins. Come to Me in trouble and when you are bowed down. Come to Me in joy. Come to Me every day that you live and I will give you all you need. Seek to know Me more and more. Knowledge of Me, being with Me, are the only way to perfect peace. They lead to eternal life.

I have a divine plan for you. I created you with special gifts and talents to be used to do My work. They are not for your own self-promotion. You, My child, are nothing except as I created you. Why try to promote yourself? It is none of your own doing. I gave you the talents you are using. You had nothing to do with it. These talents were given to you to do My work. To use these talents to make yourself feel better than your brother is indeed a sin. You must realize they are loaned to you to work for Me. As you give someone a car, or loan them a place to stay, I loan you your talents to use to work for Me. If you do not work for Me and use them to make yourself better than your brother, you are offending Me. Likewise, if I give you talents and you do not use them because you think you are not as good as your brother, you are not being thankful to Me for My gifts to you. You are not using My gifts and that offends Me greatly. Each person was created by Me to do My work. Each person has all he needs to do My work. To be envious of others is fruitless. They have their job. You have yours. You are not supposed to do their work. That is why you were not given their talents.

Do your own work. Don't be envious of your brothers. Don't hide your talents. You did not earn them. I gave you your talents. You must sing because I will it. Others must do as I will them to do. It displeases Me to give you a gift and watch you hide it and make light of it. I give the gift. You must use all your gifts. They were given to you to do My work. Your brother has his gifts. Be grateful for your brother and he should be for you. You are all chosen by Me for a special mission. You know what to do. It feels right. I plant little seeds in your heart and all you do that is for you in the end feels right. You are not to be doing your brother's work or he yours. Talk to Me that you might know just what your work is and do it.

Do not hide your talents. Praise your God Who gave you these talents. Embrace and use them. This is not pride. This is My plan. I love you. I give to each of you, My precious children, as a mother who buys special Christmas gifts for each child. To buy gifts all the same for all your children is not to respect their specialness, their individuality.

Oh, I love you, little ones, so much. Please come to Me. I am so good and I wait to be with you and share My love with you. Come now. This is your top priority. All else will work when you come to Me first. I love you. You are My chosen children. Come and be filled and I make your loads light and I fill you with the Spirit of Salvation.

All roads that lead to Me are the right roads. Praise Me for I am good and I love you, little dear ones.

10/3/93 Chicago Marian Conference 11:30 a.m.

True Presence

Messenger: Note: Early in the morning of October 6 I was awakened by the sound of knocking and the song, "Oh, the Lady is calling, she is calling you now," playing. Then the first reading at Mass that morning was about Jesus knocking.

In the afternoon I went to Adoration at St. Gertrude's Church. The Blessed Sacrament was exposed and, while adoring Jesus, I closed my eyes. I saw an image of Jesus, His face turned sideways. The image lasted about two minutes, then faded away slowly. As it faded an image of a monstrance came into view. This was signifying Jesus' True Presence to me and His calling me to spread devotion to Jesus in the Eucharist and adoration before the tabernacle.

That same night, after Communion at Mass in Dayton, I heard a voice from behind me say "Rita." I turned around and no one was there. I have had many images of doors. Jesus has called me by knocking to write these letters for you. You are being called to open your hearts and let Him dwell within you. He loves you so deeply. (See also the November 2 message.)

Jesus: I am the Lord, thy God and you shall not have any gods before

Me. Come and be with Me, child. I make your heart filled with joy. I comfort you. I sanctify you. I make you light and you turn only to Me in your prayers and cry out for My mercy, My grace and My love. All is upon you, little ones. All in this world is so useless. My hand is set on you to do My work. I need you free to be with Me here in My church. Remember My face, then the monstrance. You, My child, will see Me. I will make Myself known to you. You must come every day and be with Me, by yourself. One hour for us each day. Do not short Me. Be here for Me. I long to be with you and share Myself with you. Turn not away and toward other things. My concerns are your only concerns. Turn to Me and be attentive to all I tell you. All else is of no account.

I am your God and I love you. I need you to deliver these messages. You must stay fixed totally on Me. Be here that I might work in you, little one. I cannot make you come. I am telling you that which I desire. Do whatever it takes to be with Me alone each day. Pray to Me constantly. You are not to be of this world. That is why you feel like a misfit. You cannot do this work and be worldly. You must let go and trust entirely in Me.

I am truly with you, little one. We are as true lovers. I wait for you and you want so much to be with Me. You know how you long to be here. You must see how Satan puts other things in your way. You must outsmart him and realize I want you with Me in church. All else is insignificant. You have now seen My face from the side, child. It is Me, Jesus, Who loves you. You are not losing anything. You are gaining My love and our relationship. Hold on to Me, child. Totally trust and be with Me. Nothing else is of any account. I am your God and I am jealous. I want your time— here. I want your time in prayer. I want you—alone. All else is insignificant. I fill your heart with all good things and I am there in every step you take.

I am Jesus, Son of the Living God. Come, child, I wait and I wait for you. Don't keep Me waiting. I beg you to come. Tell others you are busy. Your love awaits you and I am God, child. One hour alone with Me each day. No excuses. I want to be with you, child. I want to show you more but you do not come long enough or you sleep. Be with Me, My child. I wait, I wait, I wait. I want you with Me. I love you. Listen to Me and be not afraid.   10/6/93

You Are Soldiers of My Love

Jesus: You, My child, are My messenger to reach many. You must come and be with Me every day. I am truly here in the tabernacle and I wait for you to be with Me. By day and night I am here and I am alone and I wait for My children to come and sit with Me. Don't write when you come. Just come and be. Talk with Me. Tell Me your cares, then just sit and be with Me. Let Me fill you with My light and My love. You are My precious child. I wait by day and night. I want you alone with Me. See Me in a smoke screen. Just you and Me present to each other. You must be alone to feel Me.

I am Jesus, Son of the Living God. My hand is with you whence you go and I never leave your side. I make your days flowing with milk and honey. I light your path and give you direction and I use you as the light in a dark world. Others do not come to Me but My light shines in the world out of you. You must come to be filled with My power, like charging a battery. You come, you get plugged in and then you go about the world, lighting it with My most precious light. This world needs you to shine in the darkness. It needs your smiles to the bowed down. You are a beacon on a cold, dark night, but it is only in your presence with Me in front of the tabernacle that you are charged. I give you such power. I give you all good things. I come to you and you are made whole. Your wounds are healed and your heart dances on a cloud of lightness. Only I can give such things to you. Come and I will give you such things that you cannot imagine in your earthly minds. My heart is on fire with love of you and I pour out My gifts to you when you are here. Oh, what silly, silly children stay away when I am God and I can give you all you need.

Little ones, stay fixed in Me. Come and be with Me. Make Me the center of your life and all will work for you. You are indeed in this world, but not of this world. You are My soldiers in this dark world. You are not soldiers as the world knows soldiers. You are soldiers of My love and I need you in My army.

I fortify you when you come and sit with Me and go to the world. They know My presence through you. Never, never stray from Me. You need My fortification to stay afloat in the world. I love you, little ones. Come and be with Me. Let Me shine through your eyes and smile with your lips and act through you to your sick brothers.

I am the divine healer. I can only reach some through you if you come to Me and allow Me to work in you. Some will never know Me if you do not come and get refueled with My love. I need you, day and night, to shine in the world. I am He Who operates out of you. Will you come and get your supplies? I am He Who fills you. You are My soldiers. I need you, little ones. Remember, I am in you and I am using you, but My love for you never dies. I am holding your hands while you do My work.

I love you, little ones. Come to Me and be filled by My love. My love is your power in this dark world. I need you.   10/8/93

Turn All Things Over To Me

Jesus: I am your precious Jesus and I am very close to you. You may not see Me but I am here. The time you are spending with Me pleases Me greatly. I am your precious Savior. I am with you in all you do. I make your days days to do My work.

Each day unfolds as I have planned and you are being used all through the day. Continue to come and just be with Me. Tomorrow you must come and be with Me or your day will not work for you. Plan your things so your time before Mass is free. There is no reason not to spend one hour with Me. Let everything else in your life go, but spend one hour with Me in private prayer. Look at it from My side. Nothing I do matters if you do not sit with Me for one hour. I fill you up, I spit you out and you are fire to the world. Energy is transmitted through you when you are charged by Me. My work is endless for you. You must totally turn all things over to Me and know I am this close to you always. I am making your days unfold for Me. You are talking and acting and teaching in your very being. I love you so and I need you to do this work for Me. You need to be alone with Me. All else is in My hands. People will come to you and things will work out. Don't make any decisions on your own. Spray your holy water. Wear your scapular and crosses. Do as you are doing, but come to Me every day in the tabernacle. Talk to your children. Have time for them. These are all that matter. Time is so short. You are bearing witness through your lives how you are. You are to be totally filling yourself. You are charged by Me. I will be by your side, guarding your every step. I need you all so much. So much. Spend your days with Me and then go about doing My work. I have so much for you to do. All you have to do is be and I will be working through you. Put all distractions aside. Leave all problems so you are free to love, smile, speak and witness.

Give Me your problems and be free. Surrender everything to Me. Do not belabor one thing in your head. It is fruitless and it keeps you from doing My work. I will take care of all problems. You smile and live with Me in your soul. I am the joymaker. I make you happy and you light up My world. I work in you and many are reached. You must never get bowed down. I need you on fire, being generated by Me. Give Me the burden. Free yourself of its contents. I will make it work out. This will teach you My trust and you will be strengthened for the days ahead. Many will fall apart. You will know My trust and love because you are learning now. I am Jesus, your Savior, and I love you, child. Would you refuse God? One hour is the key—Mass, Communion and being with your children. This is My command: love God and love one another and I will dwell in your hearts and you will have peace and comfort in your hearts. He made them His soldiers and they were not soldiers as the world knows soldiers, they were soldiers in an army of love which transmitted peace.

10/9/93

Learn to Be Christlike

Jesus: I want you present to others, loving and spreading My word. Child, it is pride to think you never get uptight. You must, in humility, accept your shortcomings and learn from them. How can you become closer to Me at every moment? How can you act more as I want you to? How can you become more holy? Strive to be holy as I am holy. Strive to act like Me in your stress. I died on the cross in perfect peace. You can have peace always if you stay fixed on Me and trusting in Me.

Every hard occasion is indeed a blessing to learn how I would act. If you do that which is so hard, it is divine. If you do that which you tend to do, but it makes you ashamed, that is human. Run and do not get weary. Fly on eagles' wings. Trust at every moment in the hardest battle when you are tired and under pressure. That is when you get the most grace. I know what the world would do. Do not be like this world, be like Me. Do that which is the hardest. That is whence the most grace and learning come.

How can I teach you My ways? I teach in trials. These are lessons you need to learn. Like taking a test, you can pass or fail. See that you do as I would do and it is passing the hardest test. It is the school of being most like Christ. Will you get a good grade on your test or will you go the easy way, the worldly way, crumble under duress and then crawl on your knees to Me, bowed down and asking for My forgiveness.

The way to Me is a hard way, but the rewards are great. All roads that lead to Me are paved with happiness, joy and peace. Other roads lead to misery and destruction. The way to Me is hard. It is turning the other cheek, it is smiling to those who are unloving and mean. It is being as I am, ready to do the holy thing at any time. What test have you been given today and how is your grade? Have you learned a valuable teaching from Me or are you upset with yourself for giving up a golden opportunity to be saintly? The world tells you to do to your brother before he does to you. Oh children, this is not My way. I stood and was silent when they persecuted Me. Oh little babies, the way of the world leads to hate, unrest, destruction. My ways are golden. They lead to peace, love and unity. I love you all so. Come to Me and I will give you My ways. My ways are hard, but the rewards are golden!

I love you.   10/10/93

Be With Me

Jesus: You are My child and I love you. I am with you in all you do. Trust in Me and feel My presence in you. Come to Me and be with Me. Relax, let go. I want to fill you. Be still, just you and Me, present together. There is no life without Me. I breathe life into your soul and you are filled to the brim. I make your life flowing with milk and honey. I am the God of this universe. I wait to share time with you. This is where it all is. Relax, this is your golden hour. Don't spend it thinking you should be anywhere else. You are with Me, alone here, and I am God. Think how you would be if a king were here. Well, there is not a king that comes close to Me. Treat Me with royalty, reverence. I am God and I am truly present in the tabernacle. I am your Savior, your lover, your best friend. This hour fills all the moments of the rest of your day. Do not waste one moment in enjoying all of its fruits. Soak in your time with Me. You are a battery ready to be charged. I charge you and you operate on this charge all day. Each moment must be focused on Me or you are unplugging yourself from My power and your time is useless. Focus on Me. Think hard. See Me and My face. Feel Me within your heart. I am your God and I love you so. Choose life that you might live. I give you My life. The life of your soul is in Me and I am ready to give it to you. My child, be with Me. Quit writing. I long to be with you. You are so dear to Me. I love You. Jesus.

10/11/93

The Good Shepherd

Jesus: Come to Me, My little lamb. You are so dear to Me. I make this day for you to enjoy My air, hear the birds, see the glory in the autumn day with all its beautiful color. You are so favored. If I make this for you on earth to enjoy, how much more I will give you in heaven. I am the God of this universe. I am in everything I have created. I have given you all the little worms and all the leaves. I have given you all that you see that is in nature. I am such a good God and I love you so much. Trust in Me and know I never leave your side and I am present in all you do. But you must come and be filled by Me. I appreciate your sacrifices. The very hairs of your head are numbered. I make the crooked ways straight and I bless you in all your trials. Every day I sit and am attentive to all your cares, like the greatest lover. I watch by your side and I never slumber or sleep. I am there, watching you and guarding you and I tell you all the little promptings in your head. How would I know if I am not right with you always, guarding you from the trouble ahead? How many times I push a truck from your path. By all rights, you should be dead, but who knows how you and the truck did not crash in the same space. I do. I made you come out of it unharmed. I guarded you.

I wait for you. I long for you. I am He Who never leaves you and never takes a vacation. I tell you all you need to know in your head. I am not talking to some and not to others. I am talking to all in the silence of their hearts. I do not love some of My children better than others. I love you all so much. I wait and wait for each child to come and when they stay away and hurt, I am most hurt. I am the giver of all good gifts, yet you go to empty wells for that which you need and never find except in Me. I am the Good Shepherd. I know Mine and Mine know Me and I make Myself attentive to all My sheep. Some wander and insist on staying away. I try to get them to come home but they must graze other lands. Their hearts ache and they wander in darkness, never feeling satisfied, always searching, always unsettled, but never finding that which is right before them.

Oh children, I love you. You are lost and I seek you so diligently and you stay far from Me. You do not even speak My name. I am the Good Shepherd. You are little lost lambs. I want to hold you and caress you and take you to your home. I want you not to worry but to follow Me and you do your own things and are miserable inside. Come that you might have the life I give, life eternal, a life that is not even able to be understood by you, but is so much more than the most beautiful day. I watch. I wait. I never leave your side. You are little fearful lambs. What do you have to fear? Join My flock, feel My love, know My face and all I have to give you.

You wander in a valley of darkness, ready to fall or bump your head or be really dumb, but you take the lumps and proceed on your willful little ways.

All works out in My plan. I am the Good Shepherd. I love My sheep. I watch out for them. I tend My flock. I sit patiently by you and I prompt you on what you must do but you do not listen. You do your own will. You create your own problems. You do not sit quietly with Me. Please come. I am waiting. Be converted to My ways and you are fed. I am the Good Shepherd. Come, little scared sheep. Come to Me and be saved.

10/15/93 1:45 p.m.

My Child, Don't Listen to Satan

Jesus: You are with Me, child. Lighten up and feel My presence. I am your true Savior. I am with you in the silence. You are doing as you should. Breathe in Me and out fear. No matter what happens, you have Me as your savior and lover. All else is insignificant! Trust in Me, My little scared baby. Release all fear. Satan is the king of fear, doubt, hate, division and worry. I am the master of love and union and strength. All things work in Me. Focus on Me and My entire divine presence here. You are finally with Me, little one, all alone. What a golden opportunity and Satan is trying to create problems in your mind to keep us apart. Let go of all his prompting. Be with Me. I love you so. Your problems are nothing. I am here. I will protect you from his lies. Be with Me, little one. I love you so. Put all doubt and worry aside. I am your God and I love you so.

10/16/93

I Am He Who Walks by Your Side

Jesus: The way to Me is the way of the cross. Stay fixed on Me. Pray. Sacrifice and be with Me. This is the way and the only way. The world tells you to go and find gratification here. I say nothing on the face of this earth gives you any gratification. Gratification comes from Me and the children I have created and My light operating out of them. To seek senseless gratification in things leads to momentary pleasure which is useless. You must find all things in their relationship to Me. To seek pleasure anywhere on the face of this earth separate from Me is to seek sin. I am God. My light and goodness shines in My children. Come be with Me. Come and share My love in each other. Come and know My ways are not rooted in this world. My ways are found only in Me. My ways are found in others who spend time with Me and fill themselves up with Me and reflect My presence and love in their being. Nothing else is of any account. Come and worship and be with Me. I am so good. I give you all you need. Let fear and anxiety go. It is so useless. Man cannot harm you. Your root is strong in Me. They may bruise your leaves or even bite at your branches, but you snap back because your roots are thick and prosperous when they are rooted in Me. No man has the least power over you when you are rooted in Me because no man has any power over Me. Satan gets his power from people who let him use them, but it is a false power. No one can get at the heart of you, your very essence, because I am all powerful. Smile, My child, you aren't tired. You are charged and ready for the slaughter. Slaughter you, this world does, but be of no avail to that which goes on around you. I am He Who makes you strong. I am He Who feeds you. I am He Who protects you. I am He Who walks by your side and, though the earth be shaken and the stars and sun cease to shine, I am still steadfastly by your side giving you the strength you need in this troubled world. I love you with such intensity. Focus on My love, not your fear. That is Satan. My love is power. It is there for you. Nothing can touch you now or ever. Little one, don't doubt. You let Satan in to prompt you. Cast him out. Let his teeth gnash. You needn't ever listen to his sick truths! He aims to stop you. You focus on My love. Your roots are steadfast in Me, but you must come to Me and be charged or he gets to you. You need a full battery. In this world, only the tabernacle provides this for you. I am your God and I love you, little one. Hold tight to this.

10/16/93

Do My Work

Jesus: I come and you open the doors of your heart. I enter and you are made whole. Your hungry soul thirsts for only that which I can give. Open the gates. Let Me enter and wash you with My Blood. My Blood is the Blood of salvation. Nothing in this world can compare to My Blood. It is there for you, it cleans you, it feeds you. It is your all. Come and be nourished by Me. I have all you need.

Your time is not your time. I loan it to you. I loan you your time to do My work. This is your day, but it is My day to work in you. You are doing as you ought. You feel tired and worn out and you wonder why. My work is work. It is not a puffy little job. It is a big job. It is the most important thing you do. You keep doing My work and then wonder why you are exhausted. My work is hard. It is struggling up a hill in a world that has lost its way. People are closed. The world is pulling you everyplace but to Me and then you wonder why the exhaustion. You pray many hours a day and talk many more trying to sell My wares. It is hard work. People reject you. They are closed. They are not of Me. They are all busy with their stupid earthly lives. I sit and watch and they are so blind. What good does it do a man to run down a road if it is the wrong one. Hold tight, My little flower. You are doing My work and it is tedious. It is hard work. It is the best work to do. Do not wear yourself out talking on the phone. Plant My seeds and be on your way. Others must do their own seeking of Me. You only lead them to the water. You do not have to stand around and see if they will drink or not and prompt them to do so. They must read My messages and come to Me for their feeding.

You do not feed your brothers all their food. You plant the seeds. They come to Me and they are fed by Me. Hold tight to all you are doing. It is hard, hard work. I am giving you strength. Each day is a day's work, indeed. No one but I knows how much work you do in a day. You have touched a lot of hearts in one day. Be glad as each day unfolds. Be glad I am using you as My instrument to reach many. Know that this is work. You should be tired at the end of the day. I am your God and I love you, My little one. I play the organ at Mass with you. I love the music. I love people to sing. It is of great comfort to Me and My mother for all the singing. Keep singing and playing. It is so soothing to our hurt hearts. I love to hear My children sing. I love you all so much!

Keep spreading My word and doing My work. You feel tired because it is indeed work, but I will supply you with extra energy and blessings for all you do. I need you to do this work for Me. You always bounce back and go full steam ahead. That is Me! All of a sudden you are refreshed and wonder what happened. The spirit is willing but the flesh is weak, but I have all the power. The very hairs of your head are numbered. I give you strength when you are doing My work. Oh, how I love you. I am pleased with your work. Your weariness is worth it. I will give you a bath in My love and you will go and feel like flying. I am your love, little, one. Thank you.   10/17/93

Come and Let Me Fill You

Jesus: My little ones, peace, love and joy. All this is from Me. You need to hold on to My hand and feel My presence with you. I am the way, I am the truth, I am the light. I come to you in a bed of peace.

Your light is growing dim. You need to be charged by Me. Come and be with Me, My little flower. Come and sit with Me alone. Put your trust totally in Me. Don't listen to others. I give you all you need. I am your God. You are My chosen daughter. Come and be filled by Me. I am Jesus, your love. I never leave you, even though you feel so empty. Come and let Me fill you. I am Jesus, Son of the Living God. All who are weary, come and I give you rest.

Messenger: Hosanna in the Highest.   10/18/93 Early Morning

Bring Your Children To Me

Jesus: You were blind but now you see, My child. Your doubt, your fear, is all coming from him who wants desperately to stop you. This is your cross. Trust in Me. I will make the crooked ways straight. Enemies speak to each other and I have cleaned the tattered heart. I have sent Satan on his way and you will know a peace within your soul. Continue as you are doing. It is My word you are spreading. I want this word to circulate. Take the pressure from your brow. Let loose of all anxieties. Satan is pressing down, but he has been cast into hell. Feel a release of all that pressure.

You, My child, are receiving these messages from Me. I have told you so many times you must listen to every word I speak to you. These are words of divine wisdom. You do not have such insights. Please trust in Me. I am truly by your side. I want time alone with you every day, a total giving of yourself to Me. I am the God of Jacob and Joseph and your fathers and I talk to you now. These messages are for you and I am delivering them to you. I will give you a confirmation of My word. You are so doubting. Where is your faith, My daughter? Do you think you could write this? This message must be given to all. All must know what transpires on these pages. Do all you can to duplicate these letters. I want My words to get out. You are My messenger to reach many. Have nothing more to do with your teaching. Spread only My word. Don't waste time in idle talk. You must do as you are told. Quit all your socializing. You won't save the world except through Me. I use you to reach many—not one, not two. You are going about it in the wrong way. Publicize these letters. Speak in a crowd. I give you the wisdom to speak. My time is very short. You musn't tarry around making small talk to one or two. I will tell you that which I want you to do.

I need you to do this work. One hour a day in adoration in front of the tabernacle. No excuses! Bring your children to Me. Pray with them. Read them every message. These messages are for all children, not a few. They must circulate. Obey Me and do your work. Always write each day and spend an hour with Me. Mass, Communion, your children! Strive to be holy as your heavenly Father is holy. Always do as I would do. My work is hard. It is tough work—acting as I would is the hardest thing to do—but frees you up instantly. My ways make for peace and your happiness. Strive to be holy. Never underestimate how you should act. Forgive, love, be there for your children, pray to Me, be of Me! I want My messages to get out. Don't tarry any more.

I am jealous. I want your time every day. You must be with Me. My little one, I will give you your sign. You are a doubting Thomas. You are doing as I wish and you lack trust and faith. Trust is placing yourself entirely in My hands. You are totally selfless. I am totally in charge. You work for Me 24 hours a day. You sleep because I will you to take care of yourself. You remain at peace so you witness My love within you. You must realize nothing is up to you anymore. Why fret? You are not in charge. I am doing all I will with you. You make yourself selfless. I am your God and I love you, My child. I know the workings of your heart. Your heart is ready for My work. Your heart is full of the spirit. My life is within your soul and you work for Me.

Little one, you are My servant. You do as I wish and you never fret or get anxious again. Come to Me every day. Be made selfless in My love. Rest yourself in My care. Be My baby and I am in charge of you. Turn yourself over. Surrender to the God Who loves you. You are Mine, says the Lord. I use you to do My work. You will comply because you have begged to do My will. This is My will for you. I love you so. I am the tenderest of hearts. I know Mine and Mine know Me and we walk hand in hand in this valley of tears and we embrace on this earth. You are My body. You will reach many for Me. You are My mouth, My smile, My hands to touch. You are My messenger and I need you to do your part. All My children have a very important part to play. They need you to spread the messages. I am strengthening you for what lies ahead. A sign you will receive and you will know what I say here is truly from Me, My child. There will be no doubts any longer.

Messenger: "And He came and He filled my weary soul with His voice and I heard as one crying in the desert that His ways were our truth." Why do we fumble around when His words are so clear? They are readily available through the messengers He sends and all can be opened up in their hearts by His words. Spread His light in the dark corners. Don't let Satan give you doubt and distraction. Hold tight to His hand, always there, always strong and sure for us. We asked one another for our answers when His were right before our eyes.

Oh, in our blindness we wallowed around in our darkness and we did-n't see that which was right in front of our eyes. Pray to the Holy Spirit for His gifts. He fills us with such great gifts of wisdom. Which of our brothers has this to give us? None! Oh, you little dumb ones, go to God.

He answers your pleas. He makes His will known. He is alive in the hearts of His children, as one crying in the desert. Make ready the way of the Lord!

Jesus: Prepare ye a place in your troubled hearts for the one true God, always constant and never changing, always vigilant and alive before your little blind eyes! Remove the blinders, pray for wisdom and under-standing. Pray to know those things which are given only to the wise. You are wise in the Spirit. You are wise in all matters of Jesus and the Father. You are wise in your life hereafter, but it was not your wisdom. It was the wisdom of God planted in your hearts!

Read My messages. Pray. Mass Communion and Adoration! Love Me. Love one another. Follow the commandments and I will give you the reward of My heavenly Father. The kingdom of heaven will be yours and you will have everlasting happiness, not of this world, but of the world to come.

Messenger: Alleluia! Praise to the one, true God. Alleluia!

10/18/93 8:20 a.m.

I Know the Workings of Your Heart

Jesus: I come. I am He Who writes to you. You question, you ask and you want proof. Will you believe then? You must trust in My words here. They are truth. You awoke with a letter, perfectly said in your mind. Now it is gone. It is gone forever, child. You hear My voice. You see My face, you believe. I am talking to you. Do you hear My voice? Does this make it better? Child, child, I am upset with your questions. Who do you think gives you this wisdom? Now you hear My voice. Are you satisfied? You write too slowly when I speak. You will hear Me in your head from now on, but you must write faster.

I am Jesus, Son of the Living God. You see and you believe. I am with you all day. I am ready to deliver these messages. You must sit and be with Me. I am He Who wants to use you. You are afraid. Don't be. It only comes from love of Me. You only want to do My will. I know the workings of your heart before you do. You are tender and young at heart. I am He Who sits and waits by your side. You could write a whole message, you can speak it as I speak to you—no erasers, no mistakes. You can't write like this. You must contemplate and put your sentences together. Try to write about some story. You can't do it. Child, child, you are so lacking in faith. If I moved My lips and appeared to you, would you believe?

My ways are hard. I am indeed talking to you. You must have faith. Showing Myself is the easy way and then you know, but did I really show Myself? My way for you is to write My letters.

Come unto Me, all who labor and are heavily burdened, and I give you rest. I give joy to the troubled soul, peace to your belabored heart. Come and be filled with Me. My presence is upon you. I love you intently. Rest, little one. I will show you your sign. You will not doubt Me again. I love you.   10/19/93

Circulate These Messages

Jesus: Child, I have longed for and waited for you here. Totally focus on Me and My light beaming into your soul. Put aside Satan and all his prompting to not publish these letters. It is indeed he who drums up doubt. He doesn't want you to know he is there creating all that in your head. Doubt, doubt, doubt!

Do you hear My voice, child? I am talking to you in an audible voice. I want you to write all I tell you, little one. I am truly here in this tabernacle, body and soul. I am with you, little love. Do not get upset and bowed down. You know I have been talking to you for two years. Read your letters. One letter tells you that you couldn't write it. Satan does not want you to spread these messages. I do. Put him in his place. By the Body and Blood of Christ, I cast out Satan and all his evilness and I command him to leave in Jesus' name. Go and begone!

I am your true Jesus, the Savior of this world. I am ever by your side and I am loving you in all your doubts and trials. I never leave you, little one, even for a split second. I love you, in your doubt. Pray for faith and trust in Me. These are two virtues you should ask God to give you. Beg for them. They are gifts. You strengthen your trust in God when you practice trust in the face of adversity. I am your Savior. I am He Who saves you. I protect you from Satan's lies and he has no power over Me or you if you focus on Me and My divine wisdom. I am the God of Jacob and Joseph and all your Fathers and you are never alone. I watch you as I did them and they for all their lives were taken care of, even if they never knew it. You are taken care of, little one, and I want you to know it.

As a child of God, you are cared for by your birth father and birth mother and loved with the greatest love. You are Our child, too, precious, beautiful, full of God's love and you are truly favored. Know your specialness and your dignity. Know your uniqueness. Feel warm and secure in My love and then you will run and not get weary. You will shine like the brightest stars in the darkest night. Your lights are bright lights in the night, but you must be feeling good inside to do this. Satan wants you bowed down. You can't shine when you are bowed down. Shine as a beacon light in the darkest night. Let all who see you praise Him Who is your Father. You are a reflection of Our love for you if you keep yourself holy. Strive to be holy as your heavenly Father. In all things, do that which is the saintly thing. I love you so much, little one. Come and rest in Me.

You are being called by Me to be here. Don't doubt—that is Satan, I tell you. He wants to stop your letters. You are taking messages from Me for your brothers. Listen and write what I tell you. You must get them out, I tell you. You tarry too much. I want My flock to return to Me. Your messages are of My love and My waiting for them. They need to know this. The harvest is ripe. Their hearts are longing for these words that I give to you. You must do your part now. Have no fear. I make you selfless. You are serving Me. You are not doing it for yourself! This is for My honor and glory and for love of your brothers. I don't want any doubts. Do My will, child. Circulate these messages. I am a jealous God and I want My children to return to Me. I have so much to give them. They will be attentive to these letters but you must circulate them now, child. Do not tarry. Do not doubt. That is from the evil one. He wants to stop My letters from reaching My children. I love you and I know I can count on you to do My will. You said you would do My will. This is My will for you. The harvest is ripe. You have the seeds. I provide water and sunlight. They will drink if they are thirsty. They will feed if they turn their hearts to Me. You provide the seeds. I provide everything they need. Many will answer My call through you if you circulate these messages. Come and do My work now! Don't be afraid. Don't even think. This is not trust in Me or faith in Me when you worry and look for proof. My proof is found in reading these messages. You do not have such wisdom. Child, I am God and these messages were written by Me. That is why they are so simple. I love you all so much. Be selfless and obedient. Don't look for proof and answers. I will provide you with all you need to do My work. You must be free in heart. This only comes from total trust in Me. The time is right and the harvest is ready. Go and do your work. Be obedient. I need you to do My work. You are My hands. You are My sower. You are My instrument. You are only as I am in you. Be selfless and unattached to any glory or persecution. You must do My work and remain selfless but steadfast in My love. I beckon you to follow My commands. My love is there. My truth is there. You needn't worry. The harvest is ripe and you are the sower. Do My work, My child. I go in you to reach My children. I love you

Do not get anxious. Get closer to Me. Pray constantly. You must remain in Me in total trust to do this work. I have primed the pump with many letters of trust and faith to you. I have sent you letters about fear. You were prepared for this, My child. Remain only in Me. Every day at least one hour in front of the tabernacle. Don't think. Your proof is in the truth in these letters. Go now and do as I command you to do. I am your strength. I am your power. I am your might. I am all you need.

10/19/93

Come to the Source of Love

Jesus: You, My child, are doing as you ought. You think you have to do it all. Let it happen. I do it for you. It is My grace in your heart that makes your relationship with Me grow. You don't have to do it. I tell you what to do. I talk to you. I tell you about Me. You crave to know more about Me because you love Me. I will feed you. You don't have to do the feeding. I will reveal such things you could never find in a million years, a million books. I can tell you in an instant. You are not in charge. I am telling you all you need to know. Don't get bowed down, trust in Me totally.

Messenger: My dear Jesus, please write to me if You so desire. I am an empty vessel waiting to be filled by You and the Holy Spirit. I am Your child. You are my Father. Dear Father, please instruct me in Your will. I wait as a child for my direction. I wait on You, Father, Son and Holy Spirit. Come and do with me at this moment as You will. I am Yours, totally Yours. Use me as You wish. I give my life to You.

Jesus: You are the child of My Father. The Holy Spirit guides you in all your letters. God fills you. Write, child, as you are told. We are one in God. We are here to help you. Put yourself in My presence and be saved by Me, your beautiful Savior. I am the God of this universe. You are My precious child. I come to you that you might have life. Live in Me and be present to the Father. I am Jesus, Son of the Living God. I wait for you and I want you here with Me. Don't ever wonder about this letter. Just write as I dictate. I will be here for you until the end of the earth. I am Jesus of Nazareth. I am He Who was born of Mary that you might have life eternal.

I came to be here for you, you alone. I came for each of you individually. I am a personal God. You must see Me as present to you alone, as being your beautiful lover, Savior, and being there just for you. My heart aches at the indifference of My children. I love My children as you do and I am offended by them, by their lack of interest in God. They have no place for Me in their lives. I hurt so badly because I am a good God and I have so much to give them. I have all they need, but they ignore Me and act as if I don't even exist. This wounds My Sacred Heart. I cry by day and by night, just as you feel such pain when your children have forgotten you. They look at Me as a person who is not there for them when I am ever there. You know what I mean if you have experienced pain with your own loved ones. These are My loved ones, beloved children of My Father, and they are totally indifferent to God. What agony to be waiting for someone and they never come when you have done so much for them. I ache at their indifference and preoccupation. Come little babies, come home to where your heart longs to be. Come to Me. Let Me fill you and lick your wounds. Let Me minister to you. This world is hard and full of hate in people's hearts. I am gentle and kind and ready to love at any second. The world does not feed the soul. I cannot make My willful children come to Me. I give them a free will. I honor their freedom. Love does not demand its way. It yields to the other. I give to you. You choose Me or reject Me, My little babies. If you reject Me, you are rejecting the life for your soul. I am indeed saddened by all this. I am so sorrowful for their actions.

I am the author of love and I have all you need to know. Come to Me and I will teach you the greatest lesson—how to love! Do you want to be happy in your hearts? Then you must love God and love each other. I can teach you all you need to know, but you must come to be taught. Love is the key to Me, to each other, to eternal life. Love is the key to life. You have the potential to love as I instruct you. Will you use this key to unlock the hardened hearts or will you continue in your blind ways. Nothing will give you peace in your heart like love. Love frees you from others' hatred. Love gives you all you need. I am He Who teaches love. All love comes from Me first. Any love that is being transmitted on this earth had its origin in Me. Why go to others to find love? Come to the source. I am the source. You get love directly. It is true, it is powerful, it is from the author of love and it is yours for the asking. Come to Me and I will fill you with My love that you might love each other as I do. I love you. Will you come?   10/20/93

I Am A Personal God

Jesus: I am Jesus, Son of the Living God. Talk to Me the same everywhere. I am there, wherever you are. I am your closest friend. I am by your side. Turn to Me all day, every minute. Talk to Me when you are alone at home. Realize I am present to talk to you just as in church. I go with you everywhere you go and I am by your side. I want you to be present to Me, to talk to Me, to feel Me as physically with you. You never go alone. You carry Me in your heart. You are My temple. I dwell within you. Profess your love to Me, the Father and the Holy Spirit. Profess your love to Us often. Talk to Us. Ask for guidance. Pray to Mary, your Mother. She is always ready to help you if you pray to her. You need these helps in this world. Don't ever feel alone or frightened. You have a team with you, a team who have all the power. You can't lose ever if you call on the Power. You can have peace and joy in your heart at all times when you realize you are never alone. You have a team to help you who love you! Feel like a well loved child who is surrounded by caring adults. They do not worry. They are in heaven. They just operate and never fear or worry for their needs. You are cared for and surrounded by God the Father, God the Son, God the Holy Spirit and the Blessed Mother. You do not worry or fear. We are with you all day. You are surrounded by a sea of love!

10/21/93

Be A Baby

Jesus: Wait on the Lord and He will grant your heart's request. For I was hungry and you gave Me to eat. I was naked and you clothed Me. For I am the God of all nations, the Father of all justice. I make the winding roads open and My ways are straight and clear. Have no fear, My child, for I go before you to open the way. Your anxiety is useless. You worry and fret when I never leave your side. Oh, little one, how, indeed, I love you!

Do not let your mind wander and focus on other things. I am God and I am talking to you. Little one, little one, you are not a baby. Babies do not worry. They do not let themselves get so full of fear. Babies just have fun. They know all they need and they simply ask for it. You are so afraid to ask for what you need. You are so afraid to let go. You are just afraid, child. Do you not listen to Me? You don't do anything anyway. You are fooling yourself. I am working when you don't even know it. I have a plan. I want it carried out. You are part of My plan. Your surrender is all you need to do. Making it work out is not your business. Surrender to the God Who loves you intently. I will use you. Don't get anxious about anything. I am going to make all things work for My glory.

The victory is already won. You will be okay. Surrender to Me, My little baby. Be as an infant at the breast. They wait and they are fed. They wait and they are changed. They wait and they are taken care of. I, My child, will take care of you. I need you to do My work. I want your total submission. That is your job—to surrender to Me. Take the weights off your shoulders. Go about your day in service of Me. I love you so, little one. I will take care of you. You are My baby. You I love. You will be provided for. I am your Savior. Harken to My commands, to surrender. That is your job. Pray and let go. Watch miracles grow in your life. My miracles unfold about you. "And they called and they were filled. Every minute was His to give. They only waited for His direction and life was no longer drudgery but a song—a song to sing in praise of Him Who loved them so much." Alleluia, Alleluia. 10/22/93

See the Radiance in My Face

Jesus: My dear child, I come to you as the brightest light, as a light that shines in the deepest darkness. I come with fire in My eyes and My heart. It is on fire for love of you. If you knew, you would see the radiance in My face at every moment. You must keep coming and just sitting. Long times alone with Me. No distraction. Do you see the fire in My eyes. My eyes sparkle. My heart is on fire. Keep this picture in your mind. My face glows. It is like nothing you have ever seen. Energy is emitted by My presence and when you recall the image I am now planting in your mind. My face glows and energy is radiating from Me. This, child, is power. When you recall this picture you have an instant energizer. I am the God of all the nations. I am He Who built all the worlds and all the people therein. My power is this radiance. It is endless. It is only I. Nothing else on the face of this earth has this power. See Me glowing in your mind. The glowing from My eyes. See Me on fire with love of you. Feel the fullness in your breast. Feel Me in your chest.

Messenger: The more I kiss the ground, the more I am stricken at Your majesty, the more alive You become because this is Your reality. I need to focus on You with the power and light and greatness You are, to be awestruck with the very thought of You. Pictures of You do not transmit You as You are. You are power and awe and majesty. If that was truly Your picture, I couldn't hold the picture because of the power it generated.

Jesus: Be as one crying in the desert. Make ready in your hearts a place for Him. Be holy and selfless, be true to all your inner promptings tell you. Listen with an open heart and let Me lead you on a path that leads to Me. My will for you I make known when you are open and ready to listen. But you must be quiet. You must be still. You must sit and wait. I do not do things in your time. My time is My own time. It may be when you least want a charge, but this is part of My plan. I want you obedient to Me in all things. Are you willing to put yourself aside and come and wait with Me? Are you willing to put aside your will for Mine? If you listen, you will know all that you need. I am your God. I make My way clear for you. Come and sit and be with Me. Be as an open door. What comes through the door you will not know, but you never close the door. You accept all the blessings and the sufferings as little children who have to accept what their parents give them. Open your heart. I will fill you with such delights, but you must be ready for all that I give. You can't take some and not the others. I want complete surrender. My way is the only way to My heart. My heart is full of power and love. Say "yes" to all I give you. Open your heart and say, "Lord, Thy will be done."

Messenger: Doing things in God's time is like having a baby. It works out best when we wait for the time that He has planned for us. Man wants to control it. Man wants to get anxious. Man wants to do it his way. But it works out when we wait on Him and it works out for the best.

Jesus: Wait on Me, My child and I will grant your heart's request—not a request from the world but a request that is best for you in My time. My will is doing things in My time, in My way. You must wait and surrender and accept all I give you, good and bad, and know it will work out for the good of your soul in the end. I am He Who loves you, little one. I will only give you out of love. Trust in Me and have faith. That is the key to your happiness: trust and faith in Me, doing it My way, not yours, being open to all I give you. You must become selfless, child. I am your God and I know all things. I know you as you do not know yourself. Trust Me and let Me work in you and you will live your life as I want you to. I love you, little one.   10/23/93 8:00 a.m.

I Am the Divine Healer

Jesus: I am the divine dresser. I dress the fields and adorn them in a covering of frost. People go out and wonder how this just appeared, as if the cold covers your fields. But I make the grass turn white. Nothing happens in this world without My knowing it. I am this personal with you. I know more about your body than you do. I can heal a stubbed toe in an instant or I can leave it broken. Oh, child, why do you fret? Why do you not believe it is in Me you are made whole? I make the sun shine and the moon give its lights. I make the stars shine for you and you wonder what you must control next. You, child, control nothing. I am by your side constantly and I make all things work for you. Turn all your little most insignificant problems over to Me. I love you, child. I will tend to them. This is My promise and I am God. I am true. I am He Who loves you. Come and be filled by My goodness. No man can fill you as I do. I love you.   10/24/93

I Want Your Total Trust

Jesus: My dear child, when will you believe Me? You are so full of doubt and fear. You know doubt and fear comes from Satan but he sets his traps and you are the first to fall in. All I have told you about doubt and fear! They are like the enemies in a war! You must battle each and every minute of every day. Battle and win the war. I want your total trust. Turn your lives over to Me. Your worry is of no account. It changes nothing. It only keeps you bowed down and in a saddened state. I am God and I command the devils who come to you with doubt and fear to be gone!

Place your heart at My feet. Let Me spray you with a protective coat. This will ward off the evil forces that knock at your ear. Your heart must be a heart totally ready for Me. You are not disturbed by the devil's tactics. He wants you in this saddened state. Then he can get in and work on you. Spray yourself with My light, My power, My presence. You are protected and I dwell in you in a unique way. You are guarded by the angels and set ablaze by the fire of My love. It is hard to let go when he grabs at you. You must let go and let the power of My love enter in. Then you will run and not get weary. You will fly on eagles' wings and you will be doing My work—smiling, being, Christ present to all! In your eyes, they will see Me working. Your eyes must reflect My presence. This only comes from letting go of negative thoughts. It is hard to be happy when he is tormenting you. Only you can let go and give him no power. Send him on his way and he will leave as quickly as he came. He comes on out of nowhere and you are hurt. He grabs with the strongest claws and his grip is paralyzing. Do the hard thing. Recognize him and send him on his way. He will leave as quickly as he came in if you call on Jesus!

Write to Me. I want you to feel Me present and in your heart. I want you to know of My intense, intense love. Why do you worry when I am here and I am God? I am God and I love you with so much love. Focus on My love. Focus on Me. Focus on My face. Be selfless. Focus on My passion—all I suffered for love of you. Every day spend some of your hour focusing on My passion and My suffering. It makes your day's work easier. You realize how I suffered and My intense love for you. Kneel and think of My passion, sweet one. I love you.   10/26/93

How Empty the Cares of This World!

Messenger: Oh, I love You so, my precious Jesus. You are so beautiful. I worship and adore You. I love You. I honor You. You are so great. Alleluia, the holiest in the heights! Jesus, Jesus! At Your name each knee should bend and we should kiss the ground below Your tabernacle. Oh, that we should be favored to be so close to You. Our King, we worship and adore Your majesty. Bow in reverence before Him Who is our Savior, our God and our Divine Lover. Oh, Jesus, praise You, honor You. We are so favored to know You. Oh Jesus, Your name rings, the stars shine brighter, the heavens proclaim You in song and we all bow down before Your presence. Honor, glory, praise and devotion to You, our King. Bow before Him. Come before Him with the greatest reverence. All honor, all glory, all devotion be Yours, oh Lord. Teach us how we can best honor You. Sing praise. Open your hearts in song to Him Who made us. Oh Father, Blessed are You. We love You. We thank You. We, Your little children, come before our Father with honor and devotion. Oh, Holy Spirit, You Who fill us with Your love and gifts, praise and honor to You, the author of love and praise to You holy, all three in One. We are indeed favored by God.

And I came to You and You filled my weary soul. You set my feet on solid ground and I worshipped the ground before You, for You are God, the one, true, magnificent God here in our midst. You dwell among us, unworthy as we are to call You our Father, our Jesus, our Spirit. We have divine lineage because we have God as our Father.

How favored are we, His chosen children, because He handpicked each soul for His glory and love. We, in our lowliness, are compelled to love this great and glorious God, our God—our Father, His Son and the Holy Spirit—three in One! We are so favored. He cares for us. He created us in His own image and we are little less than the angels. Such honor is ours, bestowed on us by Him, our heavenly Father. Oh, Father, we do indeed love Thee so! How can we love Thee more? Open our hearts to know more of Thy ways and what, indeed, pleases You. We want to do Thy will. We want to be more like You, but we cannot even comprehend Your ways in our human minds. Mold us, fashion us into Thy ways that we might know You more and more. Oh, how great is Your name, how glorious Your works. We honor You, the one, true God, Father, Son and Holy Spirit! We love each person and we are so honored to have You as our God.

Jesus: Come unto Me, My little babies. I await you by day and night. I love you so intensely. Such praise is so pleasing to Me, such comfort for My soul. Come and honor Me. I am God and I await you with eager love. I fill your troubled soul. I nurse your tired, worn little bodies and I care for you with such love.

Oh, why do they stay away? I beckon all to come and let Me give to them all the gifts and love I have for them. But they are so foolish. Where do they go? You know they miss all they were created for—for My presence is what their souls crave.

They squander My precious time given to them that they would serve Me. Some I never see at all and it makes My heart sad for their love. I long to give to them My gifts but they do not even open their blind eyes to My being. How sick they are to be after all the cares of this world. How empty these things are. They do not matter to Me. They are like puffy air. They carry no weight. They are of no importance. They can be lost in an instant and all that remains are the things of Me.

Store up your treasures, little ones, the true treasures of gold. They are found in My house in front of My tabernacle. Are you coming or are you worrying for the things of the world? I write to you all messages that you may study and know My ways more and more. I love you, little ones.

10/27/93 8:40 a.m.

On Suffering

Jesus: You are experiencing suffering, My child, suffering that I am allowing. Accept it. Be as an open door. Take all I send you. You will have more time for Me. I do not want you busy, My child. I am the top of your life. I will send all things your way. You must stay fixed on Me. Make your life simple and joyful. Be not worn out. You are exhausted, running around like a chicken without a head. My peace is not found in business. My peace is in the whisper, in him whose voice is silent, in him who is quiet, in him who is not boastful. You must remain selfless. You do not have to promote yourself. You are of value to Me. I need you to do this work. Be calm and unattached to all that is worldly. You will let go of all that you once needed and you will need only Me. In My ways is your happiness found. Only from Me do you get peace. Release yourself from people, places and things. Be close only to Me. Your life unfolds and I am unwrapping it, little one.

Suffering. I suffered, I truly suffered for love of you! Accept your sufferings as a sharing in My passion and offer them up to Me. Accept suffering as a staircase to heaven. Each day you ascend closer and closer to Me, your divine reward.

My soul is sad even to the point of death. Come and wait with Me that you might know the love I have for you. Comfort, oh comfort! I indeed am God and I care for the pain in your soul. I suffered too. I know suffering. I know longing in My heart for souls that are dead in sin and do not come to Me. I suffer for love of thee. Come to Me that I might make you whole, that I may breathe My life into your withered soul and comfort you in your sorrow! You are My child and I watch you and feel your pain. Your pain is not in vain. It is in suffering that you share in My life! Walk My passion with Me and know Me better. The way to Me is the way of the cross. Do not put your cross down. Bear all I send to you and praise your heavenly Father Who loves you! To give up My cross is to give up Me. "Oh, but," you say, "I want to know You, Lord." To know Me is to carry My cross, not to put it down. Carry the little crosses I give you every day and you will know Me more and more for I am in your life today in that cross. Will you embrace Me or turn away? Suffer with Me whenever it comes your way. It is a gift I give to you to be closer to Me.

Oh, ye little ones, you do such foolish things and you do not know what will really light the path. You use oil or water or whatever, but nothing will light your path but My light. I give you fuel for the fire. I give you energy for your way and you go to so many stupid places. Come to Me, My babies. Make your heart an open door. Open the gates to Me and all I give you. Whatever comes in your heart from Me accept as given from

Him Who loves you. I love you so.

Now listen to My words: your longing is right for My love. You cannot comprehend My love now. Your heart longs for Me, child. That is suffering. I love for you to long for Me. I am here even when you do not feel Me. In sorrow, I am closest to you. I love you so intently. My heart is on fire for love of you. It is in suffering that I am closest. I am the light to the dark world and I come to this world in you. Will you come and let Me dwell in your soul and cast My light from you? I am the Good Shepherd. I know Mine and Mine know Me. Come little lambs, let Me hold and comfort you. I am your true love.   10/27/93 6:00 p.m.

Give My Smiles to Your Brothers

Jesus: I am here, child. Feel My presence. I am by your side. I am in your heart. I am your Savior, your lover, your all. Nothing on this earth comes before Me. I come first and all else works out. Let Me light your path and you will bless My Father in heaven. He has sent Me to you. I am His Son. I come to make it whole. Your spirit I fill, your heart I ponder. I know the ways of your heart far better than you. Come to Me. I know all you need. I give you what you need. I am Jesus, your true love. If you could even imagine a little part of My tremendous love in your earthly minds! Your minds cannot fathom Me. I am too mighty for you to comprehend. Focus on My greatness. Focus on Me as God, true God, creator of all things. Focus on My might and then think of how much I love you! This is where your dignity lies. I, in all My greatness, love you so much, My little one. That should fill your hungry soul. I wait each day to be a part of your life. God waits for you. Oh such honor I bestow on you and what? You do not come in your busy day. You have made all things so important. What is wrong with you, My children?

Come to Me and be filled by all I want to give you. You can find the time. Pray for guidance to give all the honor to Me that is My due. You just do not comprehend the picture at all. You let little problems baffle you and make you mean to others. You rob them of My smiles when you are not focusing on Me. Do you want to rob your brothers? They are in such darkness. They need your smiles and your gentleness. Only you can minister to some of My children. They do not come to be fed. You are the minister to the world. Your light is their teacher. Your heart is My heart. They need to feel the love I give to you and then you give it to them. Their salvation may depend on how you conduct yourself. Look at the responsibility of your smiles and gentleness. You are responsible to shed light to your brothers. I need you. If you do not do it, they are not fed and they go deeper into darkness. Don't give in to yourself. Stay fixed in Me and My ways. My light, My heart, My presence—all I give to you. I will work in you if you do.

If you do not come to Me, Satan will work on you to stay bowed down. Oh, little ones, listen to My voice. Be attentive to My pleading. I give you a free will. I need you. Please come and let Me fill you so you can give your brothers what is their due. I love through you or do not love through you. I place before you life or death, the blessing or the curse. Choose life that you might live. Love Me, come to Me and you will be full to do My work. Do not come to Me and you will be unable to do My work and you will fall into the ways of the world. You are My soldiers. Be soldiers of My love, little ones. I need you to love for Me. I love you so. 10/28/93

My Passion I Endured for Love of You

Jesus: If you knew how really close I am to you, you would not doubt I am right by your side. I knew what I was going to go through at My passion. I was God. It was unbelievable, but I did it for love of you! All the beating and hitting on My head, whacking from behind, spitting, kicking, such horrible blows to My innocent body I saw. I knew exactly what would happen, but I did it for love of you!

Messenger: Dear Jesus, I am so unworthy to have a friend like You. I am so unworthy of You, God, to love little me so much. Oh Jesus, how great is Thy love for us. It is unbounded. It is full to the brim. It cannot be perceived in our human minds. How You loved us to death. Beatings, mockings, scourgings, thorns pounded into Your precious head, and big gigantic nails pounded into Your feet and hands. Oh, Jesus, each wound You suffered for love of us and You knew all along how You would suffer. Yet You continued and let them do those horrible things to You out of love for us!

Now You wait, day and night, in the tabernacle, by our side, for us to come. You wait and You are ignored and not loved, but You continue for love of us. Oh, Jesus, that I might learn to love a little like You. I am so worldly. I hold on to all that is for my gratification and You wait for my call. I hold back my all from You. Teach me to do as I ought, to do Thy will and know You better, to trust, to have faith, to be as You want me to be each minute, every day, every hour. You are to be honored, oh my

Jesus. All knees must bow to the one, true God. I am doing it only for You, dear Jesus. 10/29/93 5:30 a.m.

Find A Quiet Peace

Jesus: I am the Good Shepherd. I know Mine and Mine know Me. I care for you every day. I am hyper-vigilant. I am by your side. I never leave. Picture Me, child, sitting in your pew. Feel My presence beside you, clothed in a white tunic with a chord about My waist. My shoes are sandals and you feel Me right next to you. Do not focus on anything but Me. I am the way. I am the truth. I am the life. I know all things. You feel perfectly calm and taken care of. Nothing else matters. The world is Mine to care for. You needn't worry about anything. I want to give you My strength and My gifts. I want to give you all that I have for you. Sit and let Me fill you. Your body is filled by My light. It is the light of Jesus. You radiate a warmth from this filling. You feel My power within you and you are transformed from tightness to calmness. You experience a real letting go. Let go, My child. Let Me work on your heart. Your heart I fill with a fire of love. The heat in your heart warms your entire body. Open yourself entirely up to this transformation.

Be engulfed by the fire of My love. It is deep within your breast now. Concentrate on this aliveness within you.

Oh, ye beloved of My Father, what treasures indeed He has in store for you. You have no idea of Our ways, Our giving of love. You cannot experience such things in your human form. Try to imagine this warmth, presence deep in your soul. Try to be entirely alone with Me so I can work in your heart. Focus on My presence as heat and fire radiating in your heart. It is a place you long to be, never to leave. This is how Our love is, a place you can get totally wrapped up in and never want to leave! You must be alone to focus on this and let Me work on you. You do not do My work. I bring Myself to you. I work in your heart. You remain open, totally open and fixed on Me. Let all distractions go. Go to a totally still place and practice this. You will have a feeling as you never knew.

I love you, child. Come to Me and let Me wrap you in My arms. Let Me give you My warmth. Let Me dwell deeply in your soul. It is up to you to find this place. Pray to Me for guidance on this place. It must be totally quiet and free of all distractions. I want to be with you this way, to fill you. Nothing else matters, child. Find this place for Me. I love you so. Jesus. 10/29/93 After Mass

Open Your Hearts

Jesus: My dear child, I am all there is. None of this matters. I am God and I am truly here. I am Jesus, Son of the living God. I wait to be with you and feel close to you, at your side. Your attendance here with Me is very important. Do the holy thing. Act as I would act—to love always, to love My brothers who are in darkness. You must open your heart now to My love. Let Me fill you in all the dark corners. I am important. I am He Who is God. You must worship Me and love Me as God and forget about anyone else.

Messenger: And I opened my heart and the Spirit of God filled my soul. I felt its wonderful power and fire deep within my breast. He is here, Who is truly God. How can we not praise Him with awe and reverence? We bow before His altar and we exalt His holy name, for He is God— one, true, magnificent God, without error, unbounded in love and with- out any limits. He is God, He Who suffered such brutality for love of us. We do not deserve all He has done for us. But we thank Him, we love Him and we praise Him and His name is honored above all other names, holy and great. He is the King and we are His people. We have dignity in His might and His glory for He is might and He has done great things in us. His lowly people praise Him, worship Him. He is God, holy in the heights, truly honored, truly present. Jesus made man among us and He came to us. What honor He has bestowed on us, His lowly people. Honor and Praise to You, oh Blessed Father, Blessed Son, Blessed Holy Spirit. You are our God and we are Your people forever and ever. Amen. Alleluia.

Jesus: Open your hearts to the Lord. Hold nothing back. Open wide your hearts, My children. I will fill you to the brim. You will run and never grow weary. You will fly on eagles' wings. You are My chosen chil- dren. What do you have to lose? I am a good God and I have proven My love by My death. I would not do such a thing for you and then give you a snake. I am God, the same today and always. The same as I died for you yesterday, I gave the same love to you today. Open wide to all I have for you. It is from Him Who truly loves you and cares for you with the great- est love. My love does not flicker. It does not wane. It never changes. It is constant and it is there for you. Turn to Me in your great sorrow, turn to Me in your joy, turn to Me little ones. I am He Who truly loves you with the heart of God. What, do you doubt? See Me, My babies, stream- ing with My Blood, gushing from My whole body. This is the love I give to you. Would you not do the same for Me? I wait for you. I wait for each of you to come and love Me. I am longing for your love here with Me in front of the tabernacle. I will fill you with such good things only I can give. Praise Me. Honor Me. Come to Me and let Me be there, My beautiful ones. I love you so much.

Messenger: And they came and they were filled with such delights their minds scarce could comprehend it all, but they knew only He had this power. No other could be as He is. Praise your God. We are forever thankful for Your love. Come and fill us now. Our hearts are wide open. Our souls are yearning only for You. Oh, that You care so much for us is what is baffling. We are so favored, blessed, and we cry out, Lord, Lord, make us into Your soldiers, soldiers in the army of love, warriors with hearts as our arms, hearts filled with love that You give to us, hearts on fire with Your love. Alleluia.   10/30/93

Spread These Letters

Jesus: I come now, little baby. Open up your heart. It needs to be made ready for Me. Open as the open door. Accept all that goes in from Me. I want to talk in your ear. I do the changing. You wait and pray. I am so good. I love you so much, to My death. I love you just as much today as the day I walked in My passion. I love you and I am your God. Keep focusing on My passion, My love. Never turn down an opportunity to be alone with Me. These are the golden times. I talk to you in your heart. Your wisdom and understanding is coming from the Holy Spirit. Love Him, too. Thank Him for His gifts to you. He loves you so much and gives you so much. Pray to My Father. He is your Father, too. The most loving Father. He is there for you. Mary is your mother. Pray to them, pray, pray!

Study these letters. I am pleased with your studies today. Know all I tell you child. You must know these letters as your own name. Then you know Me more. I am revealing Myself to you in these letters. I am so loving. I have so much to give. Watch your fears fade as I permeate your life in these letters. Spread them. Do not be afraid of exposing yourself. How can you speak if you do not expose yourself. Hold not back. My truth is your shield, My love your armor. You are shielded as you go into the battles of the worldly but never was anyone armed better for the fight. It is a fight of love, of truth, of changing hearts and minds to know Me and My glorious love. Trust in Me, child. I am fortifying you for your journey. My truth is your weapon in a world that has forgotten and longs for these words that I give to you. Pray for strength and courage to do My work. I want you to be selfless and ready for all I send you. Strive to rid yourself of any self-promotion. Focus on your brothers and their needs and how you can minister to them with My words. I am the Good Shepherd. I long to bring My flock back to Me, to bring them home, to hold them and care for them and give them all they need. But they must be led back. You must do this for Me. As one crying in the desert, make ready the way of the Lord.

Come to Me in the towns and villages. Tell all My words. They are their truth. They need you to minister to their hardened hearts. Make them hearts for the Lord. Let your light shine on them. It is My light that is flowing through you to their withered souls. You are My empty shell. I am the divine dresser. I dress My children through you. The harvest is ready. Go to all and tell them the good news. I am Jesus, Son of the Living God and I am this close. I am here in this world. I speak to them through you in these letters. Tell them to open wide their hearts and be filled by Me. I am truly present in the Eucharist in the tabernacle. Read these messages in My house, in front of Me. They are from Me to you, My loved ones. Listen and know all you need. I am your God and I love you.

Messenger: Alleluia, Alleluia. Give praise to the Risen Lord. Give praise to His name. Alleluia.   10/31/93

You Feel Me In Your Soul

Messenger: Dear Jesus, my heart is on fire for love of Thee. You don't know how I wait to be with You.

Jesus: My arms surround your very soul. I like you to come to Me in the night when all else is quiet. You come and I am with you, in your soul. You know My presence with you. I am Jesus, Son of the Living God. I wait by day. I wait by night. I call you from your sleep to be in those moments of quiet with you. Come and empty yourself of all of you and feel only Me. All this is you and worldly. Let go of it. I want to possess your soul. I want to operate your body. You will become more and more of Me as I dwell in your spirit. You do not act because I act in you. But you must empty yourself to allow Me to fill you with Me. I want to permeate your very soul so your insides are filled by Me. Are you willing for this surrender? Let go of your tiredness. Let go of everything that is keeping you from being empty to Me. You don't need this sleep. You need Me.

You notice how this time energizes you. It doesn't take from you.

You don't see Me with your eyes. They are human. You feel Me with your soul. You must let go of yourself. Quit focusing on your eyes. You see Me in your soul. You feel the presence in your soul. You die to your body and you engage in a spiritual union with Me in your soul. Your body must go. Let it go. Be with Me in your soul. You don't need your body to get close to Me. You need your soul to get close to Me! Let go and feel My true presence in you.

Let go of you and open to Me, glorious Me—My light, My lightness, My tingliness. Empty yourself of all that holds you back. Find a comfortable place, one where you can let go of every inch of your body and get in touch with your soul. This is a spiritual communion with Me. It only comes in absolute silence. Anything that draws you back to the world stops this communion. You need to be in total silence and listen to My whispers. They are there and I am here but you cannot experience Me with your body. You need your soul to know Me.

You can know Me in a new way. Pray for help to be entirely caught in your spirit. Let go of the parts of the body. You do not know Me through your ears and eyes. You feel Me in your heart, you hear Me in your head. You see Me in your head, you hear the knocking in your head when I reach you. I don't use your body. I may use it, but I can reach you in your soul if you open yourself entirely up to Me. I don't need your ears for you to hear Me. I need your heart and your spirit. You think you bring in information through your senses. I do not need your senses to reach your soul. I may use your senses or I may use your mind and heart to talk to you. My ways are not the ways of the world. You may see Me, but not with your eyes. The image is just as vivid. It is from Me and you see it, eyes or not, if I want to communicate with you. I do so with your mind. Maybe your ears may think they hear Me, but how come no one else hears? What about smells? You smell roses. Someone else didn't. Was it your nose or your mind? Just as you saw in your mind, you can smell or hear in your mind or soul. I do not need your body to communicate with you.

Open your heart wide. Put the world aside. I will reach you. I will make known all I want to tell you. You must surrender and be open. You must be with Me. You must make Me your top priority in your life. I am Jesus, Son of the Living God. I will give you all you need. There is nothing in your life that is not being guarded by Me. Trust in Me, My baby. I watch you, I care for you. I am working behind the scenes in your life every day.

Surrender and be selfless. Let go of your body. It gets in the way. What you are to wear, what you are to eat—who cares? Your soul is what is important! Your body is another thing in this world. All it does is help you live here and sometimes it limits you here.

Keep your soul holy. Let Me sanctify you. Do not sin. Feed your soul. Tend to its feeding all day, just as you have been feeding your body. Your soul thirsts and hungers for Me. Are you feeding it? Oh, the cares of the world! Let's adorn our bodies, make them our temples, dress ourselves up! All can be taken away in an instant! Feed the soul. Store up treasures for your heart. Open up to Me and let Me permeate you. Let Me possess your soul. Let Me live in you! Die to yourself. I am your main concern. Come to Me all who labor and are heavily burdened and I will give you rest. I will make the crooked ways straight. I will furbish the starved soul. You will run and not grow weary. You will fly on eagles' wings. None of this worldly, body stuff matters. You know what matters! Come to Me and tend to your souls. Prepare for the life hereafter. Don't adorn your bodies as your temples. Adorn your souls with the fruits that only I can give. For My life is life eternal and you, My child, will partake forever and ever if you stay fixed in Me and My word. I love you.

Man has not seen or ear has not heard what glory awaits him who serves the Lord. Alleluia, Alleluia.   11/1/93 3:00 a.m.

Don't Ever Close Your Heart

Jesus: Put yourself in My presence and come to Me not all bowed down but as you were awaiting a King. You would rise to the occasion with such an eager heart! I am God and I am truly present to you. Come with your heart full of excitement and yearning. Come to Me and know God truly waits to be with you. Empty your mind of fear and doubts and let Me do My work in you. I am the Good Shepherd. I know Mine and they follow Me. Follow Me for nothing else matters.

What you write here is not up to you. I will fill you and you will know all I say comes from Me, the one, true, magnificent God. To you be honor, My little ones, because I have created you little less than an angel. Your mother is Mary. Your Father is God. Open your hearts to My words that I might work in your heart. Your heart is My instrument to reach your brothers. I act in your heart when I love your brothers through you. Don't ever close your heart, even for a little while. Put doubt and fear aside. Trust totally in My Sacred Heart. I am He Who is with you always, always by your side, catching you when you fall, guarding you and you doubt Me. You move away and want to run to the world for your security. Run to My open arms and let Me hold you and feel My security! I have security, but not as the world could ever give it. I am security and you know it when you open up to Me. Satan will try everything to close you down, get you to doubt. You must ask for my strength. Ask Me to take the blinders off your eyes so you can see all that I want to show you.

I show you My heart, ablaze in fire, warm and kindling. I show you this heart and you feel the heat as of an open furnace. The heart is My love. Be of the heart, My children. It is there that you learn to know Me. Let your heart be as an open door to Me. It is always open and ready to whatever I send your way.

I come into your heart and I fill you with all My gifts. You were made whole. Your chest was on fire with the love of Christ and you doubted no more because such a union was unmistakable and true.

The heart of Jesus radiates power and light. It is ablaze for you every day in the Eucharist. He comes to you as a bridegroom awaiting His bride and He gives you His love. Be ready for the occasion. Anticipate the event with great eagerness. Let yourself be open and vulnerable as a new bride. Take all He gives and do not turn away. Let yourself be filled to all the gifts you receive and have His joy, which only He can give.

Oh, if you could only know a little of what I have in store for you! The trumpet sounds and all glory you shall know at the appointed hour. You will be taken into My glorious kingdom and all your pain will cease. Your mind cannot even imagine what you will experience. Trust in Me, My babies. My love is everlasting. It never runs cold. It only gets hotter as we grow in our love. Will you put all the things of this world aside and come to Me? Let go of yourself. Let go of any doubts. Choose Me as your Savior and let no talk that is not conducive of My trust into your mind. Know I am truth, your truth—one, true, magnificent God—Who loves you and never leaves your side. Don't ever doubt Me, even a little. You are My baby. Be a baby. Let Me rock you in My arms and you will know I am truly here with you! Your fears and doubts leave like a thief in the night and peace covers you as a warm blanket and you are filled by Me, your one, true, glorious Savior. I love you. Alleluia, Alleluia.

Trust in Me, My child. Your mind can run crazy. Open yourself up to Me and trust. Why do you not see that Satan wants to stop you and that he does not want the world to get these messages. Such messages of love and comfort! If he can work on you, you will stop. Don't be fooled by him. He is the grand deceiver. He plans to trip you up, to rob your sanity and move in with his sick ways. You, My child, are strong in Me. I need you to do My work. Laboring in your head, looking for proof, not totally trusting in Me—those come from him. Step on his head. Do not doubt. Pray for My strength. Open your heart to Me and My love—no room for a drop of doubt. I am truly here talking to you, little one. Think about My passion and death. I loved you. I love you this much still today. My heart is so on fire for love of you. You can't even begin to know how much love

I have for you. Just be open to all I send you and cast your doubts away. It is your act of trusting that helps you develop trust in Me. Step-by-step you ascend the stairs and you get closer each time to trusting more in Me. It is your taking each little step that counts. Ascend My steps each day, every day. A million times a day you can trust or worry. You choose, "Do I trust or not trust?" How could you not trust after all I did to prove My love for you? Focus on My passion, on My wounds, on My love, on Me, the one, true God, Who loves you this much! You are precious to Me, My little baby. Come and let Me comfort you. Lose yourself in My arms. "And they came and they were given His peace and love deep in their souls."   10/2/93 4:00 a.m.

Pray For Your Brothers

Jesus: Do not worry what you are to wear or put on. Does not your heavenly Father adorn the fields with their glory? And you are so much more valuable. Look to the things of the life hereafter. Store up treasures in your heart for the life to come. Do not worry what you are to eat or what you are to put on. I will adorn you as I do the lilies of the field. I am Jesus, Son of the one, true God. I come that you might have life, life eternal. I never leave your side and I watch and wait for you.

Come when you are weary and when you are bowed down. Come to Me in all your troubles. I am He Who made you and loves you more than any mortal can. I care for you with such love. You cannot find such care anywhere on the face of this earth.

I am the Good Shepherd. I know Mine and Mine know Me. I set before you life or death, a blessing or a curse. Choose life that you might live and I make the crooked way straight. Enemies speak to one another and I will make all work for you who stay fixed in Me.

Your life is not yours to keep anyway! I ask you to surrender to Me. The first commandment demands that you put Me first. I wish you would choose this in your life, but many never think of Me all day. They live each day and soak in all the darkness. They are miserable inside and wonder why this fate. They feed themselves on all that TV has to offer and never come to Me for one word of prayer. If they are really good they may come one hour a week and their minds wander to their own affairs the whole time they are in church.

Oh, children, pray for your brothers. Your prayers and sacrifices may save their lives. Prayers can help a troubled soul. Do not underestimate the power of prayer. Your brothers are engulfed in so much darkness. They will never see the light except through you or they may never be touched if you do not pray.

When the world is getting weary and you want to let it all go, come to Me. I know your struggles in this world. I know how you go, as it seems, unrewarded. Believe Me, you are not unrewarded. Your reward awaits you in heaven and it is adorned by the angels! Look at your sick brothers. Your prayers today may save their souls. There is so much sin. It is a way of life and it is very acceptable to sin in the open. It wounds My Precious Heart to see My children run amok. They are so willful!

Come and be humble, come and soak Me up. Come to My light. We'll go with you as the beacon to the bowed down. You must do your part daily. I can only work in you if you are open to Me. I need you. The cry for My brothers is urgent. They are so blind. They do not even have an inkling what is happening. I am He, the divine dresser. I dress the fields. I care after your souls. I care for the souls of such little ones. I care for their empty hearts. I am Jesus, Son of the Living God.

Begone Satan! You have no place here. I command you to leave! I watch after you, My child. You come and I care for you. He will not harm you because I alone am tending to you. He is ugly. He is cunning. He wants to trip you up, but I watch by day and night and guard you on your way. You are never unattended, little one. My love for you is so great. When will you realize this? You do not have to worry for I am with you always.

Pray for My dear ones. They do not know how I love them and want them to return to Me. I am your Jesus. Come and be with Me. I love you so!

My heart is ablaze for love of you. It is always that strong. It does not die and it does not flicker. It is consistent in all the love I feel. When you are weary, focus on Me and how I loved you enough to die for you. I love you this way today, child. Feel the warmth deep in your soul. Focus on My love with you, alive in your soul. Communicate with Me on this level. I am here eager to be with you. Open yourself for all I pour into you. Put aside the cares of your mind and focus only on Me, your true Lover. God made man for you, little one. I am He Who gives your heart rest and joy. I am the true Savior of this world, come to this earth to save each one of you.

Messenger: Dear Jesus, at Your name each knee must bend. You are holy. You are Great. You are Perfect. You are the Savior of the World. You make the way straight. You fill us with our needs, yet some never bow to You. They bow to all the earthly things. They make them their gods and they worship them in their hearts. Their hearts have turned to stone and they know nothing of Him Who made them and waits for them. They choose to turn their backs and walk away and wonder, yes wonder, what will fill the ache in their soul. They flounder around from place to place and, like hungry dogs, are never fed, but they do not want to turn their hardened hearts to God.

Jesus: You feel as if your efforts are useless. You have waged a war against Satan and his lies. Your battle is hard. The drudging path is all uphill, but your efforts and prayers are not in vain. I see your works and they are having great effect in hungry souls. Without you they are in total darkness. Keep our candle burning. I need you to light a fire and not worry about the results. You are to stay fixed in Me. Don't worry for the results. Your life is being spent in My service and it pleases Me greatly. Continue even though you are not seeing results. I assure you you are touching many by your life.   11/3/93 4:15 a.m.

Love the Unloving

Jesus: Today I want to talk about your enemies. To be like Me you must never have any enemies. Does that sound impossible? Every soul is a soul created by Me to love and be loved. When My children are willful and allow Satan to be in control, they become very sinful and do very many unloving things. So why love them if they are sinful?

These children need My love more than anyone. All My children need My love, but these children become engulfed in darkness. They continue to only look for their reality in the dark corners and make their world reflect only darkness. This gives them the room to continue in darkness. Darkness to them makes sense. They are surrounded by it. But you come along and you may be with them and you love them. Your light, in contrast to all their darkness, shines out. It makes their dark world have a ringer in it, so to speak. It stops and they take notice. What is this? I hate you and you love me? All I see on TV is surrounded by hate. Their hearts are hate. They look at darkness only. They see only hate and you come along and love?

They must take notice of your love in this dark world. What sets you apart, they ask themselves? They may struggle with admitting I am what makes you different, but indeed they must, if they want to really know, admit it is the God in you that makes you love when everything else in their life is hate.

So you think your kindness means so little? To a person who only sees darkness, your kindness is as a bright light in the darkest night. The darker the night, the more your little light shines.

If people are ugly, who wants to be nice to them? But, you say, why love the unloving? Because that is the way Christ would do it. It is your little light shining in the darkness that makes them have to take notice. Let your light shine. It is I Who shine from you. That is how I reach My sick children in the darkness. They will never come to Me. You may be the only touch they receive from Me. But your touch will not go unnoticed. It is powerful and carries much weight. Even when they continue to hate you, you continue to love. That is My way. Not to get upset in the ugliness of others. That is their way. That is not My way. When they hate you and persecute you for My sake, remember your reward will be great in heaven.

I am here, little one. Listen to Me. You do not and never will understand My ways, but My life I give to you as a model to live by. Study Me and know how I am. My ways I make clear to you. To love the unloving is indeed a challenge, but your love may save their souls. Be of Me in all things. Do not get attached to the ugliness of your sick brothers. You know what powers them. Do not get pulled in by their hate. It is not of me. Continue and love and pray for strength. This is My work, to love the unloving. I love you, little ones. Will you be My candle in the dark world? I give you My power and My love. It is not a big job, you say, but it is the job that preaches to those in darkness. Will you preach My love today to your unloving brothers?

To be nice to only those who already love is not hard. To be nice to those who are ugly is very hard, but the rewards may be so great for their souls. This is My true job for you, little ones. Love the unloving. They need to be touched by Me. Pray for strength and do what I ask of you and you will know a freedom as you have never before experienced. You are not reacting to their hate. You are still staying fixed in Me. Don't bow to Satan. He wants you to get mean in return. That is Satan's way. My way is the way of love. I am filled with love for you. Come and get your supplies. Spend time pondering My ways. Spend time with Me and get your strength. You need Me to go to the dark world. Without Me you get caught up in their darkness. You need your supplies. Come to Me and you will not run amok. You will run and not get weary. You will fly on eagles' wings and I will love through you. Love the unloving. That is the greatest gift you can give to your sick brothers. I love you. Come that you might do My work and minister to your sick brothers. You can't do it without My supplies. I love you. 11/4/93 5:00 a.m.

I Am The Doctor

Jesus: I am Jesus, Son of the Living God. I am with you at this very moment, ready to give My message to all. I come in honor of the lowly, the persecuted, those who do not know how precious they are to Me.

I am the Good Shepherd. I know Mine and Mine know Me. I am the living water sent down from heaven to refresh you and make you whole. Drink of this water so you may have life eternal. Look for Me in every day. I am here, little ones. You are not looking hard enough.

I come to weave a blanket, a blanket for all, to cover this scared, cold earth. I am weaving this blanket with My children that are staying close to Me. I need all of you every day to realize the urgency of My call. Your brothers are so sick and they need you. I bid you to follow Me that you may show them My ways. My ways are not the ways of this world. My ways are the ways that you find in your hearts in the silent whispers of the day. Are you coming to Me alone, to hear My whispers? I need you for My blanket. You won't be part of it if you do not come and take your part. In the silence I am speaking loud and clear to those who are coming to Me and taking the time to listen. Come and help Me cover the earth.

What good does it do a man to win the world and lose his soul? It does him no good whatsoever. The things of this world are monetary and not lasting. The things of Me are for all time, everlasting.

Take all I send you, good and bad, and do whatever I am asking you to do. I am the divine dresser. I see to the care of My fields and My fields grow and are beautiful.

I want you in My fields. I want to beautify your souls. I am waiting for you to come and be with Me. That hour I ask for is My calling you to Me. I give you good gifts during this hour and you go away with so many beautiful things. If you want your world to work, put away the things of the world and let Me tend to the care of your hearts. You only need to come, open and willing, and give yourself to Me. I do all the work and you are made beautiful, ready to do all My work for My brothers. I need you and I am calling you to come to My altar and be with Me. Make Me the center of your life. Let Me engulf you in a sea of peace and give you My love, little ones. Come and let Me hold you once again!

I want you to care for yourself because you are indeed so precious to Me. I am here to help you with your lives. Turn to Me and ask Me to show you your shortcomings. I will instruct you in all you need to know about you. Come and be entirely open and tell Me that you want to hear from Me. I want you to beg to do My will. I want you to open yourself in your little heart and let Me in to do the work you and I know you need. Surrender to Me, little babies. No matter what your cares, your solution lies in Me and how you take Me seriously. You need to spend time and you need to be so open to Me. You must learn to let Me do it My way, not yours. All your trials are gifts from Me to do My work. The teachings I give you may help all know how to get closer to Me.

I am indeed here every day in your life. It is you who miss My whispers because you do not come or do not come in silence and spend time with Me. If your life isn't working, it is because you have turned yourself into caring for your needs. I am the Doctor. I cure your sickness. I care about your getting better. I am not like other doctors. I do not have to listen to you and then guess about your case. I know exactly how to fix you. I am waiting to do it. You need only come to the real Doctor and ask for My healing cure. You would go to the doctor if you were really ill, but My sick brothers do not come to Me in their sickness. They keep doing much of the same thing which made them sick to start with and is making them sicker today. Encourage your friends with diseased souls to come to Me. I heal like no doctor ever knew possible. I know your problem more than you and I know exactly what you need to be cured. Tell them to come and sit with Me alone in church. Just as you go to the doctor, come to Me with your burdens and I will make them light. All this "stuff" is so insignificant and so unimportant. Most of your sickness is yourself. You're making yourselves doctor, turning to your own sick minds for your answers, or going to other human beings who tell you to do different things that sometimes make you sicker or things in which you stay just as sick.

Would you go to a trucker for a sick body? Why do you go to humans for a sick soul? The soul is a creation of God. It can only be cared for by Him. Go to God to care for your spirit. Go to the Holy Spirit for care of the spirit. Go to Jesus for your life. Come to The Father Who loves you. Pour out your heart's laments. Don't go to a trucker for the care of your soul! What foolishness! I wait and watch and wonder at such stupidity.

Listen, little babies, I am here night and day. You need no appointment. You come to Me and I fill you. I am giving to you when you come. I ponder your hearts and know you better than yourselves. Come in your humbleness and quit acting as if you know it all. You know little. When you hurt, you get on the phone for one or two hours and wail at your brothers who are no smarter than you.

You have a choice. You should have a place of prayer in your house, somewhere you can go and turn to Me during the day so I can give you what you need. It is so simple. You are making it all so complicated. I watch and wait. I have the cure. Come to Me. Don't go anywhere else when your heart aches and you feel doubt. Come close to Me, run to your altar, empty your cares to Me. Let Me caress your little bodies and give you My love, love only I can give! God's love! Don't go anywhere else. I would pull your phones from the walls and plug the cords into My heart. I have what you need, My scared little children. Quit this waste of time. TV and telephones. What enemies to your families and to Me! Watch your time. Write it down—how you spent it in useless ways! Give your children their due. Don't rob Me of My time. I am telling you, you will be accountable for your time and how you use it. I lent it to you to do My work. I lent it to you to serve Me. Am I the center of your life or are others gods? I want My time and I want you to minister to your families. You don't owe others your time. Anyone who calls on the phone in your home should expect you to say, "I am busy now." If they get upset then they are being very selfish. Your time is My time to be tending to those things I need you to do. Tell your friends you are busy now, and come to be with Me. Such useless time spent while people's children are ignored. Oh, you are so blind. Don't squander My time. It is valuable. You waste My time on idle talk. Every moment should be spent in service of Me. Give to Me My due and you will know in your heart how to live. You are such children. You need to listen to Me and quit acting as if you know it all. This is your downfall—your big egos. I have a plan for you. I want you to cover My earth. You must come and let Me work in your hearts.

I love you so, little ones. Come and listen to Me.

11/5/93 5:30 a.m.

You Must Want Union With Me

Jesus: I love you all. I have said so much but no one knows what is in My heart because My heart is a divine heart. I need to be the center of your lives. You need to have your own personal relationship with Me. All our love is different between us. You love Me as you do. You must come and have your relationship with Me.

I am here and I wait for you day and night. You can either come or not. Most people know in their hearts that there is more. Their hearts gnaw at them with unrest that yearns to be filled and can only be satisfied by Me. A full meal, a clean beautiful house, a good friend, a lover. All leave you with the feeling it is not enough. It isn't enough because your soul craves Me and My love. Our love is as a husband and wife. We share our love and it is personal. It is different how you love Me and someone else loves Me. I wait to know you in this special way. No one can tell you what it is like to love Jesus. You must experience My love in your heart, but it comes with much decision on your part to come and keep being with Me. Time is the answer to having this relationship with Me. The gnawing in your heart is increased and you crave this union with Me. Some never identify this craving. They still look everywhere on the earth and never find their rest in Me. You will not know Me on this earth as your heart desires. This is part of the longing to be with Me forever in heaven, to know Me more, to experience Me fully. There is no longing for God in heaven. It is satisfied. Your heart is at rest. You crave this union with Me. It is very unsettling to love someone and not be able to experience it fully. I give you very intense glimpses of My love when you come.

Come to Me and know Me more. I am waiting to give you My love. You crave Me in your soul, if you know it or not. You were created with a gnawing for Me and nothing fills you like Me. Will you come and be with Me in a special way? I want to be with you. Will you let our relationship grow and grow, as your heart truly craves, or will you continue to look in dark corners for that which will never be found there. Oh, little ones, you want to know Me. You must come and give Me your all. Let Me possess you and you will know a little of My intense love. No one can talk about what our love is like — it is beyond words, beyond your comprehension, but there is a knowing that this is different from all else that you crave and it is true.

Come to Me and let your world go. It is so hard and without feeling. I am so loving and so intense. Let Me reach into your heart and love your soul. Let Me touch you the way I want to. Open yourself and be alone with Me. Experience Me, My child. You do not know what I can give you. You must trust and keep coming this way with an open soul. Open to be filled by Me in My time and in My place. Be patient. I want to love you. You must prove to Me your love for Me. Your time and desire to be united with Me will let Me know your intentions. I do not give Myself to everyone. You must want this union very much. I must be so much a part of your life that your life is so little to you. I love you so much.

Messenger: Nobody can teach me about the ways of the soul and loving Jesus and God. Only God can reveal such things to me. If I want to be close to Him, I must be as a baby at the breast.

I must be taught and cared for and fed by Him, Who knows things of love in the soul. We all crave this union, but it is only Jesus and God Who can give us what we want. We must come and beg for this from them. This is torment, to want to be so close to Jesus but not be able. I must be totally submissive and surrendering to Him and He, in His time, will reveal Himself to me little by little, if I come and wait with Him. I am like a baby. I must wait to be fed. I must wait for this love. He is in charge of giving me what He wants to. I could not, in my nothingness, take all of Him. I would pass out. I am not ready for it all. I am as a baby.

He gives me little bites—that is all I can handle—but I crave it all in my soul. Jesus, give me little bites and teach me how to know You more and more, how to serve You and please You. I know this gnawing will never be satisfied here on earth, but it will be filled to a greater degree if I keep coming to You. You will give me glimpses of Yourself which will overpower me in my earthly form.

It is this craving of the soul that keeps coming back for more and more. Now I understand My unrest. It is for love—deep, deep love of You. I crave it so. As we let go more and more of ourselves we become more and more ready for You. To experience You is overwhelming. Your power would knock us over. It overwhelms us. We can experience You more and more in the Eucharist if we give ourselves over to You and You choose when and how much You give to us. Make me open to You and all focused only on You. My unrest is for love of You. It haunts me day and night and the stalking love I feel is for love of You. I will never get enough. It is such unrest. I cannot play music after Communion. It is distractive for me and everyone there. He wants that for quiet union with Him.   11/6/93 5:30 a.m.

My Ways Are Golden

Messenger: And He came and gave them all they needed. They were strengthened for their journey. They were made His little babies and they knew they were cared for and He gave them all that they needed to be His precious children. They were heirs to His kingdom and ready for the life hereafter.

Jesus: Little child, don't worry. Your heart is all ready to be full to the brim with fear instead of love for My being with you. If you read every message I ever gave you, would you be sure or would you still doubt?

Messenger: (I smelled roses strongly.)

Jesus: I am your Savior and I am using you to write this message. I like to come to you when you come from your sleep because you are free in your heart. I am Jesus, your true love. I am He Who died and rose on the third day. You too will rise some day. You will leave behind this valley of tears and doubt and struggle and you will be in heaven. They must follow His heart and let all things that Satan uses to tempt them aside. I am Jesus, Son of the Living God. I come to you in your need and I give you strength in this troubled world. I come to show you how to follow Me, to give you My teachings, to tell you of My precious love for all My children. I want you to know, little ones, it is hard in this world today. You are pulled about by all the lies, pulled about by all the sin and all those who indeed have forgotten Me entirely. How can your life be anything but hell if you have forgotten your Master? What a horrible pit of darkness— to be void of Me and your mother. You will never know the emptiness of a heart void of Me. Think of the loneliness to be without Me every minute of every day, to be living on the edge and telling yourself your sins are acceptable. What unrest! Your heart was made for Me. Your heart craves this union with Me. Oh, such pain to be here without Me. This is the state of many of our sick friends. Your actions may be the only teaching they ever see. You don't have to talk. Silence is golden.

It takes a disciplined tongue to be quick when someone wants to argue with you. They bait you with their insults and call you nasty things and you keep silent and are unaffected by it all. Such freedom! What makes a man strong enough to know his worth in the course of adversity? What makes you stand accused and then walk away in silence, not answering their snide remarks? It takes Me. You know you are loved and Satan is attacking you through them. You stand and focus on Me and you know your worth. I am God and I have convinced you how indeed precious you are.

When others attack you with ugly words, you are strong. You don't fight (you used to be attacked and argue back). Different, isn't it? For a little voice to go off inside and say, "No matter what they say, it isn't true." I love you and I am God! Pray for them. What strength! You don't even know the lessons you teach when you let Me work inside you. Be empty to this world when you are under fire. Fill yourself with Me and walk from your attacker if you can. Then, talk to them later with love in your heart as if nothing happened. What freedom, to be fixed to Me no matter what others do! You are holding on to Me and My strength is upon you. My power does not run out in adversity. It is enhanced and you are strengthened.

Minister to your sick brothers. Teach through your actions. A soul fixed in Me is very strong. You act as I would act when I possess your soul. Your actions are not earthly or attached to earthly matters. They are holy and attached to higher things. All is insignificant when seen through Me.

The only things that matter are Me and My kingdom. If this is your top priority, the trials of this earth lose their importance and you are not shattered. Oh, little ones, I am truly here. This is what sets you apart from your brothers. This is why you respond in love and not in hate when your brothers attack you. Such freedom, such delight! Where before you stood attacked and violated, you stand strong and full of peace. It is I Who live in you. My ways are golden. They shine to those who have forgotten.

Your ways become more of Me as you choose to let Me possess your heart. Open wide the gates to your soul. Let Me in there to do My work in you. You needn't be afraid. To My own death on a cross I loved you and love you just as much today. Know My love. Know My power. Know Me as the God Who is speaking to you in this message because I love you so much. I am here, little one. Listen to My voice. Open your heart. I knock at the door and you decide to open it or keep it closed. Open to the God Who wants to dwell in your soul and make you worthwhile. I love you, little babies, with such tenderness. I am waiting to come and free you from the cares of this world.

You must open and let Me engulf your soul. It is no longer you, but I, Who dwell in you. I radiate My power and I show the world My love through you. I can minister to your brothers through you if you open up to Me. You do not have to act. I act through you. Your decision is only to love Me and be open entirely to Me in your soul, to choose to let Me fill you and possess your soul. Life is so easy when you do. The struggle is gone. You surrender to Me and I carry your load. You will know such freedom! Die to yourself and let Me permeate your soul. The rewards are peace, love and happiness, even in adversity and suffering. To remain fixed in Jesus is the ultimate weapon in this world. Your heart does not become heavy. It may be sad to tears, but the joy to serve the Lord and serve Him in your surrender is so unlike your brothers. It gives you peace. You, indeed, are set apart when I dwell in your soul. Your actions are those of Mine. You do not think you know because I act and I use you. The more you are connected to Me, the more you act from Me and your heart may be saddened, but your peace is not tainted. My heart is brimming with fire for love of you. Let Me in, My little ones, let Me bring My fire into your souls. Let Me bring My power to your weary souls and you will run and not get weary, for your God is by your side. He is inside of you. He acts through you. He is your rear guard and "fore-guard" and operates your tender body. Yes, you become of Me the more you open yourself up. Surrender to the God Who loves you. With such love, I come to permeate your soul. Surrendering to Me gives you an easy road. Open wide your gates and let Me in. I tell you, let Me into your soul. Nothing here matters. Your life hereafter is all that matters.   11/7/93 5:30 a.m.

Do Not Fear or Judge Yourself

Messenger: Dear Jesus, You know the fear from talking to everyone that I have. I give You my will and my life. I give You my all, Jesus. I give You my surrender.

Jesus: My child, do not be afraid. I am with you and I love you. Do not keep judging yourself. Let go and let Me work in you. Do not get anxious or uptight. Just trust in Me and come to Me to be filled up. You are doing well. You need not worry. I love you and I am with you.

I am the way, the truth, the life. All else is of no account, if it is not of Me. Hold your head up high and follow My lead. You needn't do anything. All things will fall into place as I lay them before you.

I am He Who comforts you. Lay ready your heart at My feet. I cherish you and I care for you. You will not be torn apart. You will be preserved by Me. Do not fret or fume or feel any anxiety. Let go and trust in Me. I need you to do as you are doing. Just write and go to church. Let Me do all the work and preparation. It will all work if you just don't think. Just trust in Me and My Sacred Heart.

I am Jesus, Son of the Living God and I wait for you day and night. Come and lay your burden at My feet and let Me hold your tired body.

I am the Alpha and the Omega, your all. You must just not fear or judge yourself. Show love to your children. They know how much you care for them. Make them so important that you spend time with them every day. You have time for this, My little baby. Slow up and smell the roses. I am truly guarding your way.

Your heart is troubled from talking to everyone yesterday. Don't give in. Just put your trust in Me. I am here and all unfolds as I have planned. You need to spend less time with others and more time with Me and your family.

You needn't fret and fume about any of this. It will all work out in My time. Just leave things for now. I am working in My time. Type your messages and get them all ready for everything to be done. Just keep doing as you are doing. That is enough for now. Do you think I write and you have to say, "Lord, do You need some help?" I don't need any help. I want things to go as they are unfolding. In My time, in My place, they will work for the right thing. All things are under My control now. Leave things alone and trust in Me. I wouldn't do all this and then not do the right thing to get them into action. Be patient and trust. I will do all I need to get the ball rolling. Do your preparations.

You are worn out and tired. I am with you, little one. Go to bed and don't fret any more. I am your loving Jesus. I will care for you. Total trust in Him Who loves all of you. Total trust. Wait on the Lord. I do not need a push. Have John read the letters, get them all ready. Do not promote any action. I will tell you what to do. Do not worry, little one, I am with you. Trust, trust and pray. I love you.   11/8/93 5:15 a.m.

Pray For My Strength

Jesus: It is not in your strength that I beckon you to come, but in your anguish and your weakness. You I love, unconditionally. Recognize your faults and come to Me and be with Me. The cares of your heart are what I want to share. Come and let Me be with you at all times. I don't love you when you are good or feel good, then abandon you when you are in anguish. I want to know your cares and I love you always. I love you the same at all times, just as when I died for you. I love you this much always. Don't think I am not pleased with you. I know how you try. Satan puts problems in your path to trip you up. You cannot control the behavior of others. You feel bad because you have problems with your family. Satan wants to divide you. Hold tight to your little ones. Remain acting as I would have you do. Do the hard thing. It is usually My way. When you feel violated and attacked, pray for My strength. Recognize Satan at work, present at that moment, and cast him out in My name. Whenever you are having a problem with anyone, know that Satan is at work there. He wants to get you, My child, and create problems for you. He wants to make you feel unworthy of Me. He wants to distract you so you turn away and don't pray. You need to pray and cast him out.

Your children are the easiest way to get to you, especially through your little ones. Be on guard when there is a problem. There, stop and pray with that child. You need your strength to fight your battle. Place your burdens at the foot of My cross now. What is past is over and you need to pray for My direction in your life. He wants you bowed down and focused on yourself. He wants to stop your communication with Me. Give him no power. Ignore him. Ask for forgiveness from Me. Pray for your children. Come and kneel with Me. Be totally empty. Empty yourself totally. Spoon out you. Let Me fill you with Me. I am filling you with My love. You are unworthy of Me, yes, but I make you My beautiful child, working constantly in your heart. Open your heart to Me now. Lay your burden aside. Practice trust in Me. I can do all things, not just some. I am truly here and ready to be trusted. The act to do so is yours or the will to doubt and stay bowed down is yours. Your will is free. You can choose to forgive yourself, knowing Satan wants you to stay bowed down, or you can choose to stay bowed down and focused on this small distraction.

To be holy is to be loving the truth. Admit your shortcomings and come to the Doctor. I wait for you, child, I bid you to come and be close to Me. I love you in all kinds of weather, in storms and on sunny days. I wait when it is cold out or when it is warm and I love you. Do you know Me a little? To know that I am always here in your weakest hour—that is when you need Me the most. Come, little one. I want to comfort you. I love you. Put your body aside. You keep telling yourself you are tired. Let your body go. Focus on Me, only Me. You are a spirit. Your body is just there to get you around. Your soul is alive in Me. Let Me fill you with My love. I am here, little one. Let Me love you and comfort you.

11/8/93 St. Gertrude's After Mass

Your Time Is So Short

Jesus: My dear child, you must turn yourself over entirely to Me. Oh, child, I am your Savior. Do not ever doubt Me. Always count on My being present to you. The days go by with such rapidness, you will soon be with Me forever in heaven.

Everyone only sees each moment as it is occurring now. There is an end to all of this and your reward waits for you. It seems hard to think of this as ever ending, but time is so short, little one. Soon all this will be over.

Fight a good fight for Me. You need to help all you can to know of Me. Keep remembering that these days will not go on forever, that this life is so short compared to all eternity.

Some day you will truly be with Me in heaven. Your life is so short compared to eternity. Here today, gone tomorrow. All that remains is how you choose to live, for God or against God!

You are responsible for all your time and your actions and how you live in service of Me. It sounds simple but people alive on earth in sin cannot see anything else but what they are doing now. Satan blinds you into thinking this life will go on and on when, in fact, it is so short compared to eternity, just a short while. It is so easy to see. Why do you get so caught up in this life here? It is so short. The batting of an eye, the dropping of a pin, and your life is over and eternity awaits. Do these short moments mean so much to you?

Listen to Me, little one. Time is so short. My light is at hand. My time is so precious because it determines your eternal life. So short, indeed.

Heed My word and listen to My voice. What you do, how you act, are so small when compared to eternity! This is no laughing matter. It is your soul that is at stake. It is your life forever and ever. Is a few years of life, holding on to such insignificant "stuff" worth all eternity? My life for you is so simple. Love God, love one another. Put Me first and all falls into line! So simple, but so hard for so many precious little ones. I tell you, until heaven and earth pass away, not one letter of My law will pass away.

Here today, gone tomorrow, and I am your God. Come to me and all will be brought to light! He made the crooked ways straight and He nourished their souls. Listen. You do not know the glories that await him who serves the Lord. Hold tight to Me, little one. Hold tight to Me and receive a divine reward forever. May My name be exalted in heaven and on earth. The trumpet blares and the Lord ascends His throne. All know His glory. Their lives were not in vain who served Him while in their lives. Their rewards are as golden gems whose splendor no one can comprehend.

Heaven and earth may vanish like smoke, but your deeds will not be forgotten. Store up treasures in the life hereafter by doing good works. Keep your eyes on your Father in heaven, Who waits and loves you so. All will be made open in the end and your life will be spent in the hereafter. What a reward for such a short test!

Messenger: Oh, Jesus, praise to You from the heights. You are so good and loving. We trust in You and Your mercy. Alleluia. Alleluia.

11/9/93 4:45 a.m.

You Are My Temple

Jesus: I came that you might have life and have it more abundantly. I am Jesus, Son of the Living God, come to earth that you might be saved. I am the Omega. I am your all. I am He Who makes the world spin on its axis. You know Me by My power. I am this close to you, little one. I know the workings in your heart. You are so worn out. You must get to bed so you can get up and write My message. What good are you to Me all worn out?

Come unto Me, all who are weary, and find rest for your soul. You come and are made whole and I wash you in My Blood—a bath in the Blood of salvation. I dry you with My intense love and you are well cared for.

You must be attentive to all. I ask this of you. I intend to use you to do this work. You must make Me your top priority. You must get yourself to bed on time. This is having no effect on you. Staying up late does very little to help you with My work. Take care of yourself, child. I truly need you to do My work.

I watch by day and by night. I am hyper-vigilant about My care for you. You never go unattended. I wait by your side always. I am in your little heart. You are My temple. Care for yourself. You are of such value to Me. Just honest care, getting the right sleep, eating the right food, doing all you need to sustain your body. You are so precious to Me. Know how I care for you, but you do not do for yourself. Your phone is still your big enemy. It feeds your ego and takes up time. Don't talk at night. You need to go to bed to do this work for Me.

Messenger: I smelled a really strong smell of incense. Then it went away.   11/10/93

I Come First, Child

Messenger: I was at church to play the organ at a family funeral. It was a new organ for me and I had not yet practiced two songs. He told me to come to Him and forget the music. I was ashamed that I wanted to put the music before Him. He said, "When I call, you come."

Jesus: Come to Me! Stop it, I tell you. Don't run amok. I want to be alone with you and you are to come and be with Me. I love you with such intensity. Sit awhile with Me and let Me fill your soul. In this silence your heart is at unrest. You are busy in silence. What a sad heart! I am here and you are busy. I want you to put Me first, to put aside your music. This is your time with Me. "Well," you say, "Who cares? The Lord calls me now. For You, Lord, I would drop everything and come and run." That is the love I bid you to share with Me! My calling you, your responding without the slightest hesitation. Do you know now what I want? I want your love committed to Me first, last and always. When I call you, come, not in a little while, but right away and bid My call! I can make the heavens fall from the sky if I choose. Would you make Him Who has all the power wait on you when He calls? I am calling you now to life with Me. I fill your troubled soul and you see things from My perspective and not your own. I have all the power. What do you have to worry for? I can make it work or not work. I must be first. You must harken to My call and surrender everything to Me. Surrender this work to Me and let Me do it. Do you trust, child, or do you think you are in control? I want your time now. You are telling Me that I am first. Do not hold on to anything when I call. I come and you must come when I beckon you. You have brought Me much joy because you came. I love you so. I want so much to have time alone in front of the tabernacle with you. You crave this time now but you tell yourself you must be focused on something else.

I come first, child—first, last and always. Drop your cares and run to Me when I call thee. Oh little one, make My heart happy with you. Surrender totally to Me. Trust and let Me play the Mass. You needn't fret and fume. I am God and I dwell in you. You move about but I operate you when you surrender. I want this surrender. Let go of the last songs and see if I do them. Be with Me now, little one, in My house, the house of your youth. Many memories are here for you. Feel your past and come to Me and share your heart.

I love you. Oh, I love you. We are alone here. Come in Communion with Me. Let all go and be with Me!

Your Savior, Jesus, the Son of God.

Messenger: Dear Jesus, Your presence surrounds me. I am filled by Your glorious light. The earth does not know Your power. Every minute, every day is fleeting in comparison to eternity. Our hearts are Yours to possess. Possess my soul, oh, my Lord, that I may know You more and more. That it is no longer I who operate, but You Who operate in me. Unworthy as I am, honored am I that You dwell in me and use me for Your work! I am lowly but You have chosen to use me and I am raised to heights in Your service. Oh Lord, Thou art so good, so loving, so—what words exist that can explain You? To say words is fruitless. There are none to explain Your might. There is recognition and some knowing of You. All that You teach us, but in this earthly form how can we ever converse about You. Words do not exist to talk about You. Our hearts ache for love of You, but they cannot feel Your true love and Your might. But the knowing—just knowing a little—keeps us fixed on You. You are indeed the true treasure, the one magnificent, beautiful Lord, Savior, Lover! All that is worthy of You is beyond me but I must be in awe of You from that which I have experienced already.

Praise You. Exalt You. Honor You. I love You, the one, true magnificent God, at Whose name each knee must bend in reverence of Thee. Holy, holy is Thy Name. Hosanna from the highest roof tops. Amid the blare of trumpets, praise His Holy Name. Hosanna in the highest. Alleluia, Alleluia.

That is You. That is what You created—beauty and truth. Sunsets that are gleaming, oceans that are wide and unbounded, beauty in all that surrounds us in natural things. Need we ever wonder of Your majesty? It is beyond comprehension. It can only be created by Your might and power! Precious Savior, You, in all Your might, love us in all our flaws and sin. That is a miracle. That is beyond my understanding!

I praise You for being You—the You I know and the parts I cannot comprehend. Praise You, the one, true God!

And He sent angels from heaven to shower them with protection and love. They sang songs of praise to God and filled our world and we were lifted up for a moment to a new realm of life. A glimpse of the life to come and our hearts scarce could speak, for nothing can explain this One.

Praise You, praise You, Jesus, all day long, from the rising of the sun to the moonlit night. Praise to the one, true God in all His majesty and might. Praise Him for this proclamation.

Holy, Holy is His Name. Alleluia.

11/10/93 Funeral at St. Lawrence Before Mass

Knowing God Is Bittersweet

Jesus: It is not you who have chosen Me, but I Who have chosen you to do My work. Open your gates wide and let Me permeate your heart! You pant for the love only I can give. Your heart is knowing and warm in your chest. Oh, the bittersweetness of knowing Me a little, but not enough! To have such a treasure, but only a glimpse. To see the golden reward but be unable to embrace it! Oh, little child, I have so much in store for you. My ways are true. I am indeed here with you with all my love. I love you so. You scarce can speak. I can give you this someday— all you crave with an aching heart. Keep yourself close to My heart. I love you so, little one. (I smell roses, but when I use my nose they don't get stronger.)

Messenger: Dear Jesus, I scarce can speak in Your presence. You are truly here in my heart and filling my empty soul. In my sin I cried out and You heard and loved me just as I am. You love me the same when I fall and when I am walking tall. You look at me with love and You just love me. You don't measure Your love by my actions. You love me in spite of my actions and You are so forgiving of my sick ways. You look with tender eyes and see me with such love. I do not deserve all that You give me. But I am thankful for everything You give me. My life is found in my soul and You tend to its feeding. I fall and You pick me up as a child and kiss my wounds and love me just the same. Oh Jesus, that I could only love You more, to know how You want me to be and be able to follow through. Oh, Jesus, You are so beautiful. Thank You. Praise You. Love You with awe. I adore You, I adore You! Jesus, my Lord, my God, my all! How can I love Thee as I ought?

I sat here in front of the tabernacle and He filled me with His presence. The longer I sat, the more I was filled. He filled me to the brim. I thought of Him and His love and His beautiful face and I was filled in my heart with warmth. Oh, such love He gives to us! Oh, Jesus, Oh, Jesus! This is real. This is the life You give. It is Your life inside. Spoon out all of me and fill me with only You. Make me selfless and surrendering to all Your ways, surrendering to Your abounding love. Come, come, Lord Jesus, fill me. Fill me to the brim and over. Let Your love flow from me to others. Overflow in my soul to spill on those I touch, especially my children. Oh, Jesus, let me touch others for You. Use me to touch their hearts and souls. Not as I do it, but You Who possess me, You Who operate my heart and my soul. They are Yours, Lord. I surrender.

Messenger: (I was looking at the crucifix at St. Gertrude's:)

God the Father: This is My beloved Son in Whom I am well pleased. I came that You might have life, not as the world gives it, but as only I can give it. Alleluia.   11/10/93 After Mass

Happiness Is Not Something You Can Touch

Messenger: I am filled with the love of Jesus. My soul is filled and nourished by His Body and Blood. I have become less me and more Him as I surrender my body and soul to Him. I want to totally let go of myself. My soul is washed by His Blood and bathed in a bath of His love. My body is of no account. I can only feel God when I rid myself totally of my body and communicate with Him in my soul. My soul is made clean by His Blood and I put all my sins aside and focus on His presence and His love. To focus on my sins is to make me involved with myself, which I must totally rid myself of to communicate with Him. I am sorry, but then I move on, to focusing only on Him. I disassociate my soul from my body and communicate to Him only with my soul. My sins, my self, my body— all hold me back from being united with Him. I must be totally free of these things and focus only on communicating with Him with a soul free of such limits.

Oh, my Savior, come and wash me. Bathe me in Your Precious Blood. Come and free me of the things of life on earth so I may see You in my very soul.

Oh Savior, come and rescue me. Fill me with all that is of You so I can become more like You in the soul You created for me.

Oh Savior, help me in my struggle to know You more and more, to feel You in my daily life and to know that You are with me always here.

Oh Savior, make me fixed in You so that I may ever be closer and closer to You then in this holy unity.

Jesus: My child, you please Me, spending time with Me. I am here with you. The closer you come to Me, the more you embrace My light. If you stay far from Me, you are surrounded by darkness. My hand is upon you in the light. You are guided on your way to Me. Embrace My light and draw yourself near to Me, nearer every day. This relationship with Me takes time. It takes many times alone with Me to know Me. I am God and there is so much to teach you, but you must come to be taught. You must come and be alone with Me so I can tell you what you long to know.

There is a magnetic attraction to Me in your soul. Once you start to seek Me, you keep coming back because you crave what I have to give you. Why do you keep coming back, My child? You could go to the world but it does not feed the soul. You keep coming back because I fill your soul and you get something here that is nowhere else.

I am your true Savior and your lover. I fill you with such good things. I do not adorn your bodies or put meat on them. I do not give you money. I do not give you cars, and boats—all the things the world gives you. These things the world says you need to be secure. I give you peace and love and joy. I give you lightness and wisdom. I give you a smile for your troubled heart. I give you all things you cannot touch, but which you crave. Clothes, cars, house are all things you touch, but their presence lasts a moment and then you ask, "What do I get next for my happiness."

Happiness, my daughter, is not something you touch. It is not an item you can buy. It is a spiritual thing in your heart. Your joy, your peace, your love are all things of the spirit. Only I can feed you with the things of the spirit. Only I can feed you with the things of the soul. I created the soul and I make it work. To try to work the spirit with the things of the body is useless. It does no good. I made the soul, I feed the soul. To go elsewhere to feed the soul is useless.

Come to Me, My little ones. How I love you and want to feed your souls. I want to give you all your hearts crave. I want to fill you with My peace, love and joy. Only I can give these things. Go to the world and they will supply you with objects. These do not feed your soul, your spirit. Come to Me and I feed the spirit. I feed the soul. I give you the greatest love there is—the love of the one, true God.

Come unto Me, all who labor and are heavily burdened, and I will give you rest. Those things you seek in this world will all pass away. What I give will never pass away. What you carry in your soul goes on with you to eternity. Carry My gifts in your soul and you will soon be with Me in heaven.   11/11/93 St. Gertrude's After Mass

Eyes Are the Doorways to the Soul

Jesus: It is the eyes that are the doorways to the soul. If the eyes sparkle, the soul is full of life. If the eyes are hollow, they may be dead in sin. Watch your brother's eyes. Pray for him always. Every moment with another is an opportunity for prayer. A heart of love has tender eyes. Eyes go right to the heart. Looking into someone's eyes is one way I can touch their soul through you. If your heart is filled with only Me, your eyes radiate My gentleness and love, genuineness and wholeness. Look into your brother's eyes and pray when you do. Pray for his healing and his turning himself to Me. Persons in sin do not like your looking into their eyes because they are afraid you might see their sins. Look anyway. It is the doorway to the hardened hearts. Your eyes reflect Me and they see that in your eyes. I am the way, the truth and the life. Let Me possess you and live in your soul. Dwell in your soul, operate from your soul. What you deem important may not be important to Me at all. I want the work I want done. Your choir practice isn't important. I can make it all work gorgeously. Just do as I say. What is important is how your heart is, how My light is coming out of your eyes. The eyes are the windows of the soul. My soul wants to permeate you and shine from your eyes. Let Me possess you this day and operate from you, My precious child. I need you to do My work.

The dropping of a pin, and your life is over and all eternity awaits. Do these short moments mean so much to you? Listen to Me, little one. Time is so short. My light is at hand. My time is so precious because it determines your eternal life. So short, indeed. Heed My word and listen to My voice. What you do and how you act is so small compared to eternity. This is no laughing matter. It is your soul that is at stake! It is your life forever and ever. Is a few years of life, holding on to such insignificant "stuff" worth all eternity? My life for you is so simple. Love God, love one another. Put Me first and all falls into line—so simple, but so hard for so many precious little ones! I tell you, until heaven and earth pass away, not one letter of the law will pass away.

Here today, gone tomorrow, and I am God! Come to Me and all will be brought to light. He made the crooked ways straight and He nourished their souls!

Listen, you do not know the glories that await him who serves the Lord. Hold tight to Me, little one. Hold tight to Me and receive a divine reward forever. May My name be exalted in heaven and earth. The trumpet blares and the Lord ascends His throne. All know His glory and their lives were not in vain who served Him while in their lives. Their rewards are as golden gems. No one can comprehend their splendor.

Heaven and earth may vanish like smoke, but your deeds will not be forgotten. Store up treasures in the life hereafter by doing good works. Keep your eyes on your Father in heaven Who waits and loves you so. All will be made open in the end and your life will be spent in the life hereafter. What a reward for such a short test! Oh, Jesus, praise to You in the heights. You are so good and loving. We trust in You and Your mercy. Alleluia, Alleluia.   11/11/93 2:00 p.m.

Pray the Chaplet of Divine Mercy

Jesus: Praise God. Honor God. Worship God, for He is Holy. His mercy is from generation to generation on those who fear Him and pray to His most Sacred Heart. He opens wide the gates of His mercy and what flows forth is abundant graces to all His children. They are the recipients of His love. But, they must come and ask for this. He does not give for nothing. A person must turn to Him. Pray the Chaplet of Divine Mercy often. It greatly pleases Me. You do not realize the power of this prayer. Pray in honor of sick ones often during the day, at 3:00p.m. especially. Pray and be with Me in this prayer often through the day. It pleases Me greatly.

Your will is very strong. When will you realize I am God and I am a person Who waits for you at night. I wait by your bedside while you sleep. I wait because I love you so. You are not alone at night when you sleep. I am there. Mary is there. You are guarded by a heavenly presence—your angels. Those dear to you wait and watch you in your sleep. Strive to be holy in all you do. Make your life an act to please Me. Please Me by caring for yourself, little gem. You are far more precious than any stone. I need you ready for Me to beckon you at any time.

I love you, My daughter. I love you, My child. I love you any way you come.

Messenger: Song after Mass: Dwelling Place
"To be Your bread, to be Your wine..."

To be Your wine, Lord, come and change us. If He can change bread into His Body, He can change us into His Body dwelling within us. Possess me, change me, fill me, permeate me with Your dwelling within me. I am no longer me, but You Who dwell in me. I am only as You live in me. What a union! We are fixed like glue, Godly glue! It never separates. Come and dwell like this, Lord, unworthy as we are. We are open to all You give us.

Song: Prayer of St. Francis
"Make Me a channel of Your grace,
Where there is hatred, let me sow Your love..."

Song: Eagles' Wings
"And I will raise them up on Eagles' Wings..."

The Father, the Son and the Holy Spirit dwell within your heart. Jesus is totally present in the Eucharist. God dwells within our hearts. The warmth of His presence is in our hearts. He is alive in our being. He is the one, true God. Our form is changed and we are made His holy people by the miracle of the Eucharist. He dwells within our hearts. He is God-made-man in us. Such honor, indeed, I can scarcely speak, for knowing Him is knowing God. He is the Alpha and the Omega, the one true presence of God and He has honored us by His presence.

Oh, Father, to know You and the Holy Spirit as much as I can! I want to know God. I want this union with God. Through Jesus You are made known to us. Oh, Father, through Jesus we feel Your love within us. A Father Who truly loves us and cares for us, Who loved us and created us out of love!

Please instruct me in all that You will share with me. I am so thirsty for You. Oh God, one, true! I love You—all three persons. Come and let me know more of Thee!

Jesus: I am the one, true God. I am Jesus, Son of God. I come to you totally present, body and soul, in the Eucharist. You are My chosen one that I choose to come and dwell in you. I am uniquely present to you here. You cannot comprehend My True Presence in your earthly form. A glimpse of My being I impart to you. You must keep begging for this intense union with Me.

This is knowing God. To know Me is to know God, for I am God. True, loving, one God. You shout for joy at such a union and you should indeed. For My True Presence is within you now in the Eucharist. You do not even comprehend what you partake in. This is so important—every day to partake in the Risen Christ, truly present within your soul!

See why you must remain holy to receive Me? I am God and I come to you. Keep your mouth holy, your hands holy, your heart holy. Be so reverent to My coming. I am God, the one true God and I come to you. You are so blessed by this union.

Spend time with Me. No prayers, just being, My being in you and your receiving Me in this union. Surrender totally to My presence and die to yourself that I may live in you. The more you die, the more I live. Let Me live through you so I can touch your brothers. The more selfless you become, the more I am able to touch your brothers through you. Beg to be emptied of yourself. Let go of this world. Be only of Me. You will see the miracle—My dwelling in your soul and acting out of you.

I am God. God has visited His people. He chooses to operate from your sick heart. Strive to become more of Me and less and less of you. Beg God for this union, joining God to your soul. Die to yourself. Let Me live and dwell in you. I want this union with you. It is an act of your will to make Me first and last in your life! I am all. There is nothing between. I am first, I am last, and there is no middle. It is only Me dwelling in you and Me operating out of you. I want to love your brothers through you. I love every one of God's children this intently but, if they do not come, how can I reach your brothers except through you? Be open as an open door. When I walk through, you greet Me with open arms. I never leave. It is a one-way door. I am in your heart to stay. Make your heart a temple for Me to live there. Keep everything ready for God. This demands holiness in all things. It is not hard. It is I Who dwell and act in you. You will cherish this union with all your heart.

Messenger: Oh Jesus, that I may know and love You more and more. Let me walk Your passion with You. Let me fight the fight for Your truth. Possess my soul and use me to do Thy will.

Praise You Father, Son and Holy Ghost.   11/12/93

I Love You to Death, Today!

Jesus: I have come to give you life, not as the world gives, but as only I can give.

Messenger: Into Your hands, Lord, I commend my spirit. The spirit is willing, but the flesh is weak. My heart is open wide and I give to You a garden ready to sprout for love of You. I am Your child. I wait for You to come and dwell in me. I am so unworthy but I long for Your presence with me.

Oh dear Jesus, You are so warm and so good. I feel Your love in my heart. I want to get closer to You but I am unable, but only as You deem possible by giving me Yourself in different ways. To be touched by You would lay me away. I want to experience all You will give me of Yourself. I long for closeness with Your Soul. I want to rid myself of me and my body and only exist here and now in Your Soul. My soul to mingle with Your Soul, to be filled with the light only You can give, on fire with Your love!

Oh, on fire with Jesus, my true love! Please give me all You will and let me know You more and more. This is the true treasure, this time alone with You. Oh Jesus, Your love is so great in our hearts. Oh, hearts of Mary and Jesus, both. Oh, God, so good to us, how lucky we indeed are!

Jesus: I come, you are filled. I reach out to you, you grab My hand. The power you feel. Feel My power through your whole body. You have been touched by the hand of Jesus.

Is there any question in your mind of My might? Open your eyes. My life is there and I am willing to share Myself with you. My whole life I will make known if you keep coming and sitting with Me.

Oh, My passion, My child! Meditate on this every day. Think of My agony to know what would happen, to see only as God could see every detail of every event that would follow. To feel the pain before it happened and know how horrendous it would be. All the kickings, whackings, not to mention the names and slanders against God. They were doing this to God! In all My dignity and honor, I would experience such vileness and take it for love of you.

My passion is a wealth of material to study. But I will reveal such things to you. The bottom line is what I suffered for love of you. I would do this today. I love you just the same. Oh, if you only knew! It feels good to tell someone when you are wronged. I was so silent. The incredible things they did and I was silent. My mother suffered so with this. She watched her beautiful baby in such anguish. She was silent. Her agony was so great. She endured this for love of you. You are so loved, child. Why do you ever think you need to go anywhere for this little human love? It is nothing. My love is all encompassing. My mother loves you intently. Forget those who shun you. Who cares? You need My love. You don't need their love. Come, get My love and then give it to the unloving. Don't worry. It may seem too hard to do but I am pushing you and the rewards for you are unreal.

It is freeing to love the unloving. It is drudgery to hate the unloving. It is far harder in the end to hate than to love. Just forgive them. They need help. They are willful and so sick and sad inside. They are to be pitied. They have to live with their sick ways. Forget them. You have work to do. Do My work! First forgive and forget others who are sick. Let them go entirely. Be steadfast in Me and I will talk with your tongue. You do not have to minister to any sick brothers. The more you become in Me, I minister to them through you and you do not do anything but become My servant.

Open wide your gates and let Me enter. I will use you and you will not even feel their sickness directed at you. Pray to be selfless. Pray to be used. Pray to be possessed by Me. You don't even have to pray to do well in a job or in handling a situation. You don't do it. Pray to be possessed by Me. It is I, then, Who act from you. Spend time thinking about Me and My life. Don't think about others and their sick ways. Who cares? Satan can do really vile things. Focus on the remedy, not the cure. The remedy is to let Me possess your soul. I handle it all. You needn't fume or fret or become anxious. I will tell you what to eat and what clothes to put on.

You are My babies, remember? Babies don't dress themselves or fix their own meals. They wait on their mothers. Be like babies. Wait on Me for the smallest details in your life. I will clothe you. I will feed you. I will comfort you. I will direct you. I will care for you. I will act in you. You must just be open as an open door. I go in and I fill your soul. You operate as I want you to. Have oatmeal for breakfast! I love you, little one.

I am Jesus, Son of the Living God. Every detail I will tend to. You live in Me and I in you. Your cares are for Me and My ways. It is I Who act for you and I Who do all things through you. You focus on Me. My life, My passion, My ways, My heart, My love, My goodness. Don't think about anybody and what they did. Just come and be with Me and let Me possess your soul.   11/15/93 After Mass

Demand Obedience of Your Children

Jesus: You are My child, My sweet one. You try so hard to do all I ask and you think it is not enough. That is Satan. He is constantly on your heels trying to trip you up. You need to let go—more to Me and less of yourself. Don't worry about anything. You are used to doing as you want. I am teaching you My will. You will not do it all right at once. I will help you let go of self and give totally to Me. As I possess you, you will surrender to Me and know how I love thee and operate in thee. You are doing as you ought.

Tell your children about Me in love. But remember, the devil is trying you all at every turn. Keep remembering that he hates you and must use your family to get to you. You pray so much and he hates that. He hates your kissing the ground in the sanctuary. I love that. I am pleased. Keep praying for help. I will help you. You still try to rely on yourself when you are under attack. Satan moves in ready to fire. You cannot ward him off alone. He is pressing in, usually by having your children try you. Then he attacks hard and you try to withstand his attack alone. You must say, "Jesus, Jesus, I am under attack. Take the devil away. By the Precious Blood of Jesus, I command him to leave." Then know he will depart.

You try to see if you can handle his attack, usually through your children, and then get upset when you must feel like a failure. You, child, don't let him attack you! Cast him out! You know when your children are attacking you by trying to disobey and do what they are told not to do. Cast out the devil. Don't try to be patient. Realize it is the devil, not your child attacking you. He is, you know, attacking you from all sides. Cast him out. Don't try to be patient with the devil. Forget it. He keeps trying you and eventually you get angry. You should get angry right away and cast him out! Don't be tried by your children. You demand obedience. Obedience teaches them about complying to your rules. They must learn how to obey you, to obey God. Tell them to obey and stop it. Don't let yourself be tried by Satan through anyone. Recognize the attack and cast him out. You are wrapped up in the personalness of your family and forget that you have the power to send Satan away. Send him away! Believe Me, he is pressing in on you from all sides. Do you think he will let you get these letters out without a fight?

I am guarding you day and night. I am there watching you. Nothing happens in your world unless I allow it. I want these letters out. Spend your days working on getting them together. I am being patient but I am tired of waiting while you do other things. You must tend to these letters until you get them out. You will not be met with resistance! I will tend to all you need. Just keep writing and getting them typed.

Oh, sweet one, don't worry about anyone or anything. Satan is using your children to get to you. Pray when you are perplexed and think of Me and My life and My passion, not the problem! Focus on My love for you, how intently I truly love you. Read My current letters. You are not reading them enough for yourself. Turn to My letters in troubles. Pray to St. Michael. You are surrounded by an army to help you. Don't give in to Satan and his sick ways. He comes in sheep's clothing but he is covering a mighty snake that means to attack you and slip you up. Cast him away. Don't try to be patient with the devil!

I love you, sweet one. Leave all things up to Me now. Tomorrow the Mass will be Mine to reach the older people. They need your songs to be touched by Me. Totally surrender. I will do it for you. Be in touch with Me every moment. When to eat, when to sleep, what to eat, who to talk to, what to do. Take a walk or exercise every day.

You are precious to Me. Keep remembering this. When you walk in raging waters, I am there. I am truly there. Cast the devil out. You are trying to calm him and put up with him. He will never give up. He gets worse. When you told your child to obey—children are willful—be stern and send Satan away. Don't bend the rule. Keep reading the 10 Commandments to your children, and studying them. Get your children to learn them. Read to them. You must spend much time with them in your teachings. Teach them. Don't teach everyone else. They can read the letters. Your children need your talks more than your friends.

I am with you and you, child, are never alone. Fall on Me, into My arms, when being attacked. Don't go there at all. Nip it in the bud. Cast him out. Don't be patient with Satan! Make your children obey you. They need to learn obedience.

I love you. I am Jesus, Son of the Living God and I live in you! Let Me live and act from your soul. I need you!

Messenger: Dear Jesus, I am finding out how I did my will and told myself, "If it was a good thing, it was Your will." I need to care to my needs so I am not tired or hungry, but properly fed. This is Your will that I sleep. My children come after You and I have the job to feed them spiritually as well as physically. It takes just as much time to feed them each day spiritually as physically and it is more important to feed them their spiritual food.

Jesus: Children must be taught to obey. You know what is best. I am guiding you. When you bend the rules with them, it is Satan starting his attack. Get rid of him and demand obedience. You are teaching them about obeying the Will of God when they learn to obey you.

It is so simple. They need to eat right, sleep right, be fed spiritually and be loved. Do all things as you know what is right. You give in because you think you don't know. You do know what to do with them. Demand obedience.

Messenger: I love You! I love You, Jesus!   11/16/93 4:15 a.m.

Do Not Plan Your Life

Jesus: Be not attached to the glory or to the persecution. Be as one who just waits and lets the Lord do all He desires.

Messenger: I am waiting for You, Lord. Come and do as Thou wilt.

Jesus: I am the God of Jacob, the God of Joseph, the God of your Fathers. How very silly to think of them as worrying. Do you not know, child, that the very hairs of your head are numbered, that life is just a breath compared to all eternity and that all your worry is in vain! I will make all things work in the end. The worry is indeed so useless. Turn yourself over to Me, body and soul. Put yourself into My hands and know the freedom of letting go. I will put all you need in your path. You must let Me operate you and do My work in you. You do not enter into it. Be surrendering and selfless so I may dwell in your heart and take up My permanent residence there. I need you in everything I have planned for you. If you begin to think, does this make sense? By whose standards will you judge? If you use the world to measure anything Godly, it will surely fail because the world does not have room for God in anything, including Kindergarten. Those poor little ones! To be taught such a sick thing at such an early age! My beautiful children, sitting in their little seats and being instructed about sex and money, void of God!

No, you surely don't want to measure your actions by the world. Where can you go? You go to Me. I wait with open arms to hail our work. Don't go to anyone but to Me. I am always there and I never steer you the wrong way. Don't go to man for only that which I can give you. Come to Me, My children, and be made whole. Come and put all your cares at the foot of My cross. Do not even think. Just know I am Jesus. I have all the power. I love you with such intensity and I am guiding you as a ship in the night. You will not crash or run into other obstacles. You will sail the seas and My beacon light goes before you.

You are My beloved. It is I you live for. It is you I died for. We are a team. We work hard each day doing the work I have planned for you. Don't stop and feel weary. My work is energizing if you do not question and measure. Have faith. Have faith. Do My work. Trust in Me. I will never forget you and you will not be left orphaned. Nay, I say, I will protect and hover over you like a mother for her newborn baby. I will guard you in every action you take. You mustn't think or measure anything you do. You must trust totally in the God Who loves you. Put your feet on solid ground. My ground is sure and steadfast. It is directed and ready for your walk. Walk with Me. Don't look back ever. Don't measure what you are doing. Trust and pray to Me. Then go about My tasks. The more you become selfless, the more I work in you and you really do very little. How can I do the wrong thing, if I am the actor? Die to yourself. Pray and meditate on Me. Don't think of anything but Me. Never try to figure out what you are to do. I will tell you, in just enough time, all you need to know. No worry, no decisions. Let go and let Me possess you. Then it is no longer you who operate, but I Who operate in you. I do not falter. I do not run amok. My ways are the ways of truth. I do what is right and I always have a success story. Did you think I would mess up? Never. I always do the thing that works out, like putting your hand into just the right glove. It goes in perfectly, no tugging or pulling, no baggy cloth. It fits to a tee and it is done with great ease.

Surrender, little ones, and spend your days praising and praying to Me. All you should seek is knowledge of Me. All else is fruitless. I have all the wisdom you need. Pray to the Holy Spirit. He is so smart! No one knows what God knows. Why go to school unless it is to His school? He can tell you in a lick all you need to know and would never know in a million years.

Oh, you are so blind and so silly. When I am here like a doting mother and I have all the answers. And you look to what for your answers? Oh, children, turn it over, I tell you! Quit running your lives. Let Me possess you and operate your very souls. You will do all you need to do with such ease. I love you all.

I am Jesus, your God. Come and be My little ones so I can work in you. Be selfless and surrender your wills to Me. Oh, little ones, I am the way, the truth, the life. All else is fruitless and to no avail. Other ways lead to destruction. Spend time with Me and I will give you all you need. Focus on Me and My life. Do not think about the world at all. It is Mine to run and you are only My warriors. You do as I command and you are obedient. I do not explain to you why you do not even think to choose a course of action. You do as you are commanded without question or pause.

Be My warrior. Be as I command and your life will be a song. You will be blessed and in the end I will lead you into the gates of paradise.

Messenger: Alleluia, Alleluia. Praise the Lord.   11/17/93

Satan Wants To Trip You Up

Jesus: I am Jesus, Son of the Living God. You must pray to cast out Satan. Stay and let Me write to you. Satan wants to trip you up. You must pray and pray hard. Put yourself in My presence and let go. You are not a baby at all. You are uptight and mad, not as I want you to be. Let go of all your anger at everyone. What good does it do you to hold on to it? You cannot be of Me and be angry. You must make an effort to forgive all you are angry at. It doesn't do you any good to hold on to it.

I am Jesus, Son of the Living God, waiting on you and you are engulfed in a sea of darkness. This, child, is the test. As long as Satan can keep you in his snare, he has you where he wants you. I am waiting for you. You are keeping yourself caught in the trap he has woven for you. What a catch! You have the will to dismiss him and send him away or to stay fixed on him. You know that you are wearing yourself down. You are not doing what I want. Play with your children. They need your time. Others do not! Satan is causing division. Let go of your anger. It is Satan using others to trip you up.

After Mass:

Messenger: In my desperation, I called out to You, Jesus, and You came and answered me. You set my feet on solid ground and I knew only You had the might to pull me from the depths of despair. Alleluia. Praise His Name for He is holy and to be honored. I clothed myself in a white robe and took off the cloak of despair and I knew the Spirit had filled me for my darkness had lifted. Only God has this might—to pull us from the pits and lift us on our way, to spread a mantle of light over us and heal our weary souls! Oh, Jesu, Jesu, You are all love. I am Your little one caught in this world. You came and rescued my tarnished little soul. You gave me milk and honey to eat and You patted me with Your gentle hand and I felt the love I longed for. Oh, Jesu, Jesu, fill us with this love. Replace our hate and anguish with a filler of divine love. Oh, love that melts all hardened hearts, that warms the cold child, that puts a smile on the stone-jawed man, You have this might. You furnish us on our way and we are made whole in Your love. Alleluia. Praise Him.

We are weak, but You are our strength. We are bowed down, but You raise us up to such heights of glory. Oh Ye, Oh Ye, Lord, God Almighty, come into our starved souls and feed us. Feed us with Your love. Let us radiate You from our very souls, Your presence within us. And You, Lord, are truly here in our hearts.

This letter gives testimony to the Spirit that filled my dark soul, that was taunted by Satan, that looks at the sick world and feels its pain. Look only to You, God. The victory is won. The fight is over! In You we find rest. We no longer look in the darkness. We focus on Your light and You energize us and give us Your peace, Your love, Your joy. You use our weak bodies for Your work and You love us just the same. In our weakness You love us as You do in our strength. Your unconditional love is always there. Alleluia, Alleluia.

Praise the Lord. Oh, Lord, what do words say that give You honor? There are none worthy of You. I can only speak in tongues to You. Oh, praise You, the song of the soul!

Praise You with this song of my soul, oh Lord. Your honor is blessed on all the earth. Alleluia. For in my desperation I cried out and You saved me from Satan. He is a liar. He is cunning and ready for attack, but You filled my hungry soul and sent him into the depths of hell. Alleluia. Praise the Lord—Father, Son, and Holy Spirit. Alleluia. You are our

King. You reign forever. Your kingdom is not of this world, but of the world to come and we will be its heirs for our life spent in service of You. Alleluia, Alleluia.

And You filled our weary souls and we knew only the God of love and might could work such wonders in our hearts. Alleluia. You, in Your goodness, have come to my unworthy heart and filled me with Your bright light, Your fire and Your kindling love. Oh Jesus, praise You forever. Alleluia.

Jesus: Cry out, My little one. You knew I was here. I never leave you. In your desperation you called out to Me, and I, by your side, comforted you. I am there in your sorrow and pain, in your trials. I am there always, not sometime. You go to man and call him on the phone. One time he acts one way, another time, another way. He wanes in and out in his behavior. You, little baby, come to Me. I am the tenderest of hearts. I wait with a bandage for you. I never change in My ways. I am loving you at this very moment as I did in your troubled soul last night. I am always by your side. The Same. You call Me and I love you, the same as to My death on the cross! I love you that way today, tomorrow and always!

Oh, little one, turn to Me in your need. I am here in your sorrow. You may not feel Me but I never go from your side. My light and My healing touch surrounds your troubled soul. I walk with you in your weariness. I do not demand a soul that is never troubled in this world. You are taunted by Satan constantly. It is in your trouble you are drawn closer to Me. What a blessing in disguise. Don't try to rid yourself of that cross. Embrace it and thank Me for the gift which draws you closest to Me. I love you in your anguish. Say thanks for all I send you, good and bad. It comes to you with My love and My love is indeed true. If you suffer, you are strengthened in your love for Me if you accept the suffering. Oh, sweet one, I loved you to My death on the cross. Do you think I would send you a snake? I send you only little petals of My love, little bits to draw you closer to Me. You come closer and we embrace and our love is enkindled.

Oh, sweet one, know all I give you is out of love. You are doing as I wish. Come to Me and let Me kiss your little wounded heart. You know I love your little heart so much. I want to comfort you and hold you in My arms. I love you so much. Trust Me and have faith in Me. Never doubt Me—ever! I am here. Love Me as I love you. We are a team. I am your divine lover. I am He Who creates you out of love. You are the heirs to My kingdom. Do you think I would ever not give the best for you?

Messenger: Alleluia. Praise our Lord and our God, our Savior and our lover. Alleluia. Oh, Holy Spirit, thank You for the gifts of the soul, gifts of my heart, gifts given that no person could ever give. How would a person give you a gift of wisdom? All knowledge that we receive is from You. What knowledge is of any account except knowledge of You?

How do we learn of God? We learn from God. Man does not know. He only knows that which God imparts to him. Why the middleman—a book, a person? Go to God yourself, man. He awaits you and wants to share His gifts with you. Beg the Holy Spirit for the gifts. He is the Spirit of Love. It is from Him, God the Holy Spirit, I have written these letters. I know none of these truths except as He has chosen to reveal them to me.

Go to Him yourself. He loves you just as much. He wants to "gift" you and you go to man for your knowledge and wisdom and counsel. Oh, how silly are we. Go to man to ask about God, while God waits for us to come to Him! It is like going to a washing machine repair shop to fix a car.

Jesus: Oh, how silly, indeed, children. Go to God to learn the truths about God. No other knowledge is of any account except as it is rooted in Him. Do not go to man when God waits. Let your hearts yearn for the time you spend in His presence and soak up all He has to give you. You, My child, are so blessed!   11/18/93 5:45 a.m.

He Is A Personal God, A Real Person!

Jesus: I come with My grace to penetrate your soul. You open your heart and I enter in. My Blood washes you clean. I dwell in your heart. I am truly present there. Amen, Amen, I say to you, unless you eat this Body and drink this Blood, you shall not have life in you. You speak from Me. What flows from your mouth is the result of My presence within you. I am He Who writes these letters. You are only My servant. I use you. I give you honor because I come to you, but it is I Who do this writing. Your hand is My hand. I am using you in this work. I want all My letters published in a book—not a few. They were written as words for all to hear. With such material, many will turn their hearts to Me. I became real to you as you read My letters. I am a real person and I want to be known as I am, Son of God, loving and true. I want to be known on a personal basis to all My children. You are only being used. I am writing to My people. You cannot stop the hand of God. You are My candidates to execute this work. I want My letters out and soon. I do not want you to waste any more time. You both have nothing to do with this. You are My servants. This is My task. I want it accomplished. Many hearts will know Me in a new way from these letters.

I have spoken to Rita with all the love I have for each of My children. I am this personal with every soul. If they come to Me they will know this. They need to read and study these letters. Your job is to get them published. I want Rita to talk to her brothers. This will be accomplished in time. The proof of this is in the contents of these letters. No person could have the insight but Me alone. I am commanding you to do this work. Do not tarry.

Do not fear. I go before you and I make ready the path. You will not falter on your way. The road will open as it should. Any obstacles I will remove from your path. It will be transacted as I have planned and you will know this by the love with which it happens.

I am Jesus Christ, Son of the Living God. I live in this world in the hearts of all. I want all to know how alive I truly am. I never go from My people's side. I am vigilant and always there. It is they who move from Me. I want them to be drawn closer to My Sacred Heart, closer and closer through the content of these letters. I am alive. I am here. I am your love. I want all to know this message of love. It is not up to you to question My ways. My ways I make known to you for I want to save every last soul. You will be a big part in helping Me do this with many souls. They are thirsty. They will drink. I love you both very much and appreciate your trust and faith in Me. My ways, I have made clear. Do not tarry. I work before you. I do the work. You will know it is Me because of its ease. If a door shuts, it is not the way I want to go. All doors are open doors in My plan. It is easy to follow.

I love you and I am truly Jesus, Son of the Living God. Your work I bless and I go with you on your way. I am as present here as I was on My death on the cross. You will not fear. You will be fearless and without worry. Be steadfast in delivering these messages to your brothers. It is their souls that are at stake. The world preaches so many awful messages. These are so powerful and will reach men's hearts. I am a personal God. I am a God of love. I am a person Who wants to love My people in a personal way. I will give them these messages through you.

Messenger: He has a plan to do His work. You don't ask why. You just do as He wants. He acts through you to minister to whom He wants, maybe only one person. You don't ask if what you did was good or not because He is doing it.

I became selfless and I surrender. The more I spoon out of me, the more He possesses me and it is He Who acts in me. If I did it, it would surely flop. If He does it, it will never flop.

It is for His honor and glory that I act. It has nothing to do with self-promotion. To be persecuted or glorified focuses on self. We must become selfless. We must act and empty ourselves. Don't ever ask if it was good or bad. We didn't do it. We are His servants.

Jesus: I am in you in this. I am working in you. I am giving you wisdom and insights to deliver My messages. I want you to speak. This has nothing to do with you. I use you. I have primed you to trust in Me and not ask any questions. It is for Jesus you act. This is your main concern: you must become selfless—totally. Drop your selves. Die to your self. Be of Me.

It is not you who act, but I Who act in you. Be selfless, child. You don't understand but when you question you are not selfless in your soul. I have planted these messages. It has nothing to do with you. I use your hand and write My words. You are a servant, My Servant. You are honored by Me that I use you, but I am He Who is acting!

Be selfless and unquestioning. Be as a baby at the breast. You wait and I do all things. Wait, baby. Wait on Me. I will use you. Be open, unattached and selfless. Be totally submissive. Do not fret or fume or worry. Let go and I will do all I need to. Just be willing. I have been teaching you about My will daily. You have studied under Jesus Christ. I would think you know some things about Me. I am the teacher. You are My people. Your life I use to teach you lessons. Your trials teach you profound truths. What gems those little trials are, gems of great knowledge from Me. Every day unfolds and you are taught by Me. You are My pupil. I am your teacher. Teach your brothers how to be My pupils in their lives.

I am the teacher of all truth. My teachings are truths of the soul. I am the greatest teacher. My school is run on My love. It is always good for you. Take your tests and receive a golden reward. Graduation is into My Sacred Heart, into the kingdom of God. I love you so!   11/19/93

Die to Self

Jesus: Die to yourself that I might live in thee, for I was hungry and you gave Me to eat, I was naked and you clothed Me. It is harder for a rich man to get into the kingdom of heaven than for a camel to pass through the eye of a needle. Remember all those words you hear in the Scriptures. They are indeed My holy words at Mass. I feed you and you are fed at Mass. I am so good to you. You must be willing to open yourself entirely to Me. Do not hold back any of yourself. I love your eagerness to give Me your all. It so comforts My aching heart. My heart aches for all those who have forgotten God. I am truly here, day and night. I watch and I wait for My little ones to be with Me, but they do not come. They stay away and tend to useless things. They do not come to Me. They are blind and totally caught up in the things of the world.

There is so much sin. People sin without even knowing they sin. It is such a habit that they do it automatically. Such wounds, habitual sin and indifference. I am God. I am Jesus, Son of the Living God. I come that you might live, that you will have life in Me, that your hearts may be ready for the Kingdom of God. And where are they? For this short time they want to be satisfied. They seek after empty wells. They run down roads that lead to destruction. They go full steam ahead in a life that has no room for God. They do not know why they were created. They are empty and hollow inside, but they continue to follow their empty lives.

Oh, little ones, you turn your backs. You listen to the sick world. I am here in all these ways but you do not want to do My will. You want to do the will of the world! Store up all these treasures here? For what? They make no difference. They are worthless to Me.

Pray, oh My children. Pray for these children in darkness! How do I reach them? Do they need a bump on their head to know that My kingdom waits and it isn't of this world? I bring My curtain down and your life is over. So sad, he who chooses to live only in this world! I have given him so many chances but he continues to sin and delights in harming his brothers. I make ready a place for all My children, so they might come and be saved. I pursue them as a treasure in the field. I open My gates. I give them every opportunity to be saved but some choose to remain indifferent to Me and caught in themselves and their sins. They make themselves their gods and are miserable inside. Only I give them what they crave. To try to fill yourself with this world is not a happy life because the soul thirsts for only that which I can give and the body holds all things of Me at an arm's distance from the soul.

The soul in its pain laments while the devil whispers words of the ego and doing one's own will in their ears. What a sad thing, to be run by Satan and not know it, to live in misery but do exactly as you want. Like blind and dumb sheep, you run into walls and keep running into the same walls. Does this feel good, little tender sheep?

Why do you do it? The things of this world give instant gratification. Then it wears off quickly. A good meal—pleasure while you eat it. Sex—an instant of pleasure—then it is gone. Drink numbs your brain and makes you depressed. Television brainwashes your mind and you go to bed the victim of those on the set who made your moods and fashioned your thoughts. This is happiness? This is emptiness.

I feel so sad for My sick ones. I want their love so much. I want to hold them and tell them all My secrets. I want to bestow on them My gifts— real gifts, not a scarf, not a piece of clothing or a muffin. I want to give them a gift of knowledge. I want them to have love in their hearts. I want to give them peace in their souls. I want to give them a relationship with Me. To know a friend who would die for you—what else could I say? I lament their souls.

Life is so short and eternity never ends. I am a loving God. Your soul craves Me like a magnet, but you fight and turn away. Such emptiness! You will never know! I am the Sacred Heart of Jesus. My heart shines bright for all My children, not a few, but you are blinded by your own wills. You are prompted by Satan to listen to his evil words. You think of your own egos and how you must do exactly as you want.

I call you to life with Me and you say no. I must be the ruler. That is why you do not turn to Me. The more you focus on yourself, the farther you move from Me. The more you focus on Me the more you rid yourself of you and the closer our union. Die to yourself that we might live. In your emptiness, you cried out and I came and your hearts were made full and you knew that you had sought your treasures down empty paths and you knew that I could fill the soul.

Pray hard for all those lost in sin. They need you today. Keep praying and offering sacrifices that they will turn their wills to Me. Only prayer will work. I love each soul and I am working for its conversion. Only prayers will help. What a beautiful reward to think you helped someone to turn his life to Me. This is all that matters. All else is useless.

Messenger: Amen. Alleluia. 11/20/93 4:45 a.m.

Study My Passion

Jesus: The thorns in My head cut through to My skull. The pain was unreal! How to describe such an experience? And I was God! Blood trickled down My face all day. It didn't dry up because, as My heart beat, it would open the wounds. Think how tender your head is if you pull a hair! The thorns pulled My hair, like the tightness of curlers, but they cut Me and when they put them on, they hammered them into My skull. This was for the sins committed in people's minds. The hatred, the anger, the sex signs, contemplating evil deeds, sneering and envy of your brothers—ugliness! The eyes are the windows of the soul. What you look at you reflect on your soul. If your eyes look at evil things, your soul is dirty. If you look on others with hatred and anger and getting even, on dirty pictures, sinful stories, bad TV and movies, what you, through your will, take in with the beautiful eyes created by God, sparkling and full of light, reflects in your soul.

Keep your eyes light and sparkling, full of love. Relax the area around your eyes so you are not looking hard and anxiously at your brothers. Let your eyes reflect My light in your soul.

My eyes were stained with the blood that poured down My head. My vision was blurred with blood and My eyes were matted with dryness. Blood came from My mouth from the blows to My head and blood came from My nose from the hitting on My head. I was beaten on My head with the crown of thorns. I was spat at in My face. Oh, such ugliness in men's hearts! It was their minds that thought such ugly thoughts and why I suffered such brutality to My head. It is paradoxical I suffered for that which they did.

Think of men cutting off women's and children's heads in Bosnia! Such hatred the devil engineers in their hearts! I suffered so many wounds to My precious, tender head. The blood I shed from My head is the blood that washes the men caught in sin from sins of the head.

Ugliness, hatred, sins committed with the mouth, the eyes, the ears! I suffered for these sins with My crown, a crown that would allow many to enter My Kingdom if they repented for their sins. I did this willingly for love of you. I saw beforehand every wound I would receive and I chose and accepted everything that was done to Me out of love of you. I love you this much!

They beat My body, My beautiful body, God-made-man. They tied Me to a pole and they beat Me. There were more than one beating Me. They took turns. I was the victim. They in their hate and anger lashed at Me, My beautiful body, tore My flesh over and over. They laughed and taunted Me. They were so happy to be so guileful. Oh, the laugh of the great deceiver! Like a thief in the night, he steals your hearts and you wonder why so hard. Where did their gentleness go? The great deceiver who laughs at hurting others.

It is the devil operating from the hearts of man! The heart is no longer kind and gentle, but merciless and debased in behavior. Oh, the great deceiver! To beat God-made-man and to laugh at his own ill deeds, to watch the blood of Jesus fly in the air and to laugh. It is by this blood that they and all others who abuse others and laugh will be made whole. I, in My love, forgave them for their deeds. They beat Me. They tore My flesh and I loved them. Can you not love your brothers when they are cruel to you? Can you forgive them and love them as the soul created by God, but dead in sin by the devil's hands? If I could love those who spit and laughed at Me and tore My flesh, who crowned Me with a piercing crown and hit Me on My head, can you not forgive him who offends you with a nasty word?

The way to Me is to study Me, to model yourself after My behavior. You must take up these crosses I give you every day. It is your love for your brothers that might save their crippled souls, dead in sin. See Me in them. Look beyond their deeds and see the God Who made them. Do not focus on their sick ways. Study My passion with Me. Study how I loved the unloving, how I loved those who persecuted Me. Study Me and My ways. Don't waste your time thinking about Satan and how he is taunting you through your brothers. He uses them to get you away from Me.

Come to Me. See Me in their hearts and their eyes. Your looking into their eyes will shed My glare of light into them. Look into the eyes of your brothers. I taught them through your look of love. It is My love and My light I cast into their dark souls. Your eyes touch, as your hands. People may not want your touching them, but your eyes touch very deeply the souls of mankind. Strive for perfection and holiness. Do not give in to yourself and think about how you have been hurt and violated. Never cry to any man. Come to Me and cry.

I will rid you of yourself and you will know no man has any power to harm you. The more selfless you become, the more you live entirely for Me, the more you realize that I am all that matters. The more you rid yourself of you and let Me in, the less power your brothers will have over you. You give them power. You think they are important to your being okay. You are okay. You are perfect as God created you. You are My child. You do not need your brother's approval. You are above the ground. You realize your worth and your job is defined. It is to let Me use you, body and soul, to do My work. This takes total submission.

Whom you touch is being touched by Me. This is your work, to live for Me so I can live in you and operate from you, so I can love My people through you. Open wide your gates and let Me penetrate your soul. For I was hungry and you gave Me to eat, I was naked and you clothed Me. "When, Lord, did I do these things...?" When you did them to your brothers, you did them to Me. Amen.   11/20/93 10:00 a.m.

Take Your Bottle

Jesus: Come to Me, you little babies, all who are weary and heavily burdened, and I give you rest. Rest, not as the world gives you rest, but in Me, your divine maker. Oh, ye wander and ye wait in a valley filled with tears and heartaches, but I say know this, little babies: I am Jesus, Son of the Living God. I am here. I am not off somewhere while you trudge this valley alone. I am right in your midst. You do not see Me but you know I am truly real and I am with you. You needn't worry or fume about while you are here. I go every step with you on your way! It isn't as if you are forgotten and you plead and I come sometimes and sometimes I don't. I am here by your side. I am always with you. You need only stop and you will feel My presence with you.

You must have faith. You must take your troubles and trust in Me, not a little, but always. You don't let anything Satan puts in your path get really in the way.

Messenger: You say this is a big one, hard as can be. But here, Jesus, my love, I stand at the foot of Your cross and I will carry out my work for You. Smiling and being there as You want me to be (smelled roses). I trust in you, Lord! Oh, Blessed Lady! I love you and Jesus.

Jesus: Life may seem tough. Life may seem an uphill battle—all the more reason you trust when you are overcome with adversity. Just don't give in to it. Let it go to Jesus and watch how quickly it works itself out. The more you trust and turn everything over, the more you will amazed. Where you operated before so perplexed, you go now and with ease the difficulty dissipates. Only My hand can do such things!

Oh, little ones, I love you, love you so. Keep focusing on Me as the doting mother, hovering over the young and you do your part. Picture yourself as a baby who is totally dependent on his mother. He doesn't get up and fix his own bottle. He waits and even takes it when it is too hot or too cold. Sometimes the mother burns his little mouth. He cries but he takes the bottle just the same. You take all I give you—hot and cold bottles, bottles that are just right. If they come from Me they are all out of My great love for you. You keep coming back. You don't say, "I think this one was too hot. I will fix my own" or "I will find another mama to give me what I need." You may cry a bit, but you come right back because you know, just as the baby, how I love you.

Turn over the hot ones to Me. Accept them as coming from Me, but don't belabor and worry and try to correct them. Just accept them in the love given and give the worries up to Me. Don't fight off the cold bottles either. Accept them, all of those I give you. When you feel I have forgotten, come to Me on your knees and beg Me to be there. You know, as a mother, I will not forget My baby and if she does forget, know I will never forget!

Turn this hot one to Me. It is only a little problem. You can trust totally in Me or worry if you finally have a big problem. Don't worry. Do My work. Know I am here in all your trials, closer and closer, loving you intently as you struggle in the valleys. Know the valleys may be low, but the peaks are there and they are so high and beautiful. It is in the valleys you learn more about Me. It is in the valleys you learn trust and faith. It is in the valleys I am right there with you, looking into your eyes. Your eyes! Oh, keep them focused on Me. Strive to be perfect as My heavenly Father is perfect. Seek after this perfection and holiness. Seek and you shall find, knock and it shall be opened unto you, for I am a God Who loves you so. You will never comprehend even the tiniest amount. The more you trust Me, the more you know Me, the more you see My Sacred Heart, so gentle, so kind, so loving! My Sacred Heart on fire! It radiates such a splendor. It shines like a hot beautiful fire. There is such mystery in a fire that is so deep and so hot. How bright is its center. How hot could it be? That is Me. My heart is on fire with the hottest fire. You wonder how hot is My center. How bright could it be? Brighter and hotter than you could ever imagine in your earthly form!

Oh, what glories I have in store for you, when you finally see it all! See all there is to Me. Little glimpses I will give you. They are special treats of My love, but you, in your earthly form, can't even handle it. My power, My light, My fire would blow you off your feet and you would be out cold! That is how I am at your side with a power pack like this and you worry about a power failure? Oh, how silly, when I am with you. Trust, trust, trust! I am here. I am the Good Shepherd. I know Mine and Mine know Me. The sheep follow the shepherd and are led where they need to go. Some go off to do their own grazing. Oh, so sad for them. Sometimes they fall and are totally destroyed! The shepherd is so sad and laments the loss of one sheep, but he tries all he can to get them and bring them back to his flock and they may graze other lands, only to find a very sorry end. Poor little lost sheep.

You, My child, are just My little dear baby. Your soul reflects the majesty and love of one Who cares for you. Your eyes are lit by My fires. Your heart is bubbling over with intense fire and this shows in your eyes, your touch, your speech, your smile. You never falter and get downtrodden even in the grandest adversity because I am guarding you. I am by your side. I love you, little one. I am Jesus, your ardent lover, come to you at every second to light your way, even when the bottle is hot. I am there in the hot one. I am there in the cold one. I am there when they are just right.

You are taunted by Satan. He hates you, but I am there and he cannot harm you. You will learn trust and faith in Me by handling your cross. Turn to Me and see Me forgiving those who put Me to death, see Me forgiving those who beat Me and tore My flesh and crowned Me with piercing thorns, see Me in all My Blood, covered from head to toe, forgiving those who did this to Me. I am Jesus, Son of the Living God. I live in your trials. I teach in your problems. Embrace all you are given and do not ever turn from Me. Turn toward Me and feel the heat, the comfort, the love!

Accept the cross. It is a gift from Me so I can touch you in a special way and give you a teaching. You are taught in your crosses when you accept them with open arms. I am here with all My love. To My death I loved you. I love you no different this day.

And I came in all My splendor and you caught a glimpse of My beautiful heart. In rays of light, really aglow, waiting, waiting for you, My love, to come and be united with Me. Unity in the cross, unity in all I sent you and you did not fear and you did not lose your way. You followed the Good Shepherd over the rocks and the thistles that pricked at your little toes, but you kept going. Rocks and thistles, because He knew the way and you were following Him as you ought.

The hills were steep, the valleys low. There were times you were dry in your mouth. There was much that was not to your liking, but you followed and followed and, in the end, a beautiful pasture, flowing with a bubbling brook, and a sunny day. Follow Me this way. Don't ask. Don't stop. Don't try to find a way out. Follow Me over the rocks, over all the dry lands, wet lands, lands that are just right. Trust in Me as little sheep. He does not go to graze other lands for he will surely lose his way. Follow, follow, follow the Master and you will never run amok, you will never lose your way, you will fly on eagles' wings. You will run and not get weary, and you will be guarded on your path, the right path that leads down all the right roads to an everlasting treasure.

My love is your fuel, My heart your light. You have heat on your journey. Stay close to the center of My heart and all you need will go with you. Alleluia.

I am the Good Shepherd. I know Mine and Mine know Me. They follow Me.   11/21/93 4:10 a.m.

Jesus On My Tongue

Messenger: Dear Jesus, this morning, as I received Communion, I cried and cried. I think it was because I am such a sinner and so full of pride. Maybe I cried for the awe that Jesus would come inside of me, maybe for the indifference of those who do not know He is truly God. Maybe I cried for Christ truly present inside of me. Oh, my dear Jesus, for whatever reason, I come to You and tell You I love Thee.

We are the daughters and sons of God, created with dignity and honor, but we still remain in our lowly state as humans. He honors us with His presence because of His intense love for us. That is the only explanation. Out of His love we are honored that He enters into our bodies and we become His temples.

Oh, God, how great You are and how honored we are by Your presence! Words are not there to express my feelings so I cry from unworthiness to You. Come and possess my soul. Make me more and more holy. Show me my flaws and the errors in my heart. Let me love as You fashion and shape me into what You want me to be.

You, Oh Lord, are the potter. I am lowly and ready to be molded by Your hands. Make me selfless and unattached to all that is worldly so I will be Yours to use and live in. Let me die to self and live only in You. Imperfect as I am, You come and dwell in my sinful heart and I am changed by Your touch.

Come, come, wash my sins away. Bathe me in Your Blood. Dry me with Your love and hold me under Your wing so I may never feel afraid again. I want to be as You want me to be. I open myself up entirely to all You want to do.

Alleluia! Praise Him, Who is God, one, true, magnificent, in all His glory. I come and open myself to Him.

Jesus: Little girl, I do love you. I am truly present in your heart. It is in touching you this way I become more real to you. Just be with Me. Do not focus any more on the unworthiness. Focus on Me, Jesus, truly present to you out of love. I come not to point to your unworthiness. I come to love you, to be with you. Focus on Me in your soul, just loving you. In your brokenness I come, but I can only have a union with you if you get this point and focus on My love. This state you feel is your realization of My True Presence, God-made-man, and you see your unworthiness to Me. But you must go beyond this to union with Me. This is only accomplished by being with Me and focusing on My love. Be with Me, soul to soul, in My love. You long for My love. I come to you in your heart and I am joined with you there. 11/22/93

Come To Communion

Jesus: The devil can't harm you. No one can harm you for I am the gentlest of all hearts. I am Jesus, Son of the Living God and I am here. I am your power. I am your might. I am your all. I call you from your sleep and beckon you to write every word. I speak to you. I am speaking in My voice, child. Listen and you will hear My gentleness. That which you read in these letters is the same gentleness. I tell you that is why you are the best to read My words. You know how I speak to you. All day I talk in your head. Tell them I talk. I am as alive to you as your children. When I speak you hear Me deliver every word. Do you not appreciate such a gift? Do they want more? They get what I give you and that is a great gift indeed.

You don't ask any questions. You come and I am in charge. I tell you what I want to tell you. No man asks God for his own eagerness to know. I know your every need. I give you what you need. If I did not give it, then you did not need this information. I am the giver here. I am in charge. This is My gift to all of you, to tell you of My beautiful love. I make known to you such mysteries as man does not know. I am the giver of the information. You, My child, are right to never question or never ask. To others who ask you to ask, tell them "no," as you did. You come, you listen, I talk, you talk, but not to ask questions of your own desires. I give you what you need when you need it. Do not ask for idle information. It is not up to you to question My knowing what to tell you. Curious children, trying to control God. This is not up to them. It is entirely up to Me and I am God. I have the power and I know all things. That is all you need to know.

To possess your soul is to make you sad, child. My soul is so sad for the loss of My children in sin. You ask Me to possess your soul, then you cry and you ask why do you cry. You cry because I am sad. My heart is so sad for love of My lost children. They wander this barren desert and they thirst for Me and I want to love them and they are dying inside, but they do not come to Me to drink. My heart is so sad for My loved ones. My heart is so sad for the sins, the murders, the sins of the flesh, the hatred, the cruelty. You wonder why you cry. You cry for My sadness in you when I possess your soul. This is your uncontrollable crying when I get close to you. I am sad. Such little ones are being taught such vileness. There is such sin and no regard for Me. God is of so little account! My love is so gentle, so kind, so real. You comfort Me when you cry with Me. It comforts My aching heart.

Messenger: Oh, Lord, please possess my soul. Permeate my very being, so I no longer live, but You Who live in me. I am no longer attached to any of this world, but only attached to You. I am Yours totally and entirely, unmistaken in my identity, that I die to self and You operate out of me as You will. God, living and acting from my heart so my heart can beat and operate as You so direct it, not for self, but for Thee. Complete surrender and selflessness. You are at the helm, Lord. I am Your empty shell. You dwell in me and we are joined in this union, with Your work to do. Our hearts beat as one and we are united in Christ Jesus, our loving Lord. We, in our lowliness and unworthiness are united then to God. The one, true, magnificent God, worthy of all praise and awe of His presence, has chosen to become united with us.

What honor You bestow on those who truly love Him! Why do not all men turn their will and hearts over to Him for this union! He laments and His heart aches for the indifference of many hearts. Be sorrowful with Him for He is God, all worthy of all my love, of my all, of me and I would be a fool to hold back from this union! I am honored by Him in all His glory that He chose to unite Himself with me. Hold not back for He is God. To mix with Him is unbefitting of me, but His great love has beckoned us to be united.

Oh, the communion of the saints! Strive after this holiness. They knew what little account the things of this earth were. They knew that only He mattered. They knew of His undying love for each heart and soul. They saw His magnificence and they chose to partake in the greatness of God. We are offered no less. We are loved the same. It is us that hold back from His love. It is there for us if we ask Him for all He has to give. Ask and you shall receive Him, glorious Him, to dwell forever united in our hearts. What a union!

Every day without communion with Jesus is a loss of the greatest gift. Always come and receive Him in the Holy Eucharist. It is there that this beautiful union is brought to fulfillment. Jesus, present to us in the Eucharist in our unworthy body, what more could you seek after? Oh, so silly to let this opportunity go by. Every day come and feed your soul. It needs to eat. Jesus is truly there, Body, Blood, Soul and Divinity.

Who am I, Lord, that You should come to me and dwell in my heart? Oh, what wonder in our hearts for Thee. You are so Great, oh Lord, worthy of all honor and all praise. In Your Communion we find life, life eternal, forever and ever. God enters our body and we are cleaned by Him Who loves us so. He loves us the same today as the day He died on the cross. Alleluia, Alleluia.   11/23/93 2:10 a.m.

His Kingdom Awaits

Messenger: Jesus, Jesus, my beautiful Jesus! I come on bended knee in the night. Nothing is fitting such honor for this King. He has a kingdom to surpass all others and it is not of this world. Entry is not dependent on gold or silver, but on our deeds of love to Him, to each other. How does He love us? With the love of God. He loved us to the point of death and He loves us like that this day. We are unworthy of all His gifts for us but

He stands and waits for us at His gates.

Jesus: Come, all you beloved of the Father. I watch and wail and eagerly await your entry. This is your way home. Come to Me with your hearts pure and your souls holy for I ask you to love one another. Be kind to those who hate you. Open up your hearts and let Me dwell there so you will know Me now and forever.

Messenger: Into Thy hands, oh Savior, I commend my spirit. The days are short, the nights are long and I am called to come and be with you. You wait with open arms and bid me to come home to the home of My Father for He is honored and worthy of all praise and we are His heirs, lowly though we be, heirs to a real kingdom. Because of our divine lineage, the angels will come at the appointed hour and carry our souls off to such a reward.

Oh Lord, such a small penitence for serving You! It was indeed the best way to go and then to be rewarded with such royalty. Praise You, my Savior, for I am lowly and You have exalted me. The angels have carried me to Thee and my sight will see You, the one, true God. Alleluia. Praise the Lord.

Jesus: You come, you ask. I tell you what you need to know. Open your heart and wait for My response. My time is not your time. I have a plan. I will make all details available. Pray for this work. I want your trust in Me and in yourselves. There is much grace in trusting in My word. You must do what you think is right. I have written these letters out of love. I will give you more information. Wait and I will tell you what you ask. You must pray for your answer. I do not answer because you ask. I have spoken.

Come and behold Me, King of all. Honor, glory and praise! Know you are dealing with God, child. I tell you in My time and in My way. You must ready yourself for this undertaking. Tell all to pray and the answer will become obvious to them. Pray and seek and it will open unto you what you are to do. I want you to seek your answers and trust in My guidance. Oh, little one, I have made you be patient all along. Is it not for your own good?

I want you to pray this day. I will reveal to you all—what exactly you are to do. I am the Savior. Open up and pray for guidance on your answer. I have a plan and, if it seems easy, then it is the right way to go. Do all want this undertaking? It is with such love I give these letters to you. It is with love and I want them published. We have a focus on Him Who dearly loves us. Wait on Him and He will grant your heart's request. Wait and pray for His word. Alleluia.

The crooked ways are made straight. I want eagerness in this operation, eagerness to serve Me and My ways, to carry out My plan and feel absolutely sure you are doing this for the love of Jesus. This is an act of love. It is a labor to serve Me. Are you ready for such service? Is this your primary goal? Out of love of Jesus you come and you ask and I answer. Is your intent to serve Me with love? The same love I give to you? I want this a top priority. I want My letters to be treated with the love they were delivered in your heart. Then they are delivered to you to give to My world. All must be an act of love for Me. Such service, to come and serve Me this way!

Messenger: It is an honor to do this work for Jesus, Lord.

Jesus: On bended knee I ask you to pray from your hearts that you are worthy to do My work. I need you and I want you eager to serve Jesus, the Son of God. This is My top priority: that it is in your love of Me that you undertake My writing.

Oh, how I love you. Would you not do the same for Me? I loved you to My death. This is an honor, to work for Jesus and write His letters to be published. Do you do this work with all the honor I deserve? Do you do it from love of Me? Then I will be the one to make your work fly. I will light your paths and make your loads light. I will see to its execution Myself, if the love of God be in your hearts, if you realize it is I Who ask and you who have answered My plea out of love and service to Me. Consider it an honor to be asked to serve Me with My holy words!

I want you to realize this treasure you are working with. It is out of love of you, each one of you, I deliver My letters to you. You must, therefore, respond in love of Me that you do this work. I ask, "Will you help Me deliver My messages?" I will make your loads light and I will give you a heavenly reward. For it is I Who give you passage into My kingdom and I will reward each according to his deeds. To honor Me in this service with love pleases Me greatly and I will give unto you the keys to My kingdom. For many, many hearts will be turned around because of My words here.

Read My messages and know the true treasure you hold here. It is with eagerness I want you to do My work. It is with love and conviction. It is in knowledge of My words that you will do My work well. I love you all so much. Will you serve Me with your love?

Messenger: Oh, Lord, Lord, I want to serve You. I want to do your work.

Jesus: Then do My work. You don't do it in the end. I do it for you. I want this work accomplished, and soon. I will go before you. I will prepare the way. I will open the doors. I use you to do this for Me. Are you willing to serve Me in love and to know the treasure you hold. Read My messages so you will better serve Me. I call, you come. I do the work. You labor and toil, but I have a plan and a way to do it. I only need servants to work My plan. Will you serve Me with love and treasure My works? Do you know how much love you can give to Me and your brothers through this work? I will make your loads light. He that serves the Lord will inherit His kingdom. This reward cannot be bought. It is gained by the love in your hearts.

Messenger: Alleluia.

Jesus: It is your commitment to do this work for Me that makes you right or not right to do the work. I do the work in the end. I will work with you and all lights will be "go" from Him Who loves you and wants this plan carried out. These are My letters of love for all My beautiful people. Each letter was hand-delivered in the greatest love. You must respond in love and know what you are handling. Spend time with Me reading My messages so you know what is here and feel Me talking to each of you. Then you will know the intense love I have for each of you and you will do the best job from knowing Me and My love for you.

Thank you for responding to My call. I am Jesus, Son of the Living God, and I am truly alive with love in each letter to your hearts. I await your response.   11/24/93

Spend Time Alone With Your Children

Jesus: Dear child, you are meeting lots of trials. Hold tight to the hand of God. If on your way everything seems to overtake you, just stop and hold tight to My hand. My hand is the hand of God. I do not ever wane or move about. I am the same today, yesterday, every day. What power! When you feel overwhelmed to stop, take a breath and then remember I, Who hold your hand, have all the power. That should put everything in its proper perspective.

These have been the times of tough days. Your child needs your understanding. Do not spend time with others. Concentrate on playing games and praying with your children. Your job is still the same: Mass, Communion, adoration, writing, and your children. All else takes its place behind these. Do not spend time with others and miss the golden opportunity of being with your children.

I will help you with My work. The more you read and edit, the more it will be very beneficial for you. Be a kind person today. Let My light flow from you. There are those you may not feel as good around.

Remember Me. I am literally present at every turn. I hold your hands and you are never alone. Jesus Christ walks with you! Do not hate, do not be envious or think low of yourself. Realize the beauty of all God's children and remember your work is to spread My light to all.

You must forgive. It is hard to forgive those who are cruel to you, but your light is blocked if you hold on to any ill will. Pray for cleansing inside like an old fashioned street cleaner. It goes down the road and doesn't miss a spot. It scrubs each part of the street and then, when it leaves the street, it is so clean. Let My street cleaner go into your heart. It will clean and forgive the tiniest corners and rinse all the junk away. Then let go of it. Let go, child. You are collecting garbage by the sides of your heart. When you start to collect a little, it is easier for new garbage to mount up by the old garbage.

Do not bring up your past or feel sorry for yourself. Give up all your attachments to the past and realize the golden gems you received from these crosses. These were My teachings. The more you embrace the cross, the more you know of My ways. Don't ever get personal with yourself. Remain selfless and unattached to old pain. Everyone has suffered. Your suffering is only glory in how it brings you closer to Me. Do not discuss your suffering with others. Preach only what is in these letters. Your job is not idle conversation. It is staying fixed in My work. If the conversation goes to you personally, take it immediately back to My words. Others only need to know My teachings, not your private life. Your job is to teach that which I have taught you. The more you become selfless, the more your life will work out.

What you have suffered lately has brought you back to yourself. Stop now and ask Me to help you forgive. Talk to your children about how I am asking you to clean well the wall in your heart and you want to focus on the ways of God. Read this letter to them and then pray to ward off Satan's lies. He wants you bowed down and focused on his nasty little works so you will get tripped up. Let go. Only you can forgive. Say the Our Father. You owe no one any explanations on your life. You can help them by sharing My life as I am teaching you in these letters. The more you talk about Me and Me alone and forget yourself, the more your work will be My work. Your life is not important against My wisdom.

You need to be alone with your children. You must have time alone with them. This intimacy is what gives you all strength and direction in Me. When others penetrate this wall too much and you lack this closeness, your wall is weaker and Satan comes in.

You must pray with each other and become very united with Me. This is the strength you need in this world: prayer in the family. Be alone with your children. It builds a strong, holy wall around you. You need a united front against this world. This time is essential every day, time alone as a family. If others infiltrate this time, even on the phone, your united front becomes very weak. Playing games, praying, crafts, and music. TV in a sense weakens this wall because it is bringing in so much from the outside.

The family that prays and plays together stays together. You are most important as a family. Stay united and strong. Satan's main word now is division. You must ward off his ways to divide you. Stay united as a family. My Mother is spreading her mantle over you to keep you united. You have much help here.

Messenger: Create in me a clean heart, oh Lord. Where there is hatred, sow love. Where there is anger, let it dissipate and let my heart be filled to the brim with You. May I realize how Satan is always around trying to get us to think of sick things. May Your light fill us to the brim with love for all and may we be able to stop this infiltration of hate and division and embrace unity and love.

Alleluia. Christ has come among us and we are made His Holy Ones. Alleluia.   11/25/93 5:30 a.m.

Prepare for My Mass

Jesus: Prepare ye the way for My Mass. Let your hearts be lifted up to Me, your Divine Savior. Come on bended knee and wait with great anticipation. Where are your hearts? Are they closed off because you are so caught up in the things of this world or are they open, awaiting My tremendous event? Let your souls be ready. Rid yourself of earthly distractions. Pray for openness. On your way, think about Me and not your problems with your wives and husbands or children or workers. This is Satan at work right away to get you focused on everything but Me.

Come with your hearts ready. Anticipate this event in eagerness. Turn your minds off and focus only on My love. Yours is a special gift, to come to receive Me in Communion! Oh, to be so close to receive God on your tongue! Who are you that God comes to you? Focus on My love. Ask God's forgiveness for your sins so you will be more pure. Once you have remembered your sins and confessed them, then forget them because they bring you back to yourself. Forgive yourself as He does.

Listen to the words in the readings. You are fed and nourished through the sacred scriptures. Be thirsty for this reading so you will soak up its message like a sponge. Be prepared for the miracles that occur in the

Mass. Bread and wine are changed into My Body and Blood. What a miracle! I am truly present! This is a glorious event when this happens. Only I have the power. The priest becomes Christ truly present, changing ordinary bread and wine into My Body and Blood. Be a witness!

You are going to be changed, this day, November 26, 1993. My hand has touched you and the path you now proceed on is the will of My Father. You will be selfless and unattached to all that is worldly. You will be focused on My work here and My union with you. Open all your cares to My Sacred Heart and leave yourself behind. Total selflessness, total surrender. I demand holiness and prayer from you. Do not focus on others and what they said or didn't say. Know I am caring for your every need and you have no reason to worry. If a cross comes, accept it as given to you from Me with much love and know it soon will pass and you will be victorious in My mission for you. You embark on My plan for you.

Alleluia. Praise the Lord. For you have said "yes" to the Father and He will bless you on your way. Alleluia. His will is My will. My love for you is so great, My child. I am your Rock, your Fortress, your Deliverer. I guard your going out and your coming in. There is nothing in your life I do not guard. I guard your every move. Have no fear. Feel a wash of peace in your heart for you need only follow Me and My work for you. Do not think. Do not question. Let Me lead the way and follow, follow, follow to be on the way that I have planned for you.

You do not worry for anything—what you are to wear or put on or eat. You do not worry. You turn your life entirely over now. Know I go with you and My mother is by your side. Do not fear. Concentrate on My love for you. It will warm you always. She is ever present for you, as a loving mother always is. She loves you very much. She loves you especially for loving her Son. She is there and she is loving you. You have a team. Fear not. Do not think of any of your earthly cares—children or whatever. All will unfold for you. Trust in Me and My ways for you. It is out of My greatest love that I use you in this task. I love you.   11/26/93 Before Mass

Do What Is God's Will

Messenger: Dear Jesus, I come on bended knee and I ask You to forgive me if I took any glory for Your writing. I am only Your servant and I do not want to receive such glory for Your works. I want to remain selfless and unattached. I want to be Your servant and I want to surrender myself to You. Please, Jesus, do not be upset for what I received or took.

This is not My goal. It is to serve You. I want to be unattached and self-less. I am Your servant. You are He Who speaks in me.

Jesus: Dear child, I am not upset with you. Satan is constantly trying to bring you down. You must remain selfless entirely and unattached to any glory. You are My servant. I am your God. I want My messages delivered. I have asked you to write and you came to serve Me.

I am He Who makes Myself known through you. I am the one, true, magnificent God. At My presence all knees must bend and all should be in awe of Me there. My love is never changing. It is the same today as the day I died for you on the cross.

Don't feel fear in your heart from this exposure. I wanted them to know of My messages. You had to tell them. You did as you were supposed to and you feel fear. Just remain selfless. I love you so much, child. I love all My beautiful people and I want to be part of their lives. If they read these words, many will respond by coming closer to Me. Have no fear. Things are happening according to My plan.

I want to teach you about surrender. When I accepted the Father's will and proceeded through all the bitter cruelty before My death and then accepted My cross to My death, this was true surrender. There were not little parts of My life I wanted to enjoy and save and do instead of the Father's will. I did always, My whole life, His will.

He has a divine plan for you and you were created to carry out His wishes. To follow His will daily is His desire. His will is not one day you do it, then for five or six days you do yours. Doing His will is a by-the-minute, by-the-hour job. It is always doing what He is calling you to do. If He wants time with you, you spend it, even when you think you are too busy. He comes first. If He wants time with your children, you spend it with them, even if you get pulled away by others. I am calling you to do those things I tell you and prompt you to do in your heart. Everyone knows My will if he prays and stays close to Me. The others just do not feel right. Everyone in the world may tell you something else but you know My will because it feels right for you. It may not be easy. It may not be to your liking, but it is your feeling in your heart, "This is what He is calling Me to do."

He may give you a disease which almost forces you to come His way, but this is not force. Many, even when given helps to follow My will through sickness and crosses, still choose their own ways. One man is given a cross. He accepts it as from the God Who loves him. He learns, he grows, he is following My teaching. Another becomes bitter and hateful and hurts all those around him. He learns not one teaching and he follows Satan's lead to make him mean. When I give a lead to accept a cross, accept it!

I am teaching you valuable lessons in your crosses. Many think they are doing My will and they do many good works. Doing My will is not performing good works. Doing My will is doing whatever I am calling you to do. I may want you to do something else. When you keep choosing "good works" as you plan your own life, this is doing your work. You plan it. You are in control. You do good things and you therefore rationalize, "I am doing God's will." You are doing your will. You are picking. You are choosing. You choose good things—it is God's will. My will is only found from Me. I choose what you are to do. You follow Me. I tell you, in your heart. I tell you in your mind. I tell you in the silent times you are with Me. If you want to do My will, you have to slow down and be close to Me. Stop doing your own will. Do the will of God. You are receiving messages in your heart. You may never hear one message. You stay in your heads and tell yourself what you want to do. You gauge it, "Is it a good act?" Then you say it is God's will. God's will comes from God. It doesn't come from your figuring out what you would think is a good work and then deciding to do it.

God's will is not what you would always choose to do. But God's will is doing what He tells you, in love, to do. You love Him so much you comply with all He sends you. Doing His will is very hard. I wait to tell you what is God's will. Will you listen or will you figure it out on your own? If you want to do God's will, you have to be in communication with God. I am calling you to daily prayer in front of the tabernacle. I am calling you to Mass and Communion. I am calling you to quiet moments with Me constantly trying to listen and do God's will. Doing God's will is a full time job and it is hard enough to figure out His will in your own life. Each person needs to come and be taught by Me. Each person needs the Holy Spirit in his life. We work together to give you the will of the Father. His will is God's will. I, Jesus, want you to do the will of My Father. His will is My will for you.

God wants you to know you need God working in your life, enlightening you and being ever present to you. You will not know many things if you do not pray to the Holy Spirit. Pray to Him and beg for His gifts. It is His wisdom you seek. Don't go to people. Oh, you may get advice all right. Who does that come from? Go to people to do God's will—how silly is that one? Go to God to do God's will. Do not get discouraged. Be open to what He has in store for you. Don't figure it out and then go and ask Him if it is the right thing. Don't figure anything out. Wait on the Lord. Be close to Him. Have time with Him every day. Make Him first and last in your life. He is your all. He is your reason for being. He is Whom you turn to. He is God.

God has a plan for you. He can tell you. You must seek. Do not go to others to know the things of God. Rip the phones from the walls. Watch your conversation. It is there that Satan leads many down the wrong road. Conversation should be of Me. Now in many circles, if you talk of Me, people get up and leave. How sick they are. No one can make it in this world without constant connectedness to Me. I want you plugged into Me as you are dependent on every breath. I want you plugged in to Me with an open heart and an open line. Others do not dump garbage in My line to you. It remains open and clear. Your heart must be fixed on doing God's will. It is hard, hard work. Your time is not your time. I have loaned it to you to work for Me.

Seek to know the will of God so you are doing My work. I need you every minute doing My work. One smile may be that which turns a heart to Me. Don't let Satan creep in with worry and doubt and indecision. There is no decision. That is you. My ways are simple. Sometimes you fall. You are human. That is pride that tells you you must create the perfect image. Stay steadfast in Me and the image you create will take care of itself. You worry about everything. I tell you again, if you pray to Me and stay fixed to My heart, you don't have to do anything but let Me run your life and it will work beautifully. I don't make boo-boos. I am your most ardent lover. I want what is best for you. What you think you want may be very wrong for you and so you get it and it is a hard road to walk. You get what you want but it is drudgery and heartache. It was what you wanted, not what God wanted, and it was not right. It may have been a good thing, but not what He wanted for you.

God's way is joy, peace and love. To walk the path with God is to feel His presence and have joy even in crosses. Come walk with Me, talk with Me. Let Me run your life. Do My will. Make this your top priority. Then you will have peace and joy in your hearts. Your lives will unfold as a book to be lived and you will touch many hearts along the way. I love you so.   11/27/93

You Are Special

Jesus: I come, you wait. I am here, Body, Blood, Soul and Divinity. All power is Mine, says the Lord, for you are My chosen people. You wait and I come to you. Prepare Me a way for My coming. I come as a baby at the breast. I come into your midst, not as a mighty king, but as a little helpless baby.

You may see Me in your mind's eye. I am becoming more and more alive to you. You truly, after all this time, believe in Me. Do you feel some shame for all your doubts? I come not to shame you but to be with you in an intimate way so I might love you as I so desire. I come to love you. I entered the womb and was born a little helpless baby, God-made-man, for love of you. I lived, I walked, I grew on this earth as a little boy, subject to My parents here. I was raised like any other child. I did not come with the blare of trumpets and roll of drums. I was born in a little old stable with the sheep and cows. The only blare of trumpets came from the angels who sang in the distance. I came and lived as a child for love of you.

Look at all I have done and I do for love of you, but you still do not see how I value you. You are so precious to Me, that I, God-made-man of a woman, came to dwell on this earth as a baby and a little child out of love of you. And you doubt your worth? You look in all the corners for recognition, for promotion of self, to help yourself to feel good, when I, God, came to a woman as a baby and dwelt on this earth out of love of you. Oh, how I love you this day. It is the same as the day I was born and the day I died. My love is always the same. My love is so intense and so great that you, in your human form, cannot fathom its might, but it is so unbounded.

Wake up, My people. See what value you are to Me. God loves you this way. I am such a good God to you. I am filled to the brim with My love for you. The Father loved you, My little child, no less than that He gave His only Son for love of you. Do you understand Me at all, child? How can you, at any moment, doubt your specialness? Embrace your value to God. God the Father to send His only Son, God the Son to comply, and God the Holy Spirit to give His consent to such an undertaking, all for love of thee!

Oh, ye of little faith, quit looking for recognition in your brothers. Their affirmations are momentary and wane in time. They love you today and hate you tomorrow. When they are tired they love you less. If you use your brothers to measure your worth, your worth is never the same— some days good, some days not so good. You are the same beautiful creation of God, but your human brothers only measure by their human ways. They cannot love beyond their limits. But God can love you, only as God can, in a divine way. God's love never falters. It never changes. It is not good today and not so good tomorrow. It is the same as the day He chose to be born and die for love of you!

Oh you, so precious of the Father, out of love of the Holy Spirit, I was born to give you life, life eternal, life forever. Why would you go to a human and ask, "How am I doing? Was I good today?" Go to God. Ask and you shall receive, knock and it shall be opened unto you, seek and you shall find. My love is endless, unbounded. I proved your worth and value by My birth, death and resurrection. Do you need more than this to convince yourself of your value? Oh, little ones, come and forget yourselves. You need not ever try to measure your worth again. Come and be alive in Me. Love Me. Be busy about this task. Forget yourself. Your value has been proven by Me. Be busy about your union with Me. Forget your unworthiness, your recognition. Forget yourself. Die to yourself that you may truly live.

Go about being aware of My love for you. Dwell on how I, God, want to be close and united to you. Forget your lowliness, focus on My love. Your value was and is established by My love. Your job is to concentrate on this love.

Come and receive Me, God-made-man, every day in the Eucharist. You are so blessed, My chosen children, to receive God in your body. Who are you that He chose to humble himself and come inside of you? And then you look for recognition and value in the world. Oh, you silly ones. This will not make you feel loved and accepted. It is the wrong place to go—to any human being for the recognition the soul craves with God! When you realize that I loved you to My death, then your hearts will no longer be empty. You can be respected and loved by every soul on the earth. This is not enough for your soul. It craves the love of God. Seek ye first Me and My love and then you will be satisfied. You will feel the enormous value I have placed on you, My lowly servants. And what do I ask in return? Only love, love of God, first and foremost, then love of neighbor as yourself. All I give and then I only ask you to love back.

Can you not come to Me and share yourself in love with Me? Will you not put Me first when I am God and I have loved you to this extent? Come and be with me in Communion. Come and sit in My house, with Me truly present in the tabernacle. Out of love of you, I sit by day and by night and few ever come. Do you not think how, if I loved you so much as to die for you, I would not pour out My gifts when you come to Me?

I wait with My love when you come in the Eucharist and Adoration. I fill you to the brim. This world cannot give anything like God. Oh you, so silly, visit your friends, go to stores, buy, buy, buy. The soul is thirsty. You look in the wrong places for your compulsive cravings. It is for God. You were created to know, love and serve Him. Nothing but He fills this hungry soul. Come to Me. Your other ventures leave you dry and unsatisfied. Only God feeds the soul. The soul is never satisfied except in union with Him. You can continue your useless feats but you are pursuing them in vain. You are only momentarily satisfied and then you must look for another self-fulfilling adventure. I am Jesus Christ, Son of God. I came to this earth out of love of you. I lived and I died a brutal death that you might have life. On the third day, I rose and I gave you new life. Only I can give you this. All other adventures leave you empty with a deep yearning to be satisfied.

Come to Me, beloved of My Father, and find the light of life. Drink the cup of salvation. Come and be filled and you will have life eternal, not as this world gives you life, but as only I can give you life. Oh, so silly ones! To forget Me! So sad, My soul is so sad for all those who have run amok. Pray and sacrifice for them that they will be lead to My light. The people in darkness have seen a great light and have been drawn from the pits to the life of the spirit. Alleluia, Alleluia.

Offer your days for these brothers. Pray for their conversion. They need your prayers. They need your example. It is in your commitment to Me that they are taught. You do not take them aside and constantly bother them about Me. You live your life in My love and your life is their teaching. I shine from your eyes and live in your hearts and you radiate an energy that only I can give. You do not have to do. You have to spend your life being attached to Me, spending time with Me, and you will teach the greatest lessons of My love by just being.

Oh, I love you, My little ones. What a battle you fight every day in the world whose people have made themselves their own gods. You must remain faithful in your love of Me. Nothing will matter but this in the end.

I come, you wait. You are filled to the brim. This alone satisfies the hunger.   11/28/93 4:30 a.m.

I Control Your Hot Air Balloon

Jesus: Come unto Me all who are weary and I will give you rest. You come and I wait for you to be alone with Me. In these precious moments, I talk to you. Do you know how truly special these moments are?

I, God, talk to you and you wait for the teaching I want to give. I may not give you any or I may give you some great gift of wisdom. This is how I want your life to be: controlled by Me. You wait and know I will take care of you. I know just what you need. You must come, though, or you miss it all. You could have slept and missed My whole teaching. You come in silence in the night.

I love the quiet hours during the night. I love you to come when you could choose to sleep. This delights My Sacred Heart when you come from your sleep and you spend time with Me. You do not suffer from this sleep loss. I make you energized and you never miss it at all.

People do not realize that I do not need to give in to your body. I do not have to obey natural laws. I make people hear what I want them to hear. They may not even know what they are saying and what people are hearing. You, little flower, do not have to do it. I do it for you. I use you to do My work if you are willing. Why would I subject Myself to what you say? I can do all things. I can talk for you. I can have others hear what I want them to. I do not have to depend on these laws on earth. I am God! I can put a person on your path and you wonder how he was there at that particular moment. All the minutes and seconds in a day, and your paths just cross. No, My child, it was My miracle. It was My doing. I watch you like a doting mother and I want your lives to work for My greater good. Oh, you say, it just happened. That is not so. I was behind the scenes.

You think you are in control. Ha, ha! You don't control anything. Look at the weather. Did you control this cold? No, that is out of your control, but other things are in your control. I give you a free will. You control your will. Beyond that, you do not know the miracles I make happen in your life.

I am always working behind the scenes. I do not abandon you ever. I watch you as a doting mother. Your children I guard. If more parents knew how I guarded their little ones, they would be constantly on their knees in front of Me!

I have all the power. You have experienced My power over and over again. Little coincidences, you say. No, I am afraid not. It was Me at work!

If you want to know Me. You must seek out all the times I was especially present and something just happened and put these occurrences on a list in the front of your head. You need My special glimpses of heaven memorized. You, My child, have quite a list to make. Do not tarry. Do this for yourself. Today. Begin it in this notebook and the Holy Spirit will help you remember (1) special times when others just appeared or things just happened and (2) supernatural experiences in your life when you got a special glimpse of heaven from Me (including a dream, smelling incense, roses, seeing images, Mary, Me, the Holy Spirit). You need dates. I am very conscious of dates. Special occasions. I want you to know My presence. I want to be alive to you. I want you to see the miracles I provide for you.

If you make this list, your doubts will definitely diminish. Include the births of your children and how it all worked so perfectly. Include Me in your life. I am here. I am making things happen. Look for one in everything that happens. I am truly here in your life at every minute. I do not leave your side. I am present while you sleep, watching and waiting for you. It is now 5:00a.m. See how I am here.

Make your list today. This will enhance your relationship with Me. This will make Me really alive in your undertakings. The minute something miraculous occurs, write it down. You smell incense—write it down. This will really make Me alive to you. Even if you don't remember everything, don't miss one opportunity from here on. I am right by your side, little one. I want to be alive in your life. You need to write these things down.

I love you so much. I truly do. I wait and watch you in the night and all day lest your foot stumbles and falls. Quit thinking you are in control. All you control is your will and what I really want is total surrender. I want to run you, totally, out of love and trust in Me. I want you to become selfless and let Me possess your soul. Then your life will fly, like the hot air balloon. You are free. You are unattached. You sail the skies and you do not meet any resistance from the earth. You are above the earth. It has no power over you. You are powered by the fire of My love. You remain high and upward. I am at the helm. You only trust in Me. I watch the wind and the weather. I look out for you. You are My little babies in a hot air balloon.

Oh, babies, I want to baby you. Let go of your silly wills. This is what separates us. Let it go, I tell you. Spend all your days focused on Me. Make yourself My empty vessel. I use you and you comply. I am God, child! Do you think you are smarter than God? Then let go, you silly. I know all things and I have all the power. I can make it rain or sunshine. I can plant the right person on your way. I can make you perform phenomenal feats. Why do you want to hold on to your ways? I am God. Can you operate like God? How silly! I am able to do all things in an instant.

Give it up. Turn it over. Let Me be in you and you have a winner every time. Whatever I send you is out of the greatest love. Your trials have been your greatest teachings! Would you give your beautiful child a snake when he asks you for your help? How much more would I, Who am God, give to you, My beautiful ones.

Oh, oh, oh, I love you so, little one. You don't have any idea how deep! Come and let Me show you My love for you. This is the only way to go. I am the way, the truth and the life. He who abides in Me will have the light of life. Alleluia, Alleluia, Alleluia.   11/29/93 4:30 a.m.

Play and Pray with Your Children

Jesus: You must listen to Me and do My will. When I speak, I do so for a reason. You are My little ones and I comfort and wait for you.

Remember Satan is there to trip you up and leave you out to dry. Like a thief in the night he comes and is there.

Come to Me and wait with Me. You must learn to let go of it all for love of Me. Alleluia, Alleluia. Praise the Lord. Come and follow Me, little ones, for My burden is light and My honor great indeed!

I am the Omega. I am all you need. You come in your trials and in your joy. I love you when you are troubled. I do not love you today and then abandon you when you need Me. I know you are weak and you fall. You want to do My will and others pull you away from your children. Learn from this. Place your cares in My hands. You must have time alone, every day, with your children, praying and playing. This comes after adoration. It is a time of refueling and reflecting My love to them. Nothing is as good for your children but your time alone with them. It does so much for a child to have a parent pray and play with them.

Others in the world can find someone else. I gave you these children and they come first. Children need to be valued. They are so precious to Me. When you are spending time with your family, it pleases Me so. If you spend too much time with others and none with your family alone, it divides you. Listen to this teaching. Satan wants to divide you and knows this time is a powerhouse for getting along and loving, so he plants distraction and puts people in your way. Time alone at home, being together, playing and praying together—this is a must to a happy, united family! Tell others you are busy doing My work. This is My work for you. It is My job for you. If you had to teach, you would be there for every class. Your job for Me is being with your children. Other things don't matter. This is your work and you must show up for your job or you are not coming when I call you to work. I am the boss. I want this private time alone with My little ones every day. This is your work. This is the power behind the family. It must be united and strong to withstand the sickness of this world. Your son is gone six hours a day. He needs this rebuilding. Your daughter needs to be with you. Time with you is most important to her.

I am Jesus, Son of the Living God. I dwell in your heart. Your job is to be with Me first, then be with your children. They are children. Other adults can find other ways to get their needs met. They can come to Me and read these letters. I have spoken. Your job is as a mother. Mary is the model for all mothers. Look at the closeness between her and her Son—very close. This is My model for you. Stay tuned in and present always for them. This is your job, your time and prayer alone with them.

Satan wants division. Beware of his cunning ways. The wolf comes in sheep's clothing. Beware, he comes as a thief in the night. You are fine and then, in one second, chaos. That is Satan. He is not nice. He wants your soul and he wants your hearts. He wants to make you cold and unattached. He uses whatever or whomever to divide you: people, phones, TV. He can use a prayer meeting to divide you if you would have been better off being alone at home together. When you are together, talk about Me. Your daughter has much to say and so does your son. The biggest gift you can give a child is the importance of Me to them. I am what is most valuable in their life. If I am so valuable, I should be the topic of conversation. Your son was thinking of Jesus carrying a tree. This is beautiful. Your daughter has many messages. She should share them with you both. Read every message I give you, every day, to your children. This is your job for Me. Treat it as a job you get paid for. You get paid by Me and that is the most valuable pay!

I love the family. I want it strong. I love My children. They are precious to Me. All are heirs to My kingdom, but it is only won through prayer and sacrifice and knowledge of Me. You must share My life and the lives of the saints with your children. I am Jesus, I will heal your hurts and send you out to play. Play this day. Teach My message of love. Satan has weakened your front and now he is attacking you. Security comes in a strong family. Fortify your walls with prayer and playing together. Have time for your children. My time is not your time. I loan it to you to do My work. My work is being with your kids.

Be attentive to My commands for you. This is My will! Do as I say. You want to do My will. Then do it! Don't ask, and I tell you, then do what you want. Oh, such willfulness in My people! I tell you, "Pray with Me. Be with Me." Then you are too busy. But you say, "I want to do the will of God." My will for My people is to turn back to God. Make Him first in your life. Spend time with Me, alone. Then you are doing My will and all else will work out.

Oh, beloved of My Father, I do love thee. Listen and harken to My commands: Mass, Communion, adoration and your family. Pray together. This is My wish for you.

Alleluia. God has spoken and you must harken to the call. It is His call to make ready your hearts for the coming Christmas is the coming of Christ to your hearts. Your children come first. Presents and business are not of God. They are commercial and divide you. Parties are not fun when the little ones are left out or thrown in front of a TV or sitter. Children are God's gifts to this earth. Recognize all the value they are to you and to Me.

Messenger: Alleluia. Praise the Lord. I accept the crosses You send me because You alone know that which I need.   11/30/93

TV Has Much That Is Evil

Jesus: My dear child, I love you very much. I know how hard it is to get out of bed. Your days are going by quickly. The nights are short.

This morning I would like to teach you about many things. Try in all you do to be holy. The world is pulling you so far away from me. You can no longer be of Me and not take a stand. Your life is so different from everyone else. It is an uphill battle to just remain in the world. They have surely lost their way. You have to deny all the TV shows. You have to stay away from the movies. You have to avoid the newspaper most of the time. All the connections with the world are detrimental to your health, the health of the soul. Whatever you take in through your eyes and ears, into your brain, becomes a part of you. If you watch TV what you take in is so vile it will cripple your soul. I know you enjoyed the movies, but there are none now to enjoy. They are full of sex and sin and violence. Watching such trash puts you in an occasion of sin.

Your life here is a battle. You can no longer be of Me and not take a stand. You must take a stand to protect yourself and your children. To not take a stand in this world leads you to sin. The world is sinning, right before your eyes on the TV and in movies, in the newspaper. And they boast of their sin. You are being persecuted because you are violated by the sins of the world. Oh, how they will persecute you for your faith! You know you are doing what you are supposed to because it is a hard road to travel.

Shame on the newspapers, TV and movies that lead my beautiful children to sin. There is so much sin on TV alone, not to mention the young people who watch it constantly and then go to the movies for recreation. This is recreation? This is sick! Little kids go to school and they do not even hear My name. They are thrown into a school where it is hard to remain because the other children have been taught such sin and nastiness from home and TV. That a well fed child, fed by God, is lost and hurting in school! He is a lonely soul because the whole class is very worldly.

Poor innocent little children! Then they are fed a daily dose of sin on the TV and in the movies. What a terrible set it is—a set to teach hatred, sin, sex, violence—every evil you can name. You can see it accepted in a five minute segment on TV. What garbage for your soul!

Oh, the poor little children. I cry for their little lives. Even if parents are good, they learn just from being with others. Why worry about your children's socialization? Who needs to socialize with those going to today's schools? At their age many are engaged in so many sins, sins of the flesh constantly—sins of hate, sins of violence, lack of care for their brothers. There is little love there. Everyone is macho and full of ego!

Watching such trash. Oh, I lament My little beautiful ones. Parents, be with those children. They have a worse struggle than you. They are young and innocent and are sent to school to be taught. They are taught, all right. Sick things! Send your little child to school to be schooled in such vileness? They learn so much from each other. Look at the indifference and hate for one another, getting their own way. It is all hurting their growth. Send your innocent to the slaughter in today's schools and then if you are a good parent, spend the rest of the night trying to unteach what they have learned.

Oh, little one, all I can say to you is pray, pray, pray. Make prayer the center of your life. You need to stay so close to Jesus. Then the world does not get to you. Spend so much time with Me and pray to the Holy Spirit. Pray every day for His guidance. He is so good to you.

I love you all with the tenderest and most loving heart. I am sorry for what you are shown on TV. Don't watch it or go to any movies that you think might not be okay. Find out first. Your children don't need the movies with the big screen, sinning before your very eyes. What a way to teach sin. The devil is running the movie reels. He is sitting in your TV, glaring at you in joy. This is indeed the time the devil has infiltrated so much of your world.

Pray, pray, pray for your brothers, for the souls that make movies and TV and then promote it. They will answer for all the sins it promotes.

Then could you question My asking you to speak? Others sin openly every second on TV. I need you to tell all of My love. Would you not do this for Me to combat this awful sin? The TV has gotten even bigger—yeah, to show the sin in such size! My heart aches at little ones watching filth while their parents work!

Your children are your prized treasures from Me. You must be on guard at every moment with them. Pray and play with your children. I am calling you to alter your busy lives and go back to the basics of being constantly with them. If they are left alone with a Nintendo they are taught to act out avenged violence. Their bodies are doing violent things. It isn't enough to see the TV, movies, etc. They have to perform violent acts on these games and are rewarded by winning the game for a game of good violence. How sick can you be!?

Parents, be with your children. You don't need the TV. You need to be with the children and they need to be with you. Throw the games out. They not only teach violence, but they even make you participate to win at violence. Acting out such vileness—how sick! Your little ones need you, my parents—not a little. They need you constantly to ward off such violence, sin and untruths being taught every minute.

I love you, you little ones. Pray for the world. My soul is so sad, so sad you do not know! Your prayers comfort My Sacred Heart and help your brothers. Pray, pray, pray, pray. I love you.

Messenger: Jesus, Son of the Living God!   12/1/93 4:45 a.m.

He Never Leaves Our Side

Jesus: My dear child, I am truly here. I come to tell you My words. Listen, all you who labor and are heavily burdened, for I will give you rest. Satan is out to stop you. His power is stronger each day. You must realize he is always around trying to trip you up. None of this matters. Yesterday you had such a hard day. You are too tired and he gets to you when you are tired. I am glad when you play with the children and pray with them.

Sit and visit with Me. My time is drawing near. Be attentive and ever holy. Do not get caught up in one event here. Live each day totally unattached, doing your best, but not getting caught up in anything. The events are all passing and of little importance. Focus on the big picture. Focus on Me and My love. Focus on your overall life. Your job is writing these letters, praying and playing with the children, being with them alone each day. Do not go one day without private prayer.

I am the way, the truth and the light. No one goes to the Father except through Me. Make ready a place that I may continually dwell in your hearts. Your trials do not cut you off from Me. Keep praying and casting out Satan. Keep thinking of Me and My love for you. I do the work in your heart. I make your heart experience Me more and more. You remain open and willing. Satan wants you to give up, to get frustrated. You say things you regret. He tries you and tries you with little things and when you are tired he has a greater chance to get to you. He uses innocent people around you to attack you with angry words or looks or gestures. Do not give him any power.

Come and rest in My arms. Find shelter from the scorching sun by abiding in My shade. I am there ready with solace for your troubled and tired soul. See Me in the eyes of all your brothers. See them as My children. Try to get beyond their imperfections to the fact that they reflect Me in their souls, even when it is hard to see it. I am here. You think I move when you are tired and I am mad because you are being tested. I am closest in these trials and I am there to comfort and love you. Run to My arms. I await with the warmest hug. Cast the devil out. He is lurking around. Like a cap, he comes on and won't leave you alone. Only I can help you take him off. Cast him out by My name. Keep saying Jesus and thinking of the Blood I shed for love of you.

Two angels sit by your side. They come in the night to escort Me. I am surrounded by things like this. You do not know and you do not see what is there with you at all times. You are as a player on the stage but you are being watched and guarded by many outside forces. Stay attuned to the good that surrounds you constantly. Angels go with Me wherever I go. Mary is always by My side. You are escorted by a choir of angels. Believe Me. Satan has only limited power. He is just so irritating! He is there. He wants to trip you. I am there too, escorted by a heavenly choir. I surround you with My love and My arms are open. Run to Me and find refuge in My arms.

I love you so. Alleluia, Alleluia.   12/1/93 5:30 a.m.

Comfort the Weary Soul

Jesus: Come to Me and I will give you rest. I am the God of Jacob and Joseph and all of your ancestors. I know all things. I know you far better than you know yourself. I wait by day and by night for you to come and be with Me. Will you come or will you continue your lives without the Master? I am the Alpha and Omega. I am all that you need. Why do you remain so far from Me? Some tell themselves they are holy but they hold themselves at arm's length from Me. Open up the gates. Do not be afraid. Let yourself go. I am a person. I am a personal God. I am your best friend. I wait when you are weary and bowed down to comfort you. Will you come, or go to man for your answers? If you miss going to Me you remain without help. Man cannot give your weary soul the rest it needs. Man cannot do for you what God will do for you.

Come to Me, all who are weary and heavily burdened, and I will give you rest. I have all you need. Others cannot comfort your weary soul. If you receive comfort, it is only momentary. God's comfort is everlasting. Run with open arms to Him Who loves you and waits at the gates to comfort you. Don't go it alone. Come all the time, strength and weaknesses, and I will always be there to light your way! Turn to Me, morning, noon, night, trials and joy. Always come to your best friend.

Only God can fix the things of the soul. That is His territory. When the spirit is weakened, go to Jesus and let Him heal you. He is the doctor for wounded souls. He is all you need. Pour your cares out to Him and He loves you and pours His trust into you.

I am Jesus, Son of the Living God. Harken, I wait and I am here. I love you.   12/3/93 4:30 a.m.

Where Will You Go On the Day of Reckoning?

Jesus: I come, you wait, you are filled.

Messenger: It seems so long since I talked to You, My Lord.

Jesus: Time is so short—here today, gone tomorrow—and your reward awaits you. What glory awaits him who serves the Lord and his life is over? Where will you go on that day of reckoning? How is the state of your soul? Did you spend your life in search of a kingdom, never to find one but an idle pursuit, looking here and there for a kingdom, but never finding what you sought? The kingdom you seek is not of this world. Your life is not its own reward. Your life is being spent for the reward to follow. This life is not the reward in itself. This life is only the batting of an eye, the dropping of a pin, and the life hereafter is at hand. Where are you going, My little one? Did you spend your life in such idle pursuits, only to find that your search was in vain? Your life was empty and now what do you have to show for how you lived? Is all that mattered up like smoke in your face and you say, "Is that all there is?"

And what did you do with your little life here? When I paraded in front of you, you knew there was more to your life but you closed your eyes and told yourself, "Nay, I live for the likes of this world. Crazy are those who speak of a life hereafter." You heard, you were made aware, you had opportunities, you laughed, you sneered, you ran amok and told yourself you were all that mattered. This life was your end. You were going to have it all right here—one, glorious, true life. You were in pursuit of the treasure found in your house, at your job, in your children, in your pocket. You blinded yourself to any other possibility and continued on your willful little way. You were sought after by Him. You were probed, you were pursued, you were shown the light. I loved you your whole life. I followed you and opened My heart to you and you closed yours and spit in My face and you walked away. You walked over your brothers and you hardened your little hearts.

You pursued idle pursuits and you ran around with a worldly-focused gaze. Tunnel vision. You knew you were not in a tunnel. You knew from My pursuit of you that there was much more but you closed yourself off and went full steam ahead down the wrong road. You did not see the birds of the air or the children at play. You saw a world to be gained and a goal to be achieved. You sought an empty treasure in a barren field and when I stopped at each crossing and said, "Oh, that you would come and follow Me," you ignored My prompting and proceeded like a blind dog down the same path toward the barren field. And your heart lacked joy and it became harder and harder as you trod, but at each crossing you say, "Nay, Lord, I will find My reward here and be off."

Oh, you silly fool! To live your life for such emptiness. The only life that is is in Me. You never die. This is but a test. This is a test for you to receive a real reward. I have prodded you and tried to lead you toward Me but you spit in My face and went your willful way. Oh, little ones, eternity is so long. It doesn't end today or tomorrow. It goes on and on and on and never ends. This is a test to see how you will fare in the end. To put all your treasures in this life is to store up nothing. You take not one dime with you. All that remains is the things of the heart, your love of God and your love for your fellow man.

To follow God is to find the real reward, a field brimming with milk and honey. And you will behold the face of God! This and this alone feeds your hungry soul. All else leads the soul to barren lands. Store up a treasure of gold for the life hereafter. When you come to that crossing remove the blinders from your eyes and look at your beloved Jesus, staring right into your heart. Take the hard crust from your chest and let your heart become alive in His love. Do not pursue idle pursuits. Go down the road that leads to Jesus and at the end you will see His face! His road is well marked all through your life. Your sisters and brothers who loved Him looked into your eyes, but you wore blinders and laughed at them.

Oh, silly! A few years? For what? You don't get anything here but heartache, momentary pleasure that leaves you empty, so you numb your hearts with TV or alcohol or food or sex. It lasts only a moment, but you numb the craving in the soul. Oh, poor starved little ones, your soul can only be fed by Me. You are starving yourself to death. Your soul is withering and dying. Your victory is already won by Me Who died a brutal death for love of you! Come to Me. I knock at the door. Will you open or will you run amok down roads that lead to emptiness. On that day of reckoning when I, in all My pursuits of your soul and My saddened heart, finally have to turn you away and say, "I do not know you. I pursued you your whole life. I stood by your side. I walked by you the whole way and you never turned your head. You looked for your glory here and I waited and waited. I sent others to show you the way to the golden reward but you laughed and continued in your willfulness to the barren desert."

Oh, child, I love you. Many have prayed and sacrificed for you but you would not turn your hearts to Me. I am the way, the truth and the life.

All other roads lead to destruction of the soul. My ways are not easy, but they are filled with peace, love and joy. My ways are everlasting. Your soul craves this union with Me. You are fighting off that which your soul thirsts after. It doesn't feel good, but you close your eyes and numb your craving. Oh, turn to Me and find rest, My little ones, now before it is too late! I am as close as your breath.   12/5/93 5:10 a.m.

How Will You Write the Life of Your Soul

Jesus: Come, come, beloved of My Father. What can I do to get you to turn your wills toward Me? You have a free will. You choose your destiny. Will it be Me or your own destruction? When you sin you are hardened in heart. It feels very bad but you justify your actions. Your hearts have turned into stone and your eyes are covered with rags and you see nothing before you.

Oh, little ones, no one can reach you. My heart laments your thirsty little souls and I cry to you as one Who suffered a brutal death for love of you. And your ears! You have plugged them up and you wander in darkness on a useless path toward your own destruction.

Come, please come to Me. I am so loving. I have so many gifts to give you. I forgive the greatest sins and you are made free and filled with such love. Come, oh open your gates to Me. Let Me in. I tell you this life is but a breath in the scoop of eternity. Knowing Me is not going to church on Sunday with a closed heart. Knowing Me is living your life in Me every minute of the day. To know Me is such a reward. I am so loving and good to you. I fill you with peace and love and joy. Even in trials you are at peace. I lament your love. Please turn to Me. I am an ardent lover waiting by your side. I never move, even in the darkest hours of your life. It is you who have chosen such darkness. My ways are light, even in suffering. To know Me is to walk a lighted path. To be absent of Me is to live in darkness. I love you, little ones. Turn your wills to Me. Satan has a strong bind on you if I am not part of your life. You have become his slave and you think you are free. You are being held captive by Satan. You are not free. True freedom comes from knowing Me! What can I say that I have not said? It is your choice. You choose your own destiny. You are the author of your soul. How will you write the life of your soul? If you are to have life eternal, you must write your biography according to God. To write your own book is to lead to a bad seller. It will never go to the house of the Lord. It will go to the tomb of destruction. I am the Good

Shepherd. I lead My sheep and they follow Me. I hold them in My arms and comfort them on their way. I am loving and I care for them. Some go astray and I lament their passing because I care for them the same as those who follow Me, but they are willful and follow their own whims and they fall off a cliff and are destroyed. I lament the loss of My little sheep, but they choose their fate and I tried all I could to save them.

Oh, little ones, you choose your fate and all My promptings will not change your willful ways. But your willful ways will lead you to everlasting damnation. I can say no more.

Say the Our Father and listen to every word. It says all you need.
I love you so. Jesus Christ, your Savior!   12/5/93 6:00 a.m.

It Is In Silence That I Come

Jesus: You come and I am here with you. I am with you in all your dreams at night. I am with you all day. I never leave your side. You may move from Me, but I stay close to you always.

I am He Who desires to teach you. I use your life to teach you lessons. Oh, little one, you have so much yet to learn. Be entirely of Me and My way so you do not miss one teaching.

This world is only a breath compared to eternity, here this day, gone tomorrow. People hold on to it as if it would never die. Your brothers are hurting. Offer up all your sacrifices for their souls. Constantly pray. Offer up your day, each day, for them. Say the morning offering with your children. All the little things you do each day can be a prayer for your brothers. Offer the day for the intercession of Me and My mother. We know who of your brothers really need prayers.

You may not feel that you are doing much but your prayers, offered up to Me for My intentions, are so powerful. You do not know the power of your prayers and sacrifices. The world is in so much darkness. It is suffering and has blinded itself to Me. You can help so many people through your prayer. Never underestimate the power of your prayers and sacrifices.

I called, you came. Make ready a place in your hearts for the coming of the Lord! Do not tarry. Time is short and His birth approaches. This time before Christmas is a time to ready yourself for Him. Anticipate His birth with eagerness. The little boy, Jesus, is born to this world. He comes as a baby but His coming is such an event. What His birth, the birth of a baby, did to change all of time!

So humble, the birth of a baby in a stable, and it would change all of time. This is Jesus, Son of God, made man, come to free the world of its sin. He comes as a little baby. He is born of Mary in a little town of Bethlehem. Who comes for this event? Shepherds and cows. But a light shines in the sky to broadcast this event! This is how it is with Christ. There is not a blare of trumpet, not a roll of drums.

Jesus comes quietly at each Mass. And who comes? God-made-man— at every Mass! It is quiet. It is not boastful. But it is God-made-man, Son of God, come to dwell in your hearts. The only blare of trumpets and roll of drums are in your hearts. If you are not aware of God truly present there in the Eucharist you miss the big event. Angels stand by and sing but man, in all his blindness, may miss the momentum of this event. You come to Mass and quietly you approach His altar. Quietly you receive God! If you are not in tune with His teachings and what is happening here, you will miss the whole event! Only those who seek Him and spend their life directed at knowing Him realize what occurs at every Mass.

Oh, you little ones, I come quietly into your hearts, but it is nonetheless the significance of the event. I am Jesus Christ, Son of God. Your hearts should be pure and your tongues holy. You should come with pounding in your chest and anticipation of what is happening. Only those who know Me truly realize what occurs because I come so quietly.

I am not boastful, I am God. If you miss the greatness of this occurrence, it is your own doing. I do not sound a trumpet. I come very quietly and I steal a place in your hearts. It is your readiness and your awareness of Me that makes My coming change your life.

Ask Me to teach you more and more each day about Me. I am there, but in your busyness you might miss Me. I am quiet and powerful. The world is noisy and abrupt and without power. It is in the silence I come. It is in the whisper I am revealed to you. It is in your search for Me that your love for Me grows. The world flaunts its useless products in front of your eyes. It is boastful and flaunting, but it is worthless. I am quiet and hidden. I am here, but you must seek Me. I do not boast of My greatness. I am there in the silence, but My might is unbounded and My power endless and I am always there out of love of you. But if you listen to all the noise in the world you will not find Me. It is only in the quiet whispers that I am found. The true treasure must be sought after. Put this noisy world aside and come to be with Me in the silence. Silence is golden and I am waiting there for you. 12/6/93

Be At Joy In My Hot Air Balloon

Jesus: Focus on Me and My words here and leave your personal life out. I want My messages to get out. Do exactly as I tell you to do. Do not try to do more than I am telling you to do. You need to place total trust in Me. I will make My messages get out the way I want. I have a plan and I will see personally to its execution. You must obey My will to the letter. Otherwise your life will not make sense. This is all to prepare you for what I call you to do. You must see your end as helping others with My messages. Nothing else matters. Persecution or glory for you has nothing to do with it. You remain selfless and unattached. I am in control and I am working behind the scenes. I will personally assist this operation. These are My letters to My people. You are My servants. You follow, I lead. All details will be worked out with ease. Trust in Me and My power. I can make everything work or nothing work. No one can buck Me if I do not allow it. I want these messages out and I will see to it Myself. Do not fret or fume or think you must wonder. Leave it and your life entirely up to Me. I will be at the helm. I am He Who knows the way. Follow Me and all lights will be "go". Count on My divine wisdom and trust in Me.

Your prayer life and your life with Me is most important. You must do My will to the "t". If you make a mistake, then you learn from that mistake. I am calling you to pray and play with your children. This is a must. One day must not go by without this time with them. You are not too busy ever. Trust in Me, My little one. I make the star shine and the moon give its light. I make the baby in the womb. That alone will tell you of My might. I never slumber. I never fall asleep. I am never off on a coffee break! Trust in Me and know My ways. Follow the Master. Be selfless and yielding to all I send you. Be putty in the hands of the potter. Be ready to be shaped and molded into that which I have planned for you.

Satan is taunting you. He may try to trip you up and distract you, but I am in charge and I have the power. Ignore him and trust in Me. This is a good sign to you. You are on the right path. He doesn't bother with those who are not dedicated to Me. He constantly taunts those who dedicate their life to serving Me. He has no power. Cast him out in My name and be about your work.

I want to tell you about heaven. What is heaven? Heaven is your home. It is a place I want you to be with Me. I want you to see the glory that awaits all those who love and serve Me. The angels sing. There is only peace and joy in heaven. Words cannot describe the beauty and rewards that await you. There is no pain. There is no sorrow. There is only everlasting joy there. All those who served Me await your entry into heaven. They stand as a cheering crowd waiting your way home to Me. This is why you toil, My child. All the sufferings and struggles are so little compared to the reward. You know how good and generous I am to you. Now I am the same good and generous God and your reward is waiting for you. Do not ever fear for one minute. Your service to Me is never unrewarded. You suffer for the souls of your brothers. Your prayer and sacrifices may change a heart tomorrow. I indeed want you to pray to Me at every moment. Your life needs to be a continual prayer.

Pray the morning offering with your children for My intentions. You think too much. None of this matters here if you are doing My work. I lift your load. I carry your burden. Do you feel how simple it is and how you deliberate and make it hard. My burden is light. My light I shine on your path. My comfort I give you on a cold night. I am there with you when you go out one moment alone. Feel My presence with you always. Turn to Me and put doubt, fear, anxiety and worry aside. These are Satan's tools to distract you. You do nothing without Me. All things work for those who love and serve the Lord. It is no longer you acting, but I Who operate you. My burdens are light. Let go, surrender, be selfless. I work, you surrender. You do not do it! And thank God!

When I operate you, you make no mistakes. I carry the load and I know exactly which path to follow. You must remain selfless and let Me possess your soul. You diminish, so I increase until there is so little of you and so much of Me. Die to yourself that you might live in My love. My love conquers all. My love is unbounded. My love sees a way where there was none. I can do in one moment what you cannot do.

Heaven itself shows My might. I am such a good God. Do you even know Me a little? Pray when you are troubled. Put your burden at the foot of My cross and be on your way doing My work. Do not deliberate. I call you to action. I run the show. I lead, you follow. Being with Me is being in a hot air balloon. You sail the skies free and unattached. The wind blows and you surrender to the wind. You do not try to control the wind. You surrender. The wind is the Spirit of God. It blows you about with the greatest love. You do not fret or fume because you have been assured that this course is directed by God. You feel the gentle breeze against your face. You take in the sights. You are free and full of joy because, in My balloon, you never have to worry.

I am He Who directs you, He Who powers you. I am He Who loves you. To My death I loved you. Would I not care for you this day? Embrace Me, My child. I am the God of Jacob and Joseph and your ancestors. All you hold on to here is momentary. Only the things of Me last forever. Let go. Surrender. Let go in your balloon. Smile and be lifted up above the troubled earth. You have the secret. You are powered by My love. My love is endless and unbounded. You I watch. You I protect. You I dote after.

Let go, child. Be at joy in My hot air balloon. You are in the balloon I have picked for you. I blow you about but you never fear. I am guarding you. You fly as on eagles' wings. You run and do not get weary. You are operated by Me and I know what is best for you. It is only in love I give all things to you. You stay fixed in Me and I operate you on your way.

Oh child, be lifted above the earth. Spend time alone with Me. Focusing on Me, not anything else, is what moves you high. The more you look downward to the details of this earth, the closer you get to it. The more you focus upward on Me, the more you sail. Burdens do not carry them. I do the deciding. When you think you are putting yourself in control, cut the lines. Let go entirely. Let yourself float and feel the peace in surrender. I never abandon you. I am at your side. Trust in Me and then you fly!

Messenger: My life with Him is unfolding. It is like having a floor that suspends out into space. I keep walking and He holds me up. Like walking on water, I do not sink. I have dreamt many times I was skimming the water and only on the top. I don't fall in. No fear. It is so free and beautiful. Enjoy the sights!

Jesus: Have no fear for I am with you until the end of time. I make all things work for those who love and serve the Lord. You go and live suspended in mid-air. No props. Does your life feel like this? This summer it was roller skates you were on. The floor felt shaky. Now the floor is gone and you are suspended in mid-air. You are being kept afloat by the fire of My love. I blow you gently. You may get a strong wind once in awhile, but you know that I am close by and you will be saved. Like walking on water!

Messenger: If I try to fish all night, I catch nothing. He comes and He gets nets that are breaking. The more I try, the more I get nothing. When He does it, it is unbelievable.   12/7/93 3:30 a.m.

Children Need Time and Attention

Jesus: I am the way, the truth and the life. Those who follow My will—they will have the light of life. I give you My will so you will be the happiest. If you do not follow, you suffer. Things do not work accordingly, and it is an uphill battle. This is the day of the Lord. Rejoice in it and be glad.

If you come to me for all you need, all else works out. When you go to the world, the world does not have what you need and nothing works out. I am the God of your fathers. What they thought was important is of no importance to them now. All that goes with them where they are now are the things of God. Life for them was a short journey, and then eternity. You know, they are no longer here. Did it matter how much money, how big a house? It did matter how they treated their children, but you (their children) still carry that with you. But their money, or job, or cows, or whatever—do you even know?

What you sow today, so shall you reap. If you sow hatred, you reap hatred. If you sow love, you reap love. This is alive in the hearts of your children. You do not pass on your pretty clothes or your beautiful furniture. You do not pass on your beautiful body. You pass on how you were as a person. Like ripples on a pond, it goes on and on.

All material things wither and fade like the grass and die. Fill yourself with the things of God. These are everlasting. The love you show today lives on in the hearts of your children. The anger and hate and selfishness live on in their hearts, too. What a legacy to be given to a newborn baby—generations of hate and selfishness!

So you thought you were so important. You thought children were children and they needed food and clothing and a place to stay. What children need is love and time. They need to know about God from their first moments. Fold their hands and teach them to look to heaven. Little ones are so close to me. They are so innocent, so pure. Teach little ones about God before they get to the schools. Those first years are so important for a child. It is there they are taught for life. Don't go to work and leave these treasures at home, paid for a price of silver. Nothing is worth that money. Their beautiful eyes tell you what a treasure you possess.

Oh people, your children are all treasures in the field. Their love goes on and lives from generation to generation. You had to have money and thus started the feelings of the deprived heart. 'I was not worth my mother's time. I sat around all day with beautiful little gestures and nobody watched. I was, more or less, in my parents' way. Oh no, little one. Your parents were sick. To receive such a gift and then leave it at home and go out to work…!

I cry for the little children, left who knows where, while their mothers are off with their big jobs. Go back to basics, America. What is wrong with your heads?

God, family, love, one another. You are all off at your soccer games, in front of your TV and at your work. More money, more education, more, more, more. It is all so simple: God, family, love, one another. Each makes your hearts happy. Each gives you a far greater treasure, the treasure of eternal life. Your children receive a legacy from you, a pocket of silver or a heart of love.

A diploma and a hardened heart. What a legacy for your children! They are pushed aside and then they are run around like little packages. You must be here for this game and there for that one and then watch that TV show. Nobody even talks to each other. What about the family meal where children sit and learn about love?

Your lives are so busy—for what? God, family, love. That is what is important. Today's world teaches money and things, not God, sex, not love, indulgence. Oh, My heart is sad. Babies are murdered so some can get about their busy lives—doing what? Oh, pray for your brothers. Make your life a constant prayer. You can do more through prayer than anything else.

I am all powerful. I am at your side. I am counting on you, my soldiers of love, in a cold, cold world. Who warms the cold heart? There are so many cold hearts and those with cold hearts do not even feel the chill within their breast! They are blind and arrogant. They think they know it all. They know nothing. Love is the only answer. God must come first. I am here, little ones. I am alive in the eyes of the little children you leave behind. You miss the treasure for 30 pieces of silver. Pray, pray constantly. Your brothers need my help. Your prayers may save one of these cold hearts. Love your brothers through your prayers for them.

I am Jesus, Son of the Living God. I come to you this Christmas with a heart of love to give. The last thing in many hearts is God. They have a million gifts and games and decorations but not a thought for Christ's birth. Pray for your brothers. Make your gift to all of them your prayers. Spend more time with me and less time at the malls. Your gift is the gift of prayer. Give to the poor. Don't buy more things.

Christmas is my birth. Your gift to me and your brothers is the importance you place on God and your love. Nothing else even matters. I am Christmas. It is My birthday. And you can't find a card with Mary, My mother, and Me on it! Oh, how sad!

I ask that you come and pray, that you be an example by your lives. Do not run amok. Come to Me and receive all your gifts. My gifts are everlasting and My Heart is on fire with love of you. The gift you receive is Jesus Christ, Son of the Living God. Nothing can even come close to this gift. I am God. I come to you every day in Communion. What could be more important? Bring your children to Mass, not to soccer games. Pray with your children. Play little games with them. Talk with them. They are the true treasures on this earth.

America, you have missed the boat and now you are drowning in the water. But the worst is you do not even feel the water going down your throats. You are hard and stiff. Oh, oh pray, little ones. Pray constantly. Make this Christmas a gift of prayer for all your brothers in darkness. Sacrifice your time in prayer. Give your own children the gift of your time. Give them the gift of praying and learning about God.

Religious stores should be swamped, but most cannot stay in business. Go to religious stores for your gifts. Buy bibles—what a gift to give—and "lives of the saints." Make Christmas a time to turn yourselves back to God. What a gift—a time for coming back to God, for spending time with your family and for loving one another! And then peace will reign in the hearts of men.

I love you so. I long to share My love with you, but you, my children, are too busy. Pray, pray, pray for this world. Offer your days to Me as a prayer. Your prayers are all being heard. This is a time of My greatest mercy. Pray for the Chaplet of Divine Mercy.   12/8/93 5:30 a.m.

Priorities: God, Family, Love, Each Other

Jesus: I have spoken to you about the family because this is the way that you will receive the strength you need to fight the world. Children are being lost before they have a chance to know any different. Children are open to begin with. If you feed them garbage, that is all they know. The world is ready to indoctrinate them.

Children are the answers to our prayers. Get them young. Teach them about God. Tell them about Me. Now tell the children, they are thirsty, they need your effort to get this message to the parents. Take time with the children. You can't be off doing your own things while your children are being indoctrinated by the TV. Wake up, America! You are losing your most valuable asset—your children! They are being lost for no good reason. Your lack of time! You need to get your priorities straight: (1) God, (2) family, (3) love, (4) each other.   12/8/93 After Mass

I Long For You

Jesus: Come unto Me all who are weary and I will give you rest. Place your head upon My shoulder and I will comfort you. The spirit is willing, but the flesh is weak.

I am your all. You need not worry about what you are to wear or put on because I go with you and prepare your path. You do not falter, you do not deviate. Your ways are directed and your path is lighted by a beacon light lest you stumble and fall. I am ever vigilant and I am ready to pick you up and place you on the right path. Your steps never go far off the path because I watch you like a doting parent. Whatever sufferings befall you, I am so close that you know you need not worry or fear for I point the way and you follow. You know I am with you in adversity. You are comforted when the road is rocky. You travel with directness the whole way.

I am this close to you but you must remain fixed in Me and spend time in constant deliberation with Me. Do you understand? I never forget you. You never go from Me. We are connected by our bond of love and it compels us both to spend time with one another alone every day. This is when I most direct you. It is in joy that you come to be with Me. The time you spend with Me becomes the highlight of the day and all else must wait while you spend this time. It is at least an hour of directed prayer in front of the tabernacle. If you miss this time, you will not flow through the air. You will get caught in the traps of the earth. It is as necessary for you as eating. Sometimes, if you can't make it, you can spend this hour at home, but most of each week you spend your hour in front of Me.

I pour out to you such gifts—you do not know! Come and sit and be with Me! Sit with Me. Be attentive to Me. Listen with an open heart. Do not be eager to leave and do other things. This hour becomes so precious to you that, if you do not come, the longing in your heart for this time makes your day a disaster. It is as though you count and count on something, you plan it with eagerness, and then you run into a big traffic jam and don't get to go. It is very disheartening. This is only a small comparison to what happens when you miss our time together. You must spend the time or the fact that you miss it so much will haunt your day.

I am so loving and so good and I have so much love to give each of you. I wait for you to come so I can pour Myself out to you. So much is gained after Communion. If your time with Me is spent after Communion, you have an extra bonus but, if it isn't, it is still so good. I wait for you to come. I love you so much and I long to be with you. Will you come and share love with Me? I am your ardent lover. I am really waiting for just you. Come and sit and be with Me. Don't read your prayers, just be with Me. Float away in My love. Empty yourself of yourself and be vigilant and attentive to only your soul. Forget yourself entirely. Oh, you little one, how I love you. Please come to Me and sit with Me.

This is an hour I give to you with My most Precious Heart. My heart is ablaze and full of such love. It is as a hot furnace, on fire for love of you. Can you refuse such intense love from God? Think of this. God waits for you. He is waiting with His heart on fire and His arms open wide for you. No one can take your place. I long for you and you alone. I can love everyone like this because I am God. Do not try to understand the ways of God with your earthly minds. Man cannot fathom that which I can do, so why try? I am God - you do not understand the ways of God. But, you must know I am waiting and longing for you and your soul was created to thirst after Me. So, if you do not come, you thirst. I am Jesus, Son of the Living God. I long to be united with you in Communion. I am here, totally present, body and soul, human and divine. I am God-made-man, of a woman, come to this earth and I want to be united to you in Communion.

What could be more important ever than God waiting for you to give Himself to you. God comes to be in you. What a gift for you! And you say, "No, I must go shopping." Where are your minds? Do you not see the folly of it all. Nothing matters but Me. How could you ever miss! Oh, children, put Me first in your life. Fit Me into your days. Plan a routine. Just as you eat, you come to Me to be fed. If you do not come, you are hungry. How are you when you are physically hungry and not fed? Very crabby! Well, you are much the same way when you are spiritually hungry, but the soul has a greater pull on the feelings in the body so you are more wanting for food from Me. Your souls are very hungry for Me. Do you want to starve your soul? Treat it like a baby. It must be fed or it cries. It will cry until it is fed. Your soul will cry when it is not fed. Only I fill the soul. All other misleadings are temporary. In the end the soul cries out, "Feed Me, feed Me." And some say, "Shut up, take some sex, have a drink, numb yourself soul!" It doesn't work! Like a baby it screams day and night and it must be fed by only God. Babies only take what they need. Your soul will only be fed by Me.

I am here always for you. I wait always for you to come. I love you this much: you are worth My being there! I long for your love. Come, little babies. Come and be fed by Me! I care for you. I wait for you. I am hyper-vigilant. I know your needs. I give you rest. Come and rest in My arms. Be fed just the right formula. I know exactly what you need, baby. Come to Me and I give you exactly what you need. Stay away and you cry. You don't get fed. You wander a barren desert with an empty stomach and nothing works because only I can feed your soul. You are wasting your life when you stay away from Me. I can do in an instant what you can never do. You are lost and can't find your way. Your way is the road that leads directly to the tabernacle. Follow that road every day and wait. I watch for your return. Come, beloved of My Father. I wait for you with eagerness. 12/9/93 3:30 a.m.

A Prayer for Holy Communion

Messenger: As I give more and more of what I am attached to away, nobody can have a hold on me. I become, more and more, the little dependent baby in His arms. I depend on Him for everything. It is hard to let go of this to be as a little baby, dependent on Him for everything.

If, when I receive Jesus, I receive God, then so, in some form, I receive the Father and Holy Spirit because how do you separate them?

And the doors to the tabernacle open wide and in it we behold Jesus, Son of God, God-made-man. His presence is to be honored, His name worshiped and adored. His glory is forever.

Jesus: I come as a little baby into your midst. I died out of love of you. I come to you today in Holy Communion. This is God-made-man, Son of God, coming in your hearts to dwell with you. Do not focus on your unworthiness. Focus on His love, just for you, to come to you today. I love you so much and God is truly in your mouth. Be close to Me. Let go of yourself. Enter into total union with Me, soul to soul. Be united with Me totally in your spirit. Forget all the cares of this world and let Me dwell in you and work in your heart. Let Me heal your weary soul.

Open wide your gates and I enter in and you remain changed, never the same because Jesus Christ, Son of God, came to you and dwelt in your soul. You are My temple.   12/9/93

Satan—Like A Worm in an Apple

Jesus: Come and let Me write to you. I awoke you from your sleep to be with you. I am your precious Jesus and I come in the night to tell you My word.

Today I want to tell you about people. Your brothers are in need of your prayers. No longer be angered by their actions. They are sick. If Satan has infiltrated their life, they do not even know it. They continue down a dark path to destruction. One person can do so much good or so much damage. Once Satan comes on the scene and acts out of another, great damage can be done. Satan works like a worm in an apple: he burrows in and keeps attacking the apple. He will go as far as he can. Finally, the whole apple becomes rotten. He burrows his way to the core. It is in the beginning when people agree to little sins that he gets in. He is no good. He is hungry to zap every last bit of life from you.

It is the same way when you allow Me to possess your soul. I operate from you to love and give to those around you. It is I Who loves and acts through you.

A person in darkness has Satan acting in him. He thinks he is free but he is a slave to Satan. How sad to be overtaken by Satan. Satan is debased. No evil is bad enough for him. The more you move away from Me, the more he gets in and uses you. His works are cunning and crafty. His game is deception, twisting the truth, outright lies, division and real heartache.

When I enter your soul, your heart is nourished and plump and red. It beats as a healthy heart and I dwell there and operate from you. I love and act to your brothers. Be of a clean heart, America. Turn back to the commandments. The first commandment alone would change your lives. I am the Lord, thy God. Thou Shalt not have strange gods before Me! If all turned their wills and their lives over to Me we would have a world of love and caring and kindness.

Why do people act this way? Why do they let Satan in? Satan convinces you. You are being cheated and you must do some selfish act. He talks in your head and his reasoning is very convincing. He works on your feelings and tells you you are being treated unfairly. He works you up. You decide to rectify the wrong and then you act. He stirs up hate and anger in the heart.

Oh, little ones, please guard your hearts. Be careful what you agree to take in. Will you listen to Satan and his ugly, selfish words or listen to Me. It is when Satan attacks that you need to recognize his paralyzing grip and cast him out in My name. Recognize it is he who is interrupting your calm life. He comes like a whirlwind and stirs up your life. There is instant chaos. That, dear ones, is Satan. Who else could do such a work of evil art? You have to be strong and recognize that what is happening is of him. He comes like a thief in the night to steal the hearts fixed on God. He wants your hearts. He wants your wills. He wants to operate you. He is cunning and debased.

When an attack occurs, identify it as from Satan and cast him out. This is so hard. He is really gripping you. Pray hard and get him out. He plans to divide you and trip you up. How does it happen so quick? How can you be called so quickly to an argument? It is very easy for Satan. He gets you when you are tired and hungry. He knows what will get to you. He is so cunning. He baits you for his kill and then you wonder what happened. Like a whirlwind, he blows no good. He enters and sweeps away your good works and you feel so empty inside. You must see his work as soon as it begins. When you are at peace and chaos starts, it is he. Pray hard, "Jesus, Jesus." Pray, focus on ME and My beautiful love for you. See Me bleeding on the cross!

You can ward off his nasty, nasty tricks. They are not nice. I love you from the bottom of My heart. Let Me operate you, little one. Open wide the gates of your heart to Me. Constantly offer your life as a prayer. Your prayers today will save your brothers.

I want to use you to do My work. I want to love through you. It is in loving we are made whole. It is in Christ's presence we are happy. Watch out for the Evil One. He aims to trip you up. If you love Me, he hates Me and wants you to be joined to him. It is a battle to gain your soul!

You are finished My child. I love you intently. Go back to bed.

12/10/93 3:34 a.m.

Come When You Are Weary

Jesus: Amen, amen, I say to you, come when you are weary and I comfort you. Don't just come in your good times. It is in stress you need Me more. I want you to come to Me. I am so close. This will be a glorious event for you all.

Let go of it. This is My way. Let go and feel peace. I am Jesus, Son of the Living God. I come in the night to be with you. Thanks and praise to My Father! I am with you now.

Little one, it is not in stress that I leave. I will be with you forever. I know times get tough. Then come to Me right away. Satan keeps gripping your mind. Remember your primary concern is peace. Do not enter into conflicts. Conflict, division, anger, hate—yes, little ones—is from Satan!

My heart is very hot for love of you. It is in your duress that I am the closest. Go about having a good time with the kids. I love you. I will come and make you whole but you must learn to let go when others taunt you. You never feel better if you say anything. You feel worse, so just let go and soak in My presence.

I am the God of Jacob and Joseph and your ancestors. They are gone. Time is so short. Nothing here matters, only love. Love one another and do My work, for the love you give this day will preach a mighty lesson. Be silent. I spoke very little under persecution. You receive a bittersweet feeling when you are attacked. It is as though it is good if you offer it up to Me.

I am with you and guarding you. I love you. Hold tight to My hand. I sustain your weary soul. I make the crooked ways straight. I am totally here and ready to rest and love you. Come into My arms, you little lamb. Let Me embrace you.

11/11/93 4:00 a.m.

Pray For Your Sick Brothers

Jesus: Oh you, beloved of My Father! You come and I am glad. My hand is upon you and you are set free from every tribulation. You are My precious child and I guard your life. Every minute I watch you lest you stumble and fall. You do not run amok because I go with you and guard you and you are free as a little baby at the breast. You are My beloved and I wait for you to come. Come unto Me and I give you rest. Your ways are made straight and your foot does not stumble for I catch you on your way. Oh, what more could you ask for, My little child?

But for many it is not enough. They search for and they seek in this barren land the milk and honey only I have. They wander, they fume, they fret, they make themselves anxious and they never find what they need. I have the key to unlock your hearts. If you will to be opened, I open you and I enter into your soul. You are no longer empty, but full. You are no longer alone, but accompanied by Me, your God. You cry out and I come to the rescue. I enter into your hardened hearts and make them soft and loving. Only I have such power and such might. Do you wonder how does He do this? I do this because I am God. I alone have the power to change hearts. I have the power to make a person dead in sin turn to a life of love, but the person must seek Me and ask for My help.

I do not beg the hardened ones to come. I prompt the hardened hearts to change. I give them ways that they cannot refuse, but they refuse anyway. It is hard for them to walk the road they choose. I remain close by their side and I teach them through you. You prove an ache in their hearts so they battle with you. If you would go away, they would be able to remain in their darkness undisturbed, so they think. But it doesn't work that way! Their own longing for God and their own denial of it causes such an ache in their heart. You who are spreading My light become a target for their unrest. It is all heaped on you and they attack you to get it to go away. But, as long as they think and argue with you, their longing does not cease and their ache is so prevalent. Be of clean heart. Follow My ways. Your soul craves this union with Me, and this union alone. Only I have that which you need! Pray for your sick brothers. Love them and show them My ways. They will hate you. They love the world. You are a thorn in their sides, but their unrest is in their own souls. It is only manifested in their attitude toward you.

They cannot attack themselves so you, who represent Me, become the target for their unrest. If they can work it out on you and win, then their unrest will go away. Don't let them taunt you. Move out of the way and they are left with the unrest. Continue to love and they must face the ache that is inside of them. If you argue with them, you become the ache.

Don't argue about Me. Just be like Me to them. Let My light flow from your soul. You don't have to say a word. Your being preaches a mighty big lesson. My light radiates from you and My power is felt from afar. I am a mighty God. You do not know whom you touch by your connectedness to Me. You touch all those around you without a word. Your being and My life within you stir up the troubled souls. You beckon them to come and savor that joy and peace of heart you possess and they refuse. What unrest for them!

Keep spreading My light. Keep being the little light in the dark world. The darker the world, the more you shine. My light is the brightest. One little light can light up the darkest night. But oh, My beautiful children, need I say it again? Your light only shines when I am the center of your life! You need to be plugged in to Me every day for an hour at least. Come in front of My tabernacle. In an emergency, you can come at home, but you come and we spend our hour together. Me and My love, soul to soul. Oh, oh, how I love you all. I want each soul to come to Me. You may be the only way I touch a brother in darkness, but I can touch them through you and love them if you love them, even when they are nasty. Just don't go there. The more you are connected to Me, the more their behavior does not affect you. You realize their pain (and it is pain, for to be absent of God is pain) and you love them because they are so disturbed.

Love My brothers for Me. Minister in your daily lives. You do not have to go out and save the world. You do not have to make it hard. It is easy. It is to be as you are, to spend time with Me every day. Mass and Communion. Be with your family. Come to Me for short periods during the day, absolutely alone with Me, 5 minutes, 10 minutes. What an energizer! Just where you are, even in the bathroom! Then just be in this world. You will be doing the greatest work. Your life is My work if you spend it for Me. Pray your Morning Offerings. Your being and your staying attached to Me is all you need to do!

Don't run from your jobs when they are hard. Stay and be at peace with their tauntings. This is a big lesson for your sick brothers. They taunt you and you receive a peace. What powers you? Well, My sick one, only God can do that! It is a heavy load, but I go with you. I showed you the way in My life. They persecuted Me and I remained silent. I was at peace to My death. This peace I give to you. Teach My lessons of love and peace. Let Me dwell in your soul. Be selfless and surrender to the God Who wants to possess you.

So, you see, you die to yourself and I am alive in you. I work through you. I act through you. I am Jesus, Son of the Living God and you are My beloved. Come and let Me run your life and you will be at peace. Peace I leave you, My peace I give to you, not as the world gives, but as only I can give. I love you, My precious ones. 12/11/93 12:00 p.m.

Your Peace Will Be Found In Trust

Jesus: Be of Me, little one. I was hungry and you gave Me to eat, naked and you clothed Me. The world will persecute you. They persecuted Me. Stay steadfast in My ways, even in your persecution. The way to Me is rocky. It is a way with thistles and brushes, but the way to Me is the way of truth!

Hold tight to My teachings. Do not question whatever I ask of you and whatever I send you. Your peace will be found in totally trusting Me. The more you turn everything over to Me the easier life will be for you. Do not question or try to figure anything out. Just accept everything as from Him Who loves you. 12/11/93 9:45 p.m.

Try To Be Saints, My Children

Jesus: I love you very much. I am glad to be with you. I am the way, the truth, the life. No one comes to the Father except through Me and the gift I give you is My life.

Messenger: Oh, Jesus, help me do Your will. I love You, God. You are so great. Alleluia. Praise You, Father, Son and Holy Ghost. Praise Your Name forever!

Jesus: Whom are you running from? Where are you going? I am He Who powers you like a power boat. I pass you in the night in your busy lives. Most are too busy to come to Me. I lament their busy lives. If they only knew the whole picture, but I give you a free will. What men do with that freedom! I could at any second snatch it back and then they would know they better mend their ways! What good is love if it is not freely given. I give that you might have life. And the life I give you is My Son.

Messenger: Praised be Father, Son and Holy Ghost!

Jesus: I come to you and you are made whole. How do you separate Me from the Father? We are there as one. You want us each in a neat little package. There isn't a neat little package. We are three in one and you cannot comprehend this! When I act, the Father and Holy Spirit act with Me because We are all God. We all love you this intently. We all loved you intently when I died on the cross. The Father gave you His only Son out of love for you. I, Jesus, died a brutal death. The Holy Spirit was there. We are all God. How do you separate Us? You might try to, but We are not separate. We are one in the same God, Father, Son and Holy Ghost. It is not clear, My little one, because you cannot understand this now.

I am Jesus, Son of the Living God. I am here with you in the bathroom of this motel, you ask? Yes, if you write here, because your children are asleep in the next room, I come in the bathroom. That is why every place is sacred, for I come to you where you are. Don't go to places that are not holy because I go with you. You carry Me in your hearts. If you do not belong where people are sinning, do not go for you carry Me in your hearts. You should remain holy at every instant. You do not get a night or afternoon off to indulge. You are to remain holy always in Me, as My little saints. Try to be saints, My children. In honoring Me, you too can become My saints. It is you who say no to sainthood. I want to call each of you to this special order. How do you commit yourself? Just this much, then the world takes over. Commit your whole heart to Me. Be attentive every moment. I am with you all at every moment and I talk to you. You don't listen. You say, "Oh, He wouldn't be talking to Me." Yes, I am. You are the one who remains at arm's length. You are the one who opens your heart just this much and then holds on to the world this much. Surrender. Let Me in to do My work in you! I will turn you into My saints. You are all chosen by Me for this mission. You say no and turn away and back to your world. I call and you give this much, like a measuring stick. You say, "This much, Lord" and then that is all. Then you run back to the world. Your world is a dry, barren desert. It is out for itself. It does not give freely. It gives to you and expects an exchange of equal value for what it gives. The world is stingy. It does not give out of love. Men in the world love you with hearts likened to Mine, but the world as a whole holds back and does not give when I ask. Most want an even exchange for all they give. Their hearts are hard and guarded and many have big brick walls around their hearts to guard against a thief trying to steal their love. They hold their hearts as an armed guard watches a bank at night. Love is not love unless you give it away. To guard your heart is to guard your love and who wants love that is guarded and doled out like money at the bank.

Guard your heart against those who seek honest pay for a little love given. A true lover gives and never expects anything in return. A true lover is one who does not demand his way, but gives for love of the other. A true lover is a person who, for the sake of the other, lays down his life for his friend. I am that lover. My heart is never guarded. It is radiant and on fire for love of you. I give and I do not ask a price for My love. I give freely, 24 hours a day. I am attentive to you and ready for your call. I love everyone this much! I love all, even in their sin! I am loving them this much even in their darkest sin! I never measure your love and then decide to love this much in return. I, God, love you as you are. I love you any way. I forgive you for any sin you have committed. I love you in good times and in bad. In your deepest sin, I am there, still loving you. I hate your sin but I love you. You are a creation of My Father. You are a temple for Me to dwell in. It is you who have moved from Me, not I Who moves from you.

My love is unconditional. It is always there! My heart is real and I blush for love of you. If you see Me this way you know the true Jesus. I watch you and I radiate love from My beautiful heart. I am all powerful and I am ablaze for love of you. Do you believe Me, My little girl? You should look at My picture. See Me in My brightness loving you with this power. If you realized My intense love for you it would knock you off your feet. How do I make you understand? Come to Me, My babies. I wait for you day and night. My love is always there in your deepest need. I am available to wrap you in this love. It is you who stay away when you most need Me.

I am here. You are not. The devil tells you God wants you away when you are troubled and in sin and it is then I am calling your name the loudest. Come to Me all who labor and are heavily burdened and I will give you rest. Not as the world gives it, but as only I can give it!

I write all these letters and then the devil says,"You never had any real love" and you believe him? Oh, if I could only make you know! I watch you with such love, little one. It is you who say you aren't enough and I think you are beautiful. I love you, just as you are, flaws and all. Like a mother who loves her children even when they are being good or have been naughty. A parent sees their beauty and still loves them. I see your beauty. I see you as the Father's creation. I see the good you do. I see you as a little child and not always obedient and without sin, but you I love anyway. I think you are cute and I love you.

Oh, dear little girl, how I love you. Don't ever think again that no one has loved you as you want. I have loved you to My death. I am waiting with My arms open wide to embrace you. It is you who do not feel and do not believe. Believe Me, I love you in a way no earthly person could ever do! I am God and I am mighty. I have made you and the most powerful thing you can think of on your earth. I am loving you with this power. It is no less the same power I have to make all things on the earth and all the people in it. I am this keen with My love. Power. Love. Open up, child. Feel it. It is you who shut down and then cry, "Nobody loves me." You do not know My love or you would never cry for love again. I pour out My love and then you overflow to others. Be open. Ask for My help to open your guarded hearts. Let My love pour into you, especially in the Eucharist. Oh, I could knock you over with My love, it is so intense.

Read this letter over and over again and make your heart open. Ask for help. I love you, little one. Power. Love. You are looking in the wrong place. This is not a joke. It is real and I am here at every moment, not like a lover who leaves and is there sometimes. I am always there, 24 hours a day. Come and open wide your gates and let Me permeate your heart and soul with this love!   12/12/93 2:40 a.m.

I Am Your Arms, You Are My Soldiers

Jesus: Come unto Me all who are weary and I will give you rest for your soul. I come that you might have life, not as the world gives it to you, but as only I can give.

I am He Who comes on a dark, cold night. I sit at your side and you are comforted. You reach no further than Me because I tend to your needs. You come time and time again and you know that in this meeting with your Lord you have solace. You do not go other places to seek your consolation for you are consoled by My meeting and you want no more. I give you a healing balm and your troubled soul is set free in the recesses of My arms and you rest from your weariness and depart from our meeting refreshed. But you travel not alone for I continue with you on your way and you know you are not alone whence you go. I go with you.

I am the Good Shepherd and you are watched after by Me. You do not fret or fume for My closeness to you gives you the security you seek. You just follow My lead and your life unfolds before you. Oh, you! Your life is precious to Me. I have plans for you and I need you to do your part. Surrender to Me and let Me lead the way. Do not become boastful and self-willed. Become as a little lamb, following the lead of the Master, not the one sheep that is lost. If you follow the Master, He knows His sheep and He cares for each of them. If they go astray by their own volition, He tries to bring them back, but they may choose in their willfulness to do their own thing and run a road of destruction.

Follow the Master. Be open to His lead. Open your hearts wide and let all He has for you enter in. He will pour in His gifts and His love. He will direct you on your way and your life will have meaning, according to the Master and for what He created you to do. Submission is the key. One person doing the will of God can do more than a million doing their own thing. I need each child to do his work. If you do not work for Me, but work for the world, your work is never done. I am counting on you, My soldiers of love, to follow the lead of the Master and do your part in this Satanic war. Your life, attached to Me, makes you My disciple against

Satan. You need only pray and stay tuned to Me and you will act as I direct you.

Die to yourself and this world. Be of Me. Let Me live inside of you and operate your body. I need you, I need you, I need you, My brothers. I need you to do this work! They may shun you and spit at you and glare at you and try to cast you away from them, but you are Christ to them alive in your heart. They need you more than any of their other foolish endeavors that lure Me out.

Be strong, My little ones. You are being called to this life. The world is not like you. You are fighting the whole way. Do not give up ever. Your presence in this world and your committedness to Me is teaching such a lesson to your brothers. Hold tight. I know the battle you fight with all around you who are blind. Keep living the truth.

Be attentive to Me. Do your adoration every day. You cannot do it without My supplies. When a warrior goes off to battle, does he leave his arms behind? Don't leave yours behind. Come to the tabernacle. I lead you on your way. You carry My supplies and you fight for My armies. "But," you say, "My hands are empty and I am traveling light into a heavy battle." And I say to you that I go with you. You are bound by My love. I give you My power to fight this uphill battle. You gird your loins and follow My lead and I am your arms. Your heart is armed with My love. My power and My grace and I go with you.

Don't look back. Don't ask Me any questions. I am directing you in your hearts. Stay steadfast and attached to My promptings. A mike you carry in your heart and I am filling you in on the other side. To hear Me, you must stay very close to Me. You never go away from Me or you will miss My strategy and you could have a mishap. You stay very close and listen with wide open ears. You are very attentive to My voice and you trust Me to know. I won't leave you ever. Even if the voice gets faint, you know that if you wait My directions will become clearer, so you wait on Me always. Trust. Faith. Love. We are bound together by these. You do not falter or run amok because you trust totally in Me. You don't think, "Oh, maybe I better help Him" and do a little of your own directing. You are like a baby on its back waiting to be picked up. That dependency I require of you. Trust totally in the Master and have faith that He will be there. You never see Me by your side. You just know I am here and never leave you. And it is My love that goes with you. The power of it all, the warmth in the soul, the light to the bowed down. My love and all its power! Rays of light and power go from My heart to you. You are never alone. I go with you always on your way!

I am the Master and you are My little ones. I bind you by My love. You trust and have faith in Me. Oh, babies, do not worry anymore. Give up this worry. Surrender to Me Who loves you and let Me lead your way. You will never run amok. Your ways will be directed and your light is My light. I light your path and you proceed on your way, directed by Me and on your way. 12/12/93 10:00 a.m.

Give Your Soul To Me To Possess

Jesus: Make ready a place for Me. Prepare the way of the Lord. I come as a baby to save you from your sins. I come and you are ready with a pure heart. Make yourself ready for Me, My child. When you have gone astray, repent and reenter into your role as My soldiers.

I forgive you for your shortcomings. Guard against your tiredness. Satan uses frustration, hunger and tiredness to trip you up. He is always lurking around, trying to divide you. Hold tight the hand of My mother and Me and pray from your heart. Make ready your heart for My coming. Keep yourself holy as the saints are holy. There is much grace to be given today. Satan wants you to focus on the bad things. He wants you to be perplexed and angry. Cast him back and do not go there! You are My light, shining in this dark world to the bowed down. How can you shine when you are bowed down yourself? The cold is a test for your strength. All is well with Me, My little one. Pray. That is your mission. Pray and be led out of the darkness into the light. My hand is close to you and it touches your soul. Your soul is being healed by the hand of Jesus Christ.

Satan is always lurking around. Cast him into hell, child. He belongs there, not trying to meddle his way into your heart. He is sly and cunning and he aims to get in like a slippery snake. He looks for a crack and burrows his way in, very undermining. He is uninvited and unwanted yet he is aggressive and doesn't give up. He has one goal: to attack those who love the Lord. The only way to fight him off is through adoration, Mass and Communion. You need the tabernacle. I miss this time with you, but I am still present to you in a special way at this farm. May your heart be released from the clutches of Satan. He wants you irritated. Pray with an open heart and give your soul to Me to possess.

I love you. Amen. 12/13/93

Accept Your Life, Crosses and All

Jesus: I come, you write. I am Jesus, Son of the Living God. Who are you that I come to you? You are indeed special and I love you! I am your Savior. I come and make My ways known to you. If you listen and are attentive to Me, I teach you My ways. My teachings are given in your daily life. Everything that happens in your life is from Him Who loves you. I allowed what is happening to you to happen and I am He Who cares so much for you that I died a brutal death for you. When you realize that all day you are being taught, you will learn My valuable lessons. You, My child, are going to school each day. What are you being taught? You are being taught My ways.

When you get up today and something happens, you must accept what I send you and ask yourself, "What am I being taught here by Him Who loves me?" If you look at your everyday occurrences as teachings from Him Who loves you, they are accepted and you are not bucking yourself.

I am the teacher for your life this day. You are My pupil. Will you learn your lesson today or will you fight that which is happening and will happen anyway? I have a divine plan for you. I want to use you to do My work. If you do not work for Me, My work is not done. How many lives will be untouched tomorrow while you feel sorry for yourself? How many teachings do others miss while you are unsure and act badly? You must accept what is happening to you as given from a most loving God. You are on your way to sainthood. You are being tested in fire. What comes from the fire is a sinner or a saint. You either love Me or you don't. In this world today you cannot straddle the fence. You have to take a strong stand if you are on the side of the saints! There is no way you can live in this world and be mediocre.

The commitment you make to accept your life, crosses and all, to look for My teachings and to stay close to Me, is the most important commitment you make. I want your commitment. I want your total commitment to Me. I came and died for you that you might live. I ask you now to live in Me in this world. Be the light to the bowed down. Be the heart to the afflicted. Be Me to all those you meet. Smile My smiles, love your brothers, look beyond their hardened hearts to the creation of the Father. Look into their eyes and see Me in them. Don't miss an opportunity to be Me to your brothers. All this I have instructed you in lessons: being loving, putting aside your self pity, releasing yourself of doubt.

You ask, "When, Lord, do I have time for My work?" I say to you that this is My work for you! If you do not do this work, you have missed the boat. The gift I give you is My life. The gift I give you is My love! I ask you for your life. I ask you to die to yourself that you might live in Me!

Give Me your life and I will guard you in all you do!

You will run but not get weary for I am by your side. You will fly like an eagle and you will sail the skies adorned in My love. It is you who fight the Master. It is you who do not accept My way for you. This causes resistance. This causes you stress. Accept all I send you. Know I watch your coming in and your going out. Know that I am a teacher Who loves My pupils. I am here to teach you lessons.

Messenger: What are You teaching me today, Lord, in this trial? Thank You, thank You for Your great love, Lord. I accept all You send me and want to do Your will.

Jesus: "But, Lord," you say, "what about my job? What about what I want to do? What about me, Lord?" You, My child, have a free will. You can totally leave Me out of your life and do exactly as you wish. How is your life this way? Miserable! You are created to know, love and serve Me. To serve other lands and other people is to bump the reason you were created. You are met with so much resistance. You cut the line which I have given to you, or you plug it up so you don't hear. I give you a line to Me and instruct you each day in your heart. To plug up the line and do your own thing is to live a life of misery. Your soul craves this union. It is a pull stronger than any appetite you have. It is the pull of the spirit on you. You are bucking a bull when you plug up the line to Me.

Your life is not free and you are not happy. You wander in darkness with a hardened heart and wonder what will show you a better life. You are never at rest for you are always on the move, looking for that which begs in your chest to be answered. But you put a towel on the line and try to turn off the ringer. I call, you don't listen. You become good at tuning Me out. You live your life always holding that towel on the phone. What a pain that is, to be given a direct line to God and to cover it up with a towel!

Little one, I am here, every minute of every day. The more you open up yourselves to accept Me, the louder the telephone rings. You get into synch with Me. You hear Me. My life for you is not a secret. I am here constantly directing you and teaching you. It is you who cover up My line. It is you who live in a noisy, busy world that blocks My whispers in your heart. What are you being taught today?

I am very much a part of your life, every minute, every second. I am here. You have a pipeline to God. You can realize this and become more aware of My constant presence in your life or you can cover up My line! But, child, this is an act of the will on your part. You have to put the towel on My line and hold it there. You are never free. One of your hands is tied up on the phone, holding the rag on it. The other hand is always busy searching for that which the other hand has covered up. What a useless task My children in darkness do, to cover up that which you are looking for. Oh, children, you are so silly. Life is so simple. You make it so complicated! Love God. Love each other. That is it and all falls into place.

Follow Me and I will give you rest. Listen to your heart. Make a commitment to the Master, He Who loves you. Accept your life as given from Me. Die, child, to yourself. Open your hands to the heavens and praise your God Who sends you such gifts. Thank Him, worship Him and surrender to the life He gives you. Spend your days seeking to do His will. Listen by a quiet brook. Come and be taught by the greatest teacher of all. It is free. His school is renowned and you will know peace in your heart. What school offers this? The world teaches many things, none of which is quiet and leads to peace in the heart. The world is noisy and boisterous. You learn lessons for things you never use. You are forced to learn foolish things and graded on their content, but the greatest lessons of all are being ignored and they are the lessons for your life.

Oh, America, you are all messed up! Come back to the basics: God, family, love. All other stuff you fill your heads with is useless! You can have a third-grade education and be happy. Some of you have never attended My school for one day. I am the greatest teacher of all. I live in your heart. My lessons are learned in your daily living. All you have to do is listen and be attentive to Me. My school is free! But you remain in darkness and search a barren desert for the treasures being revealed in your chest. Little ones, I love you so much!

Put God first and you will not search in vain. Make a commitment to Me. Make your goal a diploma in sainthood. This is all that matters. Then all you touch will be taught by the Master, for I teach through you when you go to My school. You are teaching lessons today to your brothers through your actions. Are they My lessons or are they the world's? You are busy, little one. I have work for you to do. Why sit you idle while I teach? Listen to My promptings in your heart and be of Me. This is the greatest work you can do. All else is of no account. You are My teachers in this world. See that you teach My lessons by your daily life. To do this you must come and be taught be Me yourself.   12/15/93 3:25 a.m.

Mary Is Our Mother

Jesus: Little one, you will not escape My time with you. I want to be joined to you in a special way. It is My love for you that drives you to this union. I am soft and gentle in heart. I am present in adversity. I am Jesus, little girl, Son of the One True God, Father, Son and Holy Ghost. God is One in Three. I am He Who speaks to you. Power. I have it all. Let your heart never be troubled for I am with you on your way. Throw doubt and worry and useless thinking out the window. I guard you lest you stumble and fall, but you walk alone with Me up the hill to glory. May the Father, Son and Holy Spirit be praised in their names. God is Great in all His divinity and might. He is the one to be exalted. At His name all knees must bend to the almighty and His power is endless.

This is a special right for you as you approach the 17th day. You will feel this specialness to us, Jesus and Mary, as to a pair united in a special way and present to deliver these messages. Pray for grace now.

I am calling you from the darkness to the light. Your heart is made light by the love I impart to you now. Feel it enter your soul. Nothing else matters. Focus no more on your pain. Focus on your joy for each of Us.

Messenger: Amen, Amen. Alleluia, Praise the Lord!

Jesus: You are being blessed by the Trinity and Mary. Feel the blessing, Father, Son and Holy Ghost. Specialness for you alone from Us. Praise the Father, Son, Holy Ghost and the Blessed Lady. You are entwined in their love. Alleluia.

Unity and power is here. Will you come whence I call you, child? Come and feel the unity between a Son and His mother. Very strong, very powerful, indeed! You will know a new dimension in the life of the Son, His love for His Mother. Alleluia, Alleluia.

Messenger: Mary, come and answer my plea to do Jesus' work for me. I am guided by this prompting. It is not of me. It is a prayer you write in my hand. Hold me. Bless me. Watch over me as a loving mother. I am a little child and I look for my mother. She heals my ills and cares for me like a mother. Oh, Mary, to know you! I am so empty of my closeness to you. Fill my heart with knowledge and love of you. Bless me as a mother by your hand. The mother of all! Oh, mother, great are you. Thanks for your motherly call.

Specialness I feel to this union between Son and Mother, to know the loving Son, Jesus. Oh, Jesus, how You loved Your mother. Alleluia.

To know Jesus, we must know the love that exists between Him and His mother. He has given her to us as our mother. She is truly our loving mother.

Note: When we sit in front of the tabernacle, He does not communicate just with words. He may change us internally. He gives us our supplies. He does not need words. We do not know what He gives us when we sit in front of the tabernacle in silence. He gives us gifts in our heart: healing, opening us up, wisdom. We may not hear His voice or feel what

He is doing, but He is giving us our supplies that we need to grow in Him. He doesn't have to speak. We still get gifts we do not know by His presence. 12/16/93

Keep Close To Me

Mary: My daughter, you have been given special blessings. You do not know what you received. Keep close to me. I am your mother and I love you. I am with you in a special way. Little one, you are called by your mother to this job. I am with you in it. Don't ever think I am not with you. Your mother is always with you. Stay close to me now, little one. Give me your worries and doubts.

Messenger: This Christmas I am given My Mother in a special way. She is truly our loving Mother! 12/16/93

I Communicate In Your Heart

Jesus: You come and I wait for you to be here. I am the divine healer. I know Mine and My love for you bids you to come and be with Me. But many stay away even when they know how much I long to be with them and want to give them My gifts.

My love for you, each of you, bids Me to call each of you. But do you come? Where do you go, little scared ones? You look in vain in this valley of tears for a place of refuge. You drink, eat, seek, wander—all those things which lead you to the world—while I, Who alone can quiet your stalking heart, sit without your love. I am longing for your love. I am waiting for you to come and be with Me, but you are busy, busy off doing all those little things the world calls you to do.

I am the Sacred Heart of Jesus. My heart is a raging fire for love of you. My arms are waiting for you, open wide.
I am a furnace on fire for love of you.

Do you come to get your supplies from Me? When you visit Me at the tabernacle, I am full of intense love. I am bursting with My power to give in your soul. You sit, I dish it out in big, big scoops. My light becomes your

inward flame, shining brightly for the world. You are given the light of
life, a light shining in a dark world, a breath of warmth to a cold, cold
heart. You are given interior healing. You are given the ability to be open
to Me and to grow in your love of Me. What gifts I bestow to your weary
soul!

You come empty, you leave full. "But," you say, "Lord, Lord, do I see
You? Do You speak to me? What words, Lord? I sit and You are there, My
God, but what words did You speak?" And I say to you: to a lover, do you
ask how do you speak or are you just thrilled to sit by His side? Do you
just feel the magic in being with one you love? Do you expect profound
wisdom and measure His words as proof of the value of your time spent
together?

I say to you, little child, I am as an ardent lover. Come and sit and be
with Me! I do not measure what you say to Me. I sit and wait for you to
come, day and night, and am always so happy when you come. I am the
lover Who waits for your soul to be here. How do I communicate and
become in union with your soul? Words are not the only way you communicate with your loved ones. Being present is all that matters. Few
words may be spoken. I am God and I become joined with you in your
soul. Talking, listening, etc., are human ways to communicate. Seeing,
touching and hugging are all expressions of the body for love.

I communicate in your heart. I open wide your soul and fill you with
a mystical light. You are transported to points you do not know. You still
look for your human means of expression. I pour out My gifts of love and
you do not even know how God touches you and loves you. You do not
comprehend loving in the spirit. Come and sit with Me and experience
love in your soul. You cannot put a finger on such spiritual things. How
do you touch peace in one's heart? How do you touch compassion and
love for your brothers in your soul? Can you touch the heart of Jesus? Can
you touch Me? Then why do you want Me to communicate like a human?

Do you want My peace? Do you want My love? Do you want to experience the fire of My heart? You will not do this in human terms. Come
and sit with Me and let Me have a free hand at filling you to the brim
with the things of God. Open yourself up to your soul! Do not question.
Do not become bored when you sit alone with Me. Become open and
attentive. Listen. Do not be busy. Be silent and still. Let Me act. I am
God. What could you do in My presence that could top what I want to
do for you! Be still and know I am your God. Sit with your hearts open
and your mind ready to be filled. Do not question what did I get with Him
today. Is this how you approach your lover? You are just filled in your
heart. Be filled in your heart by My presence. Come out of love and leave
walking on a cloud! Oh, how I love you. Don't bring your business to My
tabernacle. Throw away your watch. Don't time yourself with Me. Come

and sit a while and let Me work in your heart. Let Me fill you with the things of the spirit. Let God penetrate your inner being. You come, inactive and open. This is My calling!

Such insights as wisdom, peace, love, joy, yearning—all the miraculous things man could never find anywhere on earth—that is what you get here and nowhere else! Come with your hearts open and your time free to be with your lover. Do you watch the clock when you are with one you love? Time escapes you and you never want to leave. Come to Me, your most ardent lover, in this same manner. Be filled to the brim with this love I have for you. Where, child, could you buy such a gift as the Love of God!

I am one crying out to you to come and get your supplies. Do not operate in this world without your arms. Your arms are your heart filled by the fire of My love. You are soldiers of love in a dark world. Where you go I power you with My love and light and you walk this darkness with the glow of My heart. I love you, little one. Come and get your supplies. Do not measure your visits or ask what you get. I am giving to you out of My bounty. That is not in words. It is a charge in your hearts and souls.

12/17/93

Take Up Your Cross

Jesus: Pain? Oh, how I suffered! The pain was so intense, I could hardly bear it. I was so wounded and so covered with blood. Think of a little gash and how it hurts when it begins to bleed. I bled and I bled all over. Such intense pain. Every time you experience pain, think of Me and how minute your little pain is. There was not a place on My body that was not covered with blood. There were deep wounds all over Me. My head throbbed from the crown they had placed on Me and I was forced to carry a big cross so heavy, I scarce could move it on My shoulder. My shoulder ached so badly I felt as if it was constantly breaking by the weight of the cross. But I carried it and pushed on My way. If I stopped, I was poked and pushed and hit. The crowd jeered and they forced Me on My way. What crime had I committed? Why was I forced to endure such torture? It was out of love of you that I continued that journey. I was God. I could have stopped at any moment. I was obedient to death to the demands of My Father.

Pain, child? I suffered so much for love of you! This is how I love you at this moment. In all that befalls you you must know at every moment that I know exactly what you are suffering. There is nothing that happens in your life without My consent and it comes from Him Who loves you.

Take your crosses and truly endure them. Accept them. Know that everything that happens in your life I have allowed. Accept it with the love with which I give it. You are being taught in that pain. You are suffering for yourselves and others. I endured all that pain. Did I once say, "Father, take it away?" I am your model. I showed you the way. I took it all, every last wound, every kick and smack and vileness. I took My cross and I carried it without a word. This is what I ask of you. Know that when you are experiencing pain or suffering, or being taunted by those around you, look to the Master for your course of action. I took it all, every last wound, and accepted it to My death. I did not say, "Oh, how awful." I did not complain. I walked in silence that bumpy road with a heavy cross, with My mother suffering by My side and I never complained. I accepted it all for love of you.

Carry your crosses, little ones. They are gifts from Me. Do not look for an explanation or a way to get rid of them. I will take them when I think you have had enough. It is in suffering that you experience My life more fully. It is in suffering that I speak to you in a special way. Endure it. I know every ache and pain you are experiencing. I am this close to you! Your pain may save a soul dead in sin or get a soul from purgatory. Accept all I send you and don't complain. A lot of the pain is enhanced by your rejection. A lot of your lessons are lost by your refusal to see that crosses come from Me. I give you crosses to share in My suffering. I love you so much, little ones. Know how personal I am with you: the very hairs of your head are numbered. Come close to Me and look into My eyes. I am truly here with you at every single moment. Think of Me as a person, but I am closer than any person could ever be! I am there and I know your every breath and I care about your every breath. Who could even do this for another? Others would have to sometimes think of themselves.

I am God and I can think of you at every instant. I am so close to you you do not have any comprehension. It is not a myth. I am truly present to you at every instant. Feel My presence. Make Me alive to you. Experience all I have to give you. You will know Me as your personal Jesus the more you read and re-read these letters. I write them to each of you. Only God could love you each this way. Focus on Me and you and how close I am to you. I love you so, little one. Whence you go you never walk alone. I walked a road of torture that led to My death for love of you! When will you realize what I say is true? When will you know how close I am to you and embrace Me as I so desire? You hold yourself back because you do not focus on My love for you. I would walk that path this day for you. I love you the same this moment as I did then. Oh, little one, you want to put your little crosses down so fast. Hold them and walk

awhile with Me down the road to Calvary. Be by My side and share a little in how intently I trod out of love of you.

I am Jesus, Son of the Living God. I am alive in this room with you. I
am by your side. A toothache, you say—what pain! Accept your pain. I
want you to feel that pain now. It will go away.* It is so little. Heartache
I know, heartache to love each of My children so much and be ignored
or put at arm's length! Do you know how it is to love another and not
have their love? I long for your love with Me, but you are busy. You do
not have the time to be with Me while I await thee. I am an ardent lover
Who waits for each of My children to come and experience this great
love. You stay away from Me Who is always waiting and you search this
barren desert for that which I have to give you. I watch you in this search
and want you to come home to My heart. I am waiting for you, little one.
Don't keep yourself from Me. Remember how I suffered for love of you.
When you feel a pain, remember the pain I suffered for love of you. That
is how I love you this very day. Take your cross and walk with Me. Come
and be with Me. I have that which your hungry soul craves.

I am your loving Jesus. I love you, child. You do not know. I wait to be
closer to you. You must see Me as this personal and this alive in your life!
Oh, sweet one, I love you to My death and I love you this way today. I
lament My children lost in darkness. I want to be united to you. Come
and make Me the center of your life. I wait for you!

Messenger: *My toothache is gone!   12/18/93

The World Has Become Evil

Jesus: My heart is sad and I am drawn to pain from what the children
see. Little, beautiful children watching hate among people, hate on television, brutality, right in their own homes. You live in this world and,
even though you don't watch TV, you have been numbed by how truly
evil your world has become. To live in this world is to be numbed to evil.
It is all around, like a red flag, and what is not being acted out on TV and
in movies is in games and toys, comic books, Nintendo, little action fig-
ures that depict ugly creatures with hate all over them, deformed and
mean. Even the good guys look evil! Toys are evil. Children are playing
with evil things. Ugly things—cute, ugly things. No, ugly things entirely! And they are playing with them.

A child gets a fun meal and gets an ugly action figure. Oh, how lucky!

Violence in your hamburger! You just don't even know how evil your world is because you live in it!

People watch an evil TV and read evil magazines and papers. Acts that are committed by your brothers are so evil that it is almost unbelievable. Murdering an innocent baby so a mother can have her freedom. Why not go in and murder your toddlers because they get in your way? Where does this selfishness stop? Nothing is evil enough for Satan! He aims for the jugular vein.

If you could even comprehend how evil your world has become! Men's hearts are so hard and their ways reflect the evilness in the world. People are reflecting an evil world. If you go from Me and try to make sense of this world, if you want to be a part of this world, you must become a part of the evil. There is no way you can be of the world and not be sick. The world is really sick. If the world is your main goal—and making it work— you become very sick. There is no way to straddle the fence. You are Godly or worldly. There is a division as distinct as black and white. So how can you in your families experience anything but division right down the middle—those who are for God and those who are in the world!?

The world is evil. If people choose the world, their lives become evil. They watch bad movies, bad TV in eating places, violent Nintendo games, violence while they eat. It isn't that My children are bad. They are beautiful souls created by God, but they don't want to give up their world. They put it before God, so they reflect the evil they live with minute-by-minute, day-by-day!

Those who choose Me first can no longer watch TV or go to the movies. They have trouble at their work with people in the world. People in the workplace are just people of the world. The world is evil so they accept evil things. Those of God are shocked! Language that is disrespectful, disrespect for one another, violence, hardness in people's ways, emphasis on a "me first" attitude, a "deceive and use your brother" attitude. These are anything but God-like. They are evil! You, My children, are in a very evil world. To interact with anyone who has chosen the world is to deal with the evils the world has implanted in hearts as okay.

Your battle is very hard. The division is so deep between those who choose God and those who have chosen the world. They who choose the world are blocking their aching souls, telling themselves lies about what is happening around them to stay fixed to the world. The truth is so distorted in the papers and on TV. What is right is made wrong and what is wrong is made right. Deception, over and over again! Evil wins out as being okay at the movies. In this particular case, evil is okay. The whole movie plays up to the end which is evil, acceptable in this case. Evil is never acceptable. The truth is the truth. I am the way, the truth and the life. He who abides in Me will have the light of life. Woe to those who twist the truth and teach it to others. They are responsible for the souls of those they injure. The promoters of evil and deception will pay for their influences, not only by their deeds but also by their example and the souls they injured through their deception!

Oh, poor, poor little children, don't get bogged down by your brothers. You know the truth. It is planted in your hearts. Pray constantly and don't ever watch TV or listen to those who boast of their sick ways. Your hearts need to remain pure and fixed on Me. If you do not pray in front of the tabernacle you get bogged down in this world. Have a prayer corner for time alone with Me at home. Pray the rosary together each day to protect your family. It is your umbrella against an evil reign.

Oh, little ones, I am so close to you. You need to pray to Me constantly. Satan is out to trip you up. He is there and gets you in a split second and you wonder, with your pure hearts, "What hit me?" You know he comes like a thief in the night and without warning attacks, hard and fast, your little hearts. Then he tries to make you feel guilty for what he just did to you! And sometimes, My sweethearts, you listen to him. Cast him out by the precious Body and Blood of Jesus! Keep these words on your lips as your defense and then see Me bloodied from head to toe for love of you.

Watch your children. If he is this cunning with adults, think how he attacks the young and innocent without a whimper. He hits them hard. They see TV and games and other children who are mean and their innocent minds get distorted views of the truth while they are still tiny babies. An evil world makes evil hearts. It is a sick world. It raises a sick culture which has sick children.

Oh, what a setup! You have a chance, America. You have Me and I am here with you every day in the Eucharist. I have all the power. Satan does not have My power. He uses people and gets their power. Guard against his ways. You are under attack from the very culture which bore you. You have a chance. You have Me and I have you. With My might, one person fixed to God can lead an army. Never, ever, doubt your commitment to Me. It is a 24-hour, minute-by-minute commitment in this world. You need never to let your commitment to Me down for a split second. I am He Who sustains you in an evil world. You, America, don't know how truly evil your world has become. You are about to be shaken off your rocker. How can such evil continue?

Prepare the way of the Lord. I will come like a thief in the night and those who stay fixed to their evil ways will be swallowed up. Prepare your hearts for your God. He is all that matters. The world is very, very sick. Don't go to the world to feed your heart. It will swallow it up and you will be heartless. This world is heartless. Oh, little babies, protect your children. Teach them about Me at their first day here. I am all that matters. Other teachings will not save your soul. Your children need to be taught about God. Pray to the Holy Spirit every day. You need to receive all My gifts. He will make your way clear like a snowplow on a winter evening. You will see the road clear ahead, but only by the direction of the Spirit. Pray for His gifts and profess your love to Him. Love My Father and the Holy Spirit. They want you to profess your love to Them. We are three persons in God. Love each of Us!

We love you so. Know Us all and pray to Mary. You need her strength against the devil. She is ready to battle with you in this evil world. You are in battle. You are under attack. Your supplies are given in front of the tabernacle in quiet moments alone with Me. I give you your arms to fight this evil war. If you do not come, you are going into battle without ammunition. You need your arms. Come to Me and let Me give you your supplies. Your children need your committedness to Me. The world needs every last soul to be holy to fight this battle. It is a heritage you pass on to others when you come and pray with Me.

You are the light to the darkened night. You are little but mighty because you are powered by God and His light is the brightest light. Be vigilant. Do not put down your guard. You are under fire by a sick world. When you are fired at, it is sudden and abrupt. You are not warned. You are just fired at. Come to Jesus to get your arms. Only He can give you what you need. Oh, how I love you. I love you to My death. I love you with intensity. I am your Savior, your one, true God. Alleluia. You have warded off another attack!   12/19/93

Angels Will Read the Message

Jesus: Who will read the message? Angels will read the message. I will be by their side. I want the messages out. I want them out, I tell you. I want My people to hear all I am telling you. I want, not a few, but all to hear these words. They are private revelations given by Me to My people. The souls are, oh, so hungry for this one. They need to get these messages.

I am one crying in the desert. Make ready the way of the Lord. Prepare ye a path for the Master. He comes as a child in a stable. His people are asleep. Where are they and what are they doing with their busy lives? The angels will read the messages. They will rock the heavens and all will know My love and My might. From the housetops, shout this. Proclaim,

"The day of the Lord is approaching. Make ready a path for Him." Will you comply with this demand to deliver a message to My people?

Time, child, is so short. You must ready all with My words of love. They are half asleep and dazed. They walk this earth with blinders on their eyes. My day will rock them off their rockers and they will know it is I with Whom they deal. No mistake will be made as to what is happening. All will see My power and My might. From the heavens shall come a sign and all will know from whence it comes. And the days that follow will be days to prepare men's hearts for My coming. I will not come unannounced. I will come with My power and My might and you will know what you will behold. Men will turn their hearts to Me with these messages. Get them out, I tell you, for their need is very great. I am patient and yet I am demanding. Ready yourself for this day of the Lord. I come as a baby into your midst, the angels sing, the choirs of heaven rejoice and you will know soon that I am very close to you all. Indeed you will know!

What awaits those in their feeble hearts! They run after such useless things when I, God, am talking in these letters. They think their world is their end. What an awakening they will have—a wide awakening!

I knock to make ready for My coming. You hear Me knock on your door in the night. Make ready this path so My people will read these letters of love. I am mighty and worthy of such praise. My people must realize My love in My intense might. What sign do you need? Do you think these messages were for your ears alone? Such power and wisdom in Rita's purse? This is not the idea. They are for all! My ease goes with you in all your undertakings to get these messages out.

Slow, too slow, I tell you. Shout My message from the housetops, that I am Lord and I am coming in your midst as a baby, but, with such might! My time is at hand. You tarry too long, My little ones. Time you do not have. This world is crazy! People are so busy at the malls. Oh, what foolish ones. I come as a baby into your midst. This is My birthday and whom do you worship? You worship idols! It is all such a sick world. Make ready My path, My little ones. Time is so short and you must not tarry any longer for into your hands I place My words for the world. They are mighty, little ones. Read them! What do you do with these words? Do you want proof? Look at Me hanging on the cross. It is out of this love of you I died a brutal death! Do you think I would not go to this extent to save the souls of My loved ones? Why would I come to this earth, give My life for all My beautiful creatures, and then, at this stage of the game, not send some mighty medicine to cure My sick little ones? You possess the mighty medicine. I mixed it with such love and I hand-deliver each message to shake My people to My love. The heavens will rock and the Son of Man will appear on a cloud and the glory of the Lord will be shown on high!

Get busy, you little people. The angels declare My words are given here. This is My gift to My people—distinct, clear letters proclaiming My love. Are you listening? Do you think I would not try everything to save My beloved ones?

Oh, I will go to any extent to save these little ones, so ornery and so stupid in their ways, so sinful in this evil world, but so precious to Me. I will come in My glory and I want every last soul.

I am God. Why would I not speak to you? I wait for you. I wait, I wait, but you are all so blind and dense. What you do is so silly. Your ways here have become sick and your hearts have become hard. But shout it from the housetops! I loved you to My death! I love you all in your sickness. I want you united under the mantle of My mother, praying and honoring God.

America, turn yourselves around before it is too late. Come and heed My harkening. Come, come, My children. Time is so short and a lot of mending must be done in your hearts. You have hardened them and now they must come back to life. Only I can give you this life in your hearts.

Heed My words here. I am gentle and kind in heart. My heart is a heart of love. I have hand-delivered these messages to My people and you are My delivery boys. Get them going, little ones. You tarry too much.

My gift to My people is My love this Christmas. I am showering all at this Center with grace this season. The devotion there pleases Me, but more must flock and they will be changed from hardened hearts to hearts for God. I am God, little ones. I came and I died a brutal death. I am calling to you all to deliver this now. Make this your top priority so they will hear My message of love and know the love I have for them. Do not tarry. Do this today, little ones.   12/20/93 2:40 a.m.

A Prescription for Smooth Sailing

Messenger: I sit in front of the tabernacle. I am sun bathing. I am then suspended above the earth. My ways are free and I fly and float about. A wind may come but my balloon does not fall. It may blow a little but it remains high. I am high in the Lord. I am above the world. I am free and unattached. I am transcended into the things of God. He propels my balloon and I worry not on my way. I am free and carefree. He has the helm. I am the recipient of His love.

When I do not come, the air goes out of my balloon and I fall to the ground. I am covered by its cloth and feel trapped in despair. Little things become big things. Big things are unable to be handled and Jesus waits and says, "Where are you, little one? You cannot operate. I am the Controller of your Balloon!"

Jesus: You know nothing about My ways. To sail the skies you need the Sky Master. You are in a balloon and know nothing about them. You must come and get to power your balloon. Doing it yourself or without Me is disasterous. You are now on the ground, covered with cloth and you can't get out.

I free you up. I suspend you in the skies. I give you life. I give you wind. I give you sunshine. You go it alone and you have no light, no life, no wind, no sunshine. You are in trouble!

Little one, have you learned your lesson now? It took a painful tumble for you to learn the lesson. My words here are prescriptions for smooth sailing. Do you want to follow or try to go it alone?

Don't go alone, little one. You have no knowledge of balloons. You know nothing of the wind and the skies. You are your own worst enemy. To go alone is worse than not going at all. The more you operate without your supplies, the more you stumble.

To do My work, you must stay refueled in My love. You can't do My work without My supplies. My work is hard work. No little softy job, little ones! It takes some mighty power and you need to get that power from Me. Come and sun bathe in My love. What a bath! Soak in My rays and come and follow Me. I am the Master, the Captain. I am He Whom you follow. You never make a decision. You do not fret or fume. You live in My love, I bathe you in My bath and you go refreshed on your way.

Come, Come, I am the Captain. You know nothing of these things. Surrender and be selfless. Spoon out the ego, children. It is a mighty trap for you. Spoon out control. It is not My way. Spoon out all that is not of Me and be selfless. The more you empty yourself to Me, the more I act and you do wonderous things.

Little ones, I am God. Why do you want to act in your weak ways? I wait to act out of you! You do not act. Let Me do it through you! The more you die to yourself, the greater your success. Be selfless and full of Me.   12/21/93

You Are Raising Your Children Without God

Jesus: This is the day of the Lord. Slowly approaches My day, My birth. I am Jesus, Your Savior. I come as a little baby to save a big world. How could such a little one save a world and all those to come? This little one, My child, is God-made-man of Mary, just a baby coming in such silence, yet He comes with the might to save the world from its sin. He comes into a little stable and He comes without any proclamations from mankind. The beasts surround Him, the King of Glory. His court is made up of cows and sheep and His bed is dirty hay. Oh, how we await the birth of a baby. Everyone is eager to know of His arrival. All is ready, yet Mary does not have a place to lay her child. There is not room for them except with the beasts of the stable. Did Mary know that Jesus would be born in such poverty? She has said "yes" to all the events that are to happen. This is her firstborn baby and there is not a place for them.

Messenger: What things we are so eager to surround ourselves with and God is born in such poverty under the eyes of animals! The choirs of angels sing, but the world is numb to the event. Is this not how it is 2000 years later? It is Christmas Saturday, yet where are the statues and the stables remembering Christ's birth? Can you find any remembrances in stores? They are too busy. You cannot go and pay except for waiting in line at the money counter, a line to buy treasures, while the Son of Man waits in tabernacles all over the world and who comes?

Is the world today so blind that its people call this Day Christmas, but who is talking about Christ? Little snowmen, reindeer, Santa Claus, little sleds, red and green, and bells and holly. Should not every little detail be tended to? The family is all prepared. Gifts are wrapped to perfection yet where is the baby? Is a picture of Christ on any paper or magazine? He, the King of Glory, sits alone in every church while people wait in line with batteries and cards and wrap. How long do they wait in that line? Does it matter? Christmas is the most important event of the year to them and every detail must be tended to.

Wake up, America. How you are fixed on such foolishness! Ribbons and bows and wreaths adorn the house from the top to the bottom, inside and outside. Sound the trumpet! But the Son of Man waits in churches all over by Himself and the busier they become, the more the faithful ones rush too.

Jesus: I am Christmas. It is My Birthday. The Son of Man waits in a tabernacle. There are no trumpets. There is not a line. He is alone! What is the first Commandment? "I am the Lord, thy God. Thou shalt not have any gods before Me." America, you have so many gods, but the true God is ignored!

My heart aches at the blindness of My children. Every detail, indeed, is tended to but the details of the heart. Adorn the body, adorn the house, decorate the trees and lights and play the music. Music to Rudolf, music to the snowmen, music to Santa, but some will not even sing a song to Christ the King. What do they think the words to Silent Night mean?

The adoration pleases Me. This is My birthday. Who will even come to Me? Very few even know what Christmas is about. Does Christ reign in their hearts or do other gods? Who will you worship this Christmas, Christ the Savior or some other god? I wait, My children, just as I do every moment of every day. I never leave. I wait for you. I am Jesus, Son of the Living God. Please come and make in your hearts a place for Me. I want to come into your hearts and dwell there. Open wide to the King of Kings. Take the blinders off your eyes. Let Me in. Your hearts have turned to stone and your bodies are numb. What has happened to My beautiful ones?

Messenger: Think of a baby, so bright, so beautiful, so alive! His face reflects the courts of heaven. His eyes are beauty in themselves! Then look at the eyes of my children 20 years later! Look at the mall—how people dress and how they act. This 20-year old at the mall is reflecting your world! Is it not the same beautiful baby that was born? But look at people standing around—looking, for what? Is there anything at the mall to feed a soul? Look how big they are, these malls! Now they have two floors. You get lost! Is there anything of God at the mall? Do you feed your face, America, on every corner, but leave your soul withering and shriveled up!

Jesus: This 20-year old is the child created by My Father to know, love and serve God, but, America, what did you teach him, when he was that little baby, about God? How was he to learn when you yourselves put God on a back burner or have no room for Him at all. You made this child at the mall. God made the baby. God gave you this baby with eyes still on heaven and you wiped the sparkle from his eyes and piped in your world. If he was fed on God and the things of heaven, if his heart was nurtured and cared for, he would still have sparkling eyes, the eyes reflect the heart within. You have taught him your ways, America. His eyes are not like those of babies. How can he look to heaven when you, yourself, know nothing about heaven? Take a baby young and give it what are the true treasures. Tell it about God. Make the Bible the book that is read and found on every table and by every bed.

America, you are missing it. You are raising children without a God. To be created to know, love and serve God, but not be taught anything about God! You, America, are responsible for taking the sparkling eyes and making them dull and changing his heart to stone. You, America are responsible for the stalking soul that goes about in such unrest, but has no training of God and no example from which to learn about God. You, America, have taken a beautiful child and made him into a bundle of unrest, nervous energy, jumpy looks, wild music. What do you feed this stalking soul? Is it sex? Is it self-indulgence. Is it drink? You gave it nothing of what it was created for and it has no source to obtain it. Children are given such unrest in their world: self-indulgent games, music, drink, magazines. And the soul lives on unattended! Such unrest stalks the young heart with no clue about how to be saved.

America, this is your child. How can he be saved? You kept him from the things of God and now he walks the malls searching with hollow eyes and a heart yearning to find that which he craves. Children are thirsty for Me. They are driven by their souls to know Me. America, what do you teach them? You are feeding them garbage and they are sick from it. A daily diet of garbage, of filth! You give them a handful of dirt for food! What would your body do if you fed it dirt? Oh, how you are hurting your loved ones, your little children. They come with a guardian angel they never know. They never even hear the word of God or, if they do, it is taught as a far-off thing in the distance. You will reach God as He is alive in your own hearts. You, America, have borne the children. You took innocent babies and slaughtered some. Then, to those who survived, you fed a daily dose of garbage!

But how could you give them anything but a hardened heart when yours was frozen in your very chest. You cannot teach what you do not know. These messages, America, are your answers. Read them to your young. Tell them about Jesus. My words are not hard to understand. You do not need much education. A second-grader could understand My messages here. What they need from you you can explain.

Where is the family circle of prayer? Where are our pictures on your walls? Where is My crucifix, by which you are saved? To My death I love each one of you, yet you do not know that My death and resurrection is of any account in your life.

This is not your life here. Your life will go on and on after your body goes. This is your test, America. You have made the test the finished product and you do not even take the test. It has become an end in itself. None of this matters here—all this materialism. I am so sad in My heart for My little ones being raised in this culture. Some homes do not even have a Bible or a crucifix.

Spread My word, My children. Teach your little ones about God. Spend time in prayer and tell your sick brothers about God. Tell them to read the Bible and pray to the Holy Spirit. He has the wisdom their souls crave. He gives gifts to those who ask. I am ready to shower you with My graces and lead you back myself. Plant the seeds. How can anything germinate if the seed was not planted. You are My sowers in a starving world. Plant the seeds to your brothers. Tell children about God. Their minds are so open. Get them young. Tell children in your family, your seed may save their soul. Tell them about My love. Don't miss any opportunity. Your reward will be great in heaven for all the seeds you sow!

Tell little ones wherever you are that Jesus is Lord and He is a God of Love. Tell children about their souls. They need to care for them and feed them. Tell them to fill themselves with good, not evil. Give them Bibles. There are children's Bibles. These plant seeds that will live in their hearts. They are My children and I love them. I need you to plant the seeds. I will provide water and sunlight. I will talk in their hearts and they will listen if you plant the seeds.

Have prayer groups for children. What a way to spread the faith! They do not see other children praying so they do not pray. I will attend those prayer groups and work in their hearts there. My power is mighty, but I cannot work in a barren desert. You must be constantly sowing seeds. Spend money on Bibles and give them to children. Give them little books about God. Tell them of My love. There is a magic in the book about God you give to a child. I will make it come alive in its life. But you must give the book. If you have any opportunity, tell children about Me and how I love them and I am by their side with such love and care for them. You can do so much for the children by doing so little. My magic will work on the little seeds you plant.

Have a light heart and ask for guidance. Submit yourselves to Me so I can reach your brothers through you! Look at how many souls you touch each day. Sow seeds of life in their hearts. They will not turn you off. They are thirsty. Give them the messages I write here. Give them the Blue Book. They will turn their hearts to God. I will work on them as they read. They will receive life from this book, life in their souls. Alleluia.

I am the son of God and I come into your midst as a baby, mighty and powerful, but little and helpless. I come to you in Communion. I am God. My power shines on your soul there. Do not go a day without receiving Me. If your children are sick, teach them to make a Spiritual Communion. The power of the Eucharist is the most powerful.

Don't miss the opportunity to go to Communion every day. Make spiritual communions throughout the day. I long to be united to you. Beg for this union. In moments of silence, come and sit with Me. At home, make a Spiritual Communion and sit with Me there for short periods of silence. I will come to you and dwell in your hearts. I yearn to be alone with you and share My love. If you have 5 to 10 minutes at home, come to Me. You will have a new energy and peace. I give you what you need. Be alone with Me and sit. Don't be anxious. Just be patient and not busy. Sit still. Let Me work in your heart. Do not expect any concrete results. I give you what you need and you do not need to feel anything. Make your life a time to deepen your union with Me. The Ultimate Work of your Heart is to be united to Me. I work. You sit in silence and in submission. You become selfless and unattached. Transcend your body and be with Me in the soul. Sit now in silence. Don't be busy. Let yourself go in a Spiritual Communion. Ask Jesus to come into your heart now. You are too hard. Be like jello, let go. Let go of everything. I will work on all that. Leave it behind and be with Me, alone.   12/22/93 5:00 a.m.

Unrest Comes from A Loss of God

Messenger: Precious Savior, I come ready to do Your work; it is You I adore, You I love, You I praise. You are so beautiful! At Your Name all knees must bend, for You are Almighty and Holy and Worthy of all Praise. Alleluia. The day of His birth approaches, Alleluia!

Jesus: My child, you are little people. You worry and you fret. Your mind is ever busy, but I am God and I go before you. Your worry and your fretting is to no avail. The very hairs of your head are numbered and I never leave your side. It is My little ones who move from Me. I never move from them. Sad is a heart that is in sin, a heart that has left Me out is void of inner peace. There is a constant rumbling inside that beckons it to turn its ways, but people do not heed the call. They cover up the promptings.

The deeper one goes from Me, the sadder is his heart. The soul knows that which it is missing. It is as though it has a memory of the presence of God, but a sadness that it has chosen to ignore Him. Satan constantly tells the heart it is the master and preaches lies in one's head! The heart hurts from this loss of union with God. The face is not one of joy. It is one of definite pain. The heart aches for the presence of God. Life loses its life, and the person now comes on a journey to get its life back. All those roads one travels lead to idle pursuits. And the restless soul remains empty, void of God. If that person, however, comes to Me, if he fill himself with My gifts, then the soul is ever at joy and has inner peace. You are created with the yearning to know, love and serve Me. To do otherwise is not a good feeling.

I am the Master. My heart is there for you, little ones. It is power, it is light, it is a flame that burns and warms your soul. You know the concept of being cold. With such chill, nothing feels good. Why would coldness feel good once you have experienced heat! Every baby beholds the face of God. The soul is given a memory with His presence imprinted on it.

Every baby, when it is born, is in grace1 and loves God! It is taken away from this place by your world, America! The devil stalks the infant heart, as it is the prey, ready to devour it. It is his glory to have its young. You were created in innocence. You behold the joy of God in your soul. You were led astray, maybe at an early age. It is so sad. You behold the life of a soul, America. Do you have the right to ruin this life, to take a little one and teach it materialism?

This little soul needs God. You need to teach it from the very first moment of life. To develop your personal relationship with God is to gift this world with the most precious gift. You will reflect the love of Jesus in your heart. Your actions will show His might. He will use you to do His work.

Your job is to know, love and serve God. If this is the goal of your life, your heart is joyous and your ways are free. Come to Me, My little babies. My life is waiting for you. I give Myself to you every day in the Holy Eucharist. You receive God. Into your lowly body I come out of deep, deep love for you. You have such dignity because I come to you. You are a creature of God. To take God from the creature is to be left with only the creature. This is a sorry, sorry state. Your face sparkles and your life shines from you when you are affixed to Me.

There is no mistaking a person void of God and a person of God. There is a radiance that shines from you, My little one, when you have been with Me. My light shines forth from your very heart. I am a mighty God and, when I possess your soul, My might cannot be covered up!

I am such a good God. I have so much to give you, all of those things which delight the soul. When I am in you, your heart knows the light of life and you walk with My joy in your heart. Do not let your light be covered, but put it on a stand to shine for all. You are the light of the world. I vest you in such dignity. I proclaim My love, deep and honoring for you, and I am God! That alone gives you such respect! That God would care for you, little one, is honoring to you!

I am Jesus, Son of the Living God and I shine from your souls. Your eyes reflect the presence of God within and you are unmistakably God's creature. You do not know how My presence shines to your brothers. There is a glow about you that is unmistakable. Your face reads the state of your soul. Your face shows the face of your heart. Many hearts with many different faces. See that your heart proclaims the goodness of the Lord, that your face reflects His Holy Name. You, then, become the little but mighty light that shines in a dark world.

Little one, oh how I love you. How I am offended by your lack of attention to Me. My heart is sad for My lost people. It laments as a mother who laments the loss of a child, a well intentioned mother, who loved and cared for her little ones, but now must suffer their indifference to her. This is only a shadow of the pain I feel for loss of My little ones. How do you understand My love for thee? To even tell you in words is impossible. My love is abounding. You in your earthly form cannot fathom it. I died a brutal death for love of you. I came to earth as a human and withstood such brutality for love of you. What more do you need, America? I sit every minute, out of love for you, waiting and waiting. God waits for you! Such honor I bestow on you and you turn your backs? I am He Who gives you your life. If you remove Me from your hearts, your soul withers and dies. It is by Me you are fed and nourished. It is by Me that your life has meaning and it is by Me that you are at peace. Living without Me is to lose your inner life, to starve your soul, to leave the soul in such a state of unrest.

America, your unrest comes from your loss of God. You indeed are noisy. You cry out in loud boisterous noises for this loss, but the louder you get, the further you go from My silence. I am found in the quiet whispers in your heart, America. I am found in quiet things. Nothing is more quiet than a trip up the aisle at Communion, but that is the food of the restless soul! It is the road on which you are fed and nourished! It is I, come to you, and I am God, little ones! God chooses to enter your breast and dwell there. What honor I bestow on you!

If a king were to come to your house, you would ready for his coming and never stop talking about it. But, little ones, listen. I am God and I long to come and dwell in you. Make ready your hearts for Me and never quit talking about Jesus, Who comes to you in your hearts. I love you so intently. I died for you, but you are blind and you turn your backs. Would you turn your backs on the king or be ever attentive? You, however, do not comprehend your specialness that I, God, come and choose to dwell in you!

My presence gives you honor. Come with your hearts eager and ready for the King. I am the King of heaven and My kingdom is far greater than any kingdom on this earth! I come to you this day. Await My coming and ready your hearts for I am He, worthy of all Honor and all Praise. I am coming to you and I am longing for this union with you. With dignity and honor I have clothed you, given you rule over all. My little ones, I love you so.   12/23/93 6:30 a.m.

God-Made-Man Is Born

Messenger: Dear Jesus, Your day is slowly approaching. Praise You, Jesus. I love You. You are great in heaven and on earth. Praise You. Oh Jesus, help us this Christmas to sow Your love.

Jesus: I am the way, the truth and the life. He who abides in Me will have the light of life. Make your ways straight and follow in My paths that you will know all My ways and I will be your Master. May you know a peace that only I can give and may your days be spent in spreading My love, for I am worthy of all honor and glory. Holy is My name. Alleluia, Alleluia.

I am Jesus, Son of the Living God. I am the God-child. Do you comprehend this? You search a barren desert for My love and I am by your side. My heart is ever present to you. Your search should be avid for Me and My ways for I am truly your God and I am ever attentive to your needs. Come and let Me lead you on your way. Let Me lead you down your path and your foot will not falter. Your steps will be made light, light in the ways of the Lord. Holy is His name and all blessings are His. Alleluia.

This is the day of the Lord, rejoice in it and be glad. Make straight your path, make ready a way for Him and open yourself up to His promptings deep in the hearts of those who serve Him.

He is so good. He is so holy. He is indeed God, little ones, your God Who comes and is full of love for you, little creatures of this world. He raises you up and you are brought to new heights in His love. You are honored in Him and He is worthy of such praise.

I am the Savior. I was born of Mary. I came for you, little ones. I come to this earth as God to show My intense love for you. I lived as a human man. I walked like you, a human creature. I then died a brutal death for you. Alleluia. Praise the Lord! In His Love we have been saved. It is through Him that we are saved and holy is His name. Praise Him. Worship Him. He will give you the Light of Life. His star burned bright in the east and the world did not even know what might come on that night! People were numbed to His coming and all were dazed. Behold, a star glowed in the east and the glory of the Lord was with us.

Messenger: Jesus, God-made-man, Son of Mary is born in Bethlehem in a stable, under the eyes of beasts. Such poverty for a mighty King! He is not a king of riches. He is not a king that comes to flaunt His wealth. He is a King for the kingdom that is The Kingdom. All other kingdoms are of no account when compared to His kingdom, yet He comes as a baby in such poverty.

Sound the trumpet, blow the horn, roll the drums! The angels are all that declare His coming—and a few shepherds. Nonetheless He comes in His glory and His might, worthy of all honor and all praise! At His presence we must bow in awe and know what a King is in our midst. It is Jesus, Son of God, King of Kings, and Lord of Lords. It is He by Whom we are saved. No other king can claim to such a feat. No other king can compare to this one.

Jesus: Remember, people. He is a King. Remember He is in your midst. Do you realize His might or do you go about your busy lives ignoring a King in your midst? How foolish, you say, to be in the presence of a King and ignore him and I say to you, "How foolish indeed, My little ones." Make your lives attentive to the greatness that you possess. Be eager with an anxious heart and a holy life. Be prepared, for a true King is with you. Honor Him and Praise Him. He is worthy of all praise. Alleluia. Praise the Lord and know His name.

Bow, My children, to this King Who walks among His people. All honor is yours today for a Savior is born and He will come as a baby. But He will save all from their sins and they will be heirs of His Kingdom. Alleluia. Alleluia.   12/24/93 6:10 a.m.

I Came This Day as a Baby

Jesus: I am the way, the truth and the life. No one comes to the Father except through Me. The gift I give is eternal life. I came this day as a baby to make ready your way to the Kingdom. I love you with such intensity. This is the reason for My coming.

If I could get inside of you and make you realize My love. I died a brutal death. I came and was born God as a man. I rose again from the dead and you don't even realize My death and how important all this is to your salvation. You doubt My intense love, no matter what I said or did. You need to keep a list every day and put on it the proof that "my Lord loves me." Make this your gift to Me and yourself this Christmas. A list every day of proof of My love for you! I love you so, little one. Cling to Me and My ways. The world is in so much darkness and so much pain.

Let go of your children and give them to Me. I am watching them for you. I promise this. You must learn trust. You are so far from Me when you do not have adoration. Go to church early and pray. You need time in front of the tabernacle. I will help you find a way to know My love and quit caring about anything but Me.

Start anew—prayer and playing with the little ones. They must come and be in front of Me. This is My birthday. Come and be with Me, this day. I want to be honored this day by you.

It is a hard road you walk, with Me. Such worldliness knocking on the door and you think you are feeling queasy. You know the truth. There is a false peace in this world of yours. So many are in total darkness. You must pray constantly when others are around you. Pray for this world. It lives a life of blindness. I am the Savior. There was no doubt of My brutal death, My birth, My resurrection. It was not pretty and it happened. I know how bad this world is and I tell you. You talk to Me and you know because I tell you of the evil ways. You, My child, must pray this day. I call you to put aside self, offer it all up as the morning offering. I know exactly what is happening and I am not going to tell you again.

Stop, now. Focus on Me and My love. Focus on the infant birth in such poverty. Focus on the brutal death—every detail—and then the resurrection. I am Jesus, Son of God. I come to you this way to deliver a message. The message is My love. Fret not what you have done or are doing. Your works and the love with which you do it please Me greatly. I am the truth, the way, the life. All else takes its place behind Me.

Do not get caught in the laugh of the great deceiver. His ways are to trip you up, to make you feel as if you are the one who needs to understand the world. The world says: "I am the world and I, in all my joy, come to tell you of my ways." No, little one, the world is not joyful. The world laughs a laugh of sin. The first commandment demands My being made the first and last in your life—your all. Everyone who is focused on the world is going down a dark road. That road is not paved with joy. It is paved with empty hearts. Only in Jesus do we have joy in our hearts. To be void of Jesus, or to push Him onto the back burner, is to be void of happiness. You were created with a soul to know, love and serve God. This is ultimate in your being. Any other pleasure is momentary and leaves your heart empty.

The world has taught the lesson that leads to such unrest in the soul. The world has given you such hardness in the heart. Love does not demand its own way. It is there and exists for others. Love is seeing your brother, even when sick, as a child created by God and finding a place for him, even when sick, in your hearts. You are above the things of this world. You are of the things of God. Then, pray to be like Him in your actions. Put aside pettiness and love your brothers despite their faults.

This, child, takes God! You cannot do this act alone. You need the power of God. This is how this world will be changed. It will be changed by your love, given to the sick and sorrowing, even when they don't know they are sick. I am Jesus, your Savior. I am here in your unrest. I hold your hand and offer Myself to you. Make a Spiritual Communion, little one.

Time will stand still and you will feel a new cleansing in your heart. Read the November 25 message all day. One month before My birthday! Make ready a path for the Christ Child. Put foolishness and doubt aside and be in union with Me. I am guarding your children.

Messenger: Alleluia, Alleluia.   12/25/93 Christmas Day

The Bridegroom Awaits

Jesus: Dear child, the Son of Man waits and you sleep in the night. I wait for you and you sleep. You know I am waiting and you are dead in your bed. Awake, My little one, when I call. You must not give in to the desires of the body. I care for your needs. Your strength comes from Me. Jump from your bed, sound the trumpet and arise, for your Savior comes in the night to bring you a message for all His children. Ready yourself, for I do not like to wait. Get up and come, child. I am God.

I am He Who made the world, He Who makes the sun shine and the baby in the womb! You make Me wait while you sleep. Rise and run, for the Lord is at hand. God awaits you and beckons you to be attentive to your calling. Sound the trumpet! Arise in the night. I am He Who comes to you. You must harken to the call. Come pronto to My request and do not tarry. I wait and I wait and I eagerly want to talk to you.

I am Jesus, Son of the Living God. Oh, child, I want these messages to reach the ends of this earth. I deliver each with such love. Will you deliver My messages to all My loved ones? They eagerly need to hear My words of love. They need to know how I feel about each one of them. They need to know that I am God. I love each child uniquely and My love is the love of God. What can you get on this earth that can compare to the love of God? You have a message declaring My love for each of My children. They are My love letters to them. Please see that they receive this letter. This is your top priority. It is a love letter to My beloved ones.

I am your Savior. I am not a myth. I am alive and I come to you. I wait in the tabernacle every day as a prisoner. Waiting and waiting in the tabernacle and who comes to be with Me? I await you, My children, to come and realize that God is in the tabernacle. I am Jesus, the Son of God, and I wait for you every day. Come to Me in your busy day. Come to Mass. Make ready your hearts and receive Me in Communion. I am there awaiting you as a groom awaiting his bride. I want to be with you, united in

Holy Communion. I am truly present there, but which of you come? I wait for each of you. I am God. I can love you each so intently you do not understand. Your brother does not make up your love to Me. I wait, you little ones. Will you come and receive your love this day?

Ready your hearts and keep them holy. God will enter there. Prepare the way for Me. Do not sin. Do not lie to yourselves and tell yourself that some sins are of no account. Every sin is wrong. I tell you what is right and wrong in your hearts. You know the Ten Commandments. Satan tells you "but in this case, you are exempt", "this is out of date, you are allowed here." No, little ones, sin is sin and your heart knows what is wrong! Keep it pure. The more you lie to yourself about evil, the more right it becomes. Oh, how sad to numb your beautiful heart and accept the things of this world that are evil as okay. Evil is evil and you must guard against any evil the world tells you is okay.

I am the way, the truth and the life. When you abide in My ways, you possess the light of life. Do not be pulled into the world and its evil ways. Ready yourself for My love. I am as a bridegroom awaiting his bride. So pure, so white, so untainted she appears, just for her loved one. Her ways are gentle and kind and she is a picture of holiness, dressed in a white gown. Dress your soul in a white gown for Me. Keep your soul clothed in a cloth of dignity, a white cloth untainted by any sin, pure as the bride who meets her groom. Our meeting is with such love.

You enter My church, you walk My aisle. Your bridegroom awaits you in Communion. I am the bridegroom of your hearts. I come with such love to enter your soul. I am He Who walks with you to be united in Communion. I am Jesus. I am your true Love. I wait for you, My child. Please clean yourself up for My arrival! Think of My coming the day before and eagerly await our union. This is the greatest event of your life, union with God. Anticipate it with such eagerness, as the wedding of our hearts. I await you, little ones. I am God. What could this world ever give you that can be likened to God's entering your soul?

I am God and I come to you in Communion. Do you wait for Me, the bridegroom of your soul? Do you wait as one who is going to one's own wedding? This event far surpasses any wedding. It is you who are missing the significance here. I am here every Mass waiting, just for you. Get dressed, purify yourself, see the priest, go to confession, guard your tongue as the opening to your soul. I enter therein and you receive God, my child. Do you not comprehend this a little?

Read My words here. They are as real as the eyes you use to read them. It is you who blind yourself to all I have to give you. You do not reach with the things of the soul. You look for explanations in bodily things. To see the soul and the things of God you must reach with the eyes of God. You must be opened by the faith I eagerly want to give you. Beg to be open to Me so I can give you all you need to know Me. This world is blurring your Godly vision. It is hard to see through the mask of evil it has created. Every day the mask becomes more dense.

I am here, little one. You must die to this world to see Me. You don't need more of the world. You need less of the world. As the world decreases, your knowledge of Me increases. Take the mask off your face. Make your hearts pure. Pray to the Holy Spirit for His gifts of wisdom, understanding, counsel, fear of God—all gifts that only He can give! Fill your hearts with the gifts of the Spirit. He will remove the blinders from your eyes and dwell in your soul. You will know a new life and I will become so much more alive to you. You, child, need the Spirit!

The way to God is through Jesus. You need the Spirit. You need the Father. You need all three. Pray to be made whole in the Holy Trinity. Pray for union with God. Pray for the things of the soul. When your soul is in order, all else falls into order. You needn't pray for things of the world. Pray to know Me more fully. Pray for unity with God. Pray for opening in your hearts. Pray for holiness. Pray for faith, hope, charity. Pray for knowledge of how to please God. These are the true treasures. All else is of no account. Don't recite prayers for worldly things. Pray for your union with God. This is what it is all about!

I am so eager to make Myself known to you. Our love affair awaits and it depends on you. I am here loving you. It is you who keep us apart. What could you find on this earth that could compare with a love affair with God, child? Your soul was created to know love and serve Me. It craves this union with Me. This appetite is stronger than any other you possess. You hold it back and make light of it because this world has taken God out. This world is messed up. I am God and you are a creature of God. You cannot take God from you or you remain only a creature. What dignity you sacrifice to remove God from yourself!

Prepare for the wedding of our souls. Your bridegroom awaits you. I am Jesus, Son of the one, true, God. I await your union with Me. Child, nothing you ever do on this earth can compare with Communion with God. If you do not behold this as something, you need to pray to know Me more. Go to the Spirit and beg Him for understanding and wisdom. Beg Him for all his gifts to enhance your knowledge of God. Beg the Spirit for His baptism. Let Him shower you with His life and you will become alive and on fire in your heart.

Your bridegroom awaits you. Prepare yourself for the wedding. Come, pure and white, and anticipate this union with eagerness. I love you so, My child. You will never find a speck on this earth that can compare with the love of God. Search, you feeble creature, for worldly satisfaction and you will never satisfy one little part of your soul. Your soul can only be satisfied by the love of God. It stalks your restless heart and is only satisfied in God. It craves God like an appetite except that it is much stronger. What is in your heart that is never satisfied by your worldly way? It is the soul that craves union with God. It constantly keeps you in a state of unrest, of searching, of seeking, of looking for more. The more is found in the Eucharist. It is the answer to the empty heart. It is the love you seek, but cannot find anywhere else. It is Jesus, child. It is your Bridegroom. Come and be in Communion with Him. He awaits you and bids you to come, pure in your heart, to the wedding—the wedding of your soul.

Messenger: I felt as if there was so much I just did not understand and I was overwhelmed by the mystery of God. I opened the Blue Book to this:

Nov. 21, 1993:

Jesus: Oh, what glories I have in store for you when you finally see it all, see all there is to Me! Little glimpses I will give you. These are special treats of My love, but you, in your earthly form, cannot even handle it. My power, My light, My fire would blow you off your feet and you would be out cold.

That is how I am at your side, with a power pack like this, and you worry about a power failure? Oh, how silly, when I am with you. Trust, trust. I am here.   12/27/93 4:00 a.m.

Be Ready—My Time Is Near

Jesus: Dear child, My ways I impart to you. You come, I direct you in the ways of the Lord. You must come and be ready for My work here. This is the most valuable job you have. Do not underestimate the importance of our meeting in the night.

I come to you. Listen and be taught for I am the Savior of this world. I come to you and you know that Jesus, the Lord, is with you. I am He Who calls you from your sleep. I am Jesus, Son of the Living God and I come to you, My child, every night.

Do you realize Whom you are dealing with? You do not know how truly lucky you are that I have chosen you to carry out My mission. Pray and be alone with Me to ready yourself for My letter.

Whatever you do to your brothers, you do to Me. Pray and be ready, for your time is at hand. I blow a mighty horn when I come. You know it is I Who send you to deliver such a message. Time is short and your redemption is at hand. Busy yourself with things of the spirit. Do not get caught in the things of the earth. Spend time with your children. Each day is approaching an end. Each day must be spent to the fullest doing My work.

Do not fume. Do not fret. Does He Who loves you with such intensity intend to leave you in such turmoil? Little one, I will never leave you. All you receive comes from Him Who loves you. You must develop trust now. Practice letting go of your doubts and problems. Practice letting yourself be absolutely absorbed in Me. I am so close to you that you needn't ever worry. Some people think it is their duty to worry. I say it does no good. I am in charge of all things. I know all things about you. It is out of love I allow things to happen.

It is in your trials that you are taught mighty lessons. Do you comprehend, My little one? You are a baby. Babies never question. They are too little and too dependent on their mothers. You must have this dependency on Me. Trust is developed by the act of your will. You will to turn everything over and put it in My hands. Turn it over. Lift it up and be about My work to you. Who, child, does this work? You need to do it or it is undone. Pray for faith, hope and charity in these tough days ahead. This I give to you, that you must beg for these virtues.

Ready your hearts for My coming. You should be about this task constantly. You need to be sowing the seeds I have given to you. To present anything but a picture of assuredness and trust in Me is to be moving away from Me.

I am here and I am strengthening you in your hearts for the days ahead. You must follow My lead in all you do. Worry is fruitless. Preparedness is your utmost concern. Concern yourself only with the things of God. Do not be led astray by anything that leads you from your focus.

Pray for your brothers constantly. It is as the unrest before the storm. There is an unsteady feeling, a nervousness as if one knows the storm is coming. This is how the world is now—it is as if you are waiting for a big explosion. You almost know the time, but no one has told you a thing. The unsteady air is telling you the message. Be ready. Be tuned into the events about to occur!

You must be tuned into trust in Me. Nothing else! Trust and Faith will be the lamp that lights your path. Your job now is not to know when, how or if, not to worry, not to fret, not to fume. Your job is to stay fixed to Me, to disregard the unsettling feeling and to take this time to become very close to Me, to use this opportunity to practice total Trust in your God, and to be about the things of God at every moment—attending Mass, receiving Holy Communion and praying before Me in adoration!

You are missing private prayer with your children. They will not come to you and say, "Let's pray the rosary, Mom." You must take time for your children. Your time alone with them now is strengthening them for the days ahead. You need time alone with them, and in private prayer. Teach them that this time is a top priority in your life. You need a united front in the family. The family that prays together, stays together. You can give them so much by demanding this time alone with them and praying as a family together.

You need to be ready for My coming. You need to pray with them. You must initiate the prayers. Your world has become very distracted with others because of Christmas. You need to quit talking to others and realize these are valuable demands that I am placing on you. You need this time with the children. They need time with God. Many will not pray without your leading the way. Talk to them about Me. They need your constant conversation about Jesus, Savior of this world!

You have a job to do and it isn't saving a mighty world. It is simple, but very important. God is always first in all you do. You need to attend daily Mass and go to Communion. You need adoration. Then you need time alone, praying and playing with the children. This is My prescription for all parents in these troubled times. Do not focus on things of the world—here today, gone tomorrow. All that I ask is for your everlasting life. Mass, Communion, adoration, prayer and time with your children. All other things you do leads to rewards in the world. They are of no account to Me. Nothing but the things of Me matters!

Ready yourself and your children for the things of God. The world preaches a false peace. You must trust Me and the message I am delivering here. I know all things. Place your trust in Me. Forget the world. It thinks that it will go on forever. You must tend to all the things of the soul. Do not go to the world for your being. See yourself as My beautiful one and recognize your need for Me at every moment. Do not question, ask, fume or fret. Just be about My work which is performing your daily duties towards Me. That is simple, you say ? It is not as simple as it sounds when the world is pulling you away from God and Satan is planting his distractions on your way. If he can keep you from prayer and time with your children, he has performed a mighty feat. I am telling you: guard against distractions that leave you no time for your little ones. They need this time as they need food and clothing. Do not underestimate this command I am giving you. Heed My words. They come from Him Who loves you and knows all things. Do not worry or be anxious. Just listen to what I tell you to do and then put all worry aside.

Child, I know all things and I know what is best. It is this simple: be about the things of Me. Forget all these other demands on your time. They are hollow in the end.

I am so close to you. Concentrate on Me as a person that is with you always. Talk to Me and focus on Me by your side, in your heart. I am surrounding you. Stay holy, little one, and do as you are told here. I know more than any person on this earth. Worry is useless. Prayer to Me is golden. It is the security you need to store for the days ahead. Forget money and treasures. Your only command is to store the things of God in your hearts and those of your children. Money, education, things—all those things you think you must have — will be useless in the end.

Harken to My word here. I am there with you and I will remain with you in all your trials. Practice trust in Me and teach it to all you meet. You are My light shining in a dark world. Your example is the way I teach. Don't go to the world for answers. Do as I say, child. Store up the things of God and don't worry—ever! I am this close to you. I will never leave your side, but you must pray constantly and be there with your children to pray and play with them.

I love you. I am He Who came and died for you out of love of you. I give you this message with the same love. Let your hearts be not troubled for the Lord is by your side. Alleluia. Alleluia.   12/28/93 3:00 a.m.

My True Presence

Jesus: I am the Good Shepherd. I know Mine and Mine know Me. I am one Who goes before you. Pave the way for the Lord. He is mighty and deserving of all praise and Holy is His Name! His might goes from generation to generation on those who fear Him. He raises the lowly to new life and the rich He sends away empty.

Prepare His way. As one crying in the desert, prepare and make ready a path for the Lord. At His name, every knee should bend and all should be attentive to His coming. I am Jesus, Son of the Living God. I come into your midst, not as a king adorned in splendor, but as a helpless little baby. I do not carry My might in front of Me. My might is there without any ado.

I am He Whose boot strap you are unworthy to tie, but I come and give Myself to you. I am a God of might, but one Who loves you so much that I come and dwell with you. I enter into your bodies in Holy Communion. I do not blare the trumpets and roll the drums, but nonetheless am I mighty and nonetheless am I the true King of heaven and earth!

My love for you gives you such dignity, My little ones. Why do you go about wailing for all you're worth when I give you worth. So much worth by My Communion with you. I come and I dwell by your side. I enter your body. I remain waiting for you in the tabernacle and you miss the great dignity that I bestow on you. Wake up, My people! The King of Glory is in your midst. He awaits you in the tabernacle. He waits for you to come and be in Communion with Him at Mass. And you sleep, you follow roads that lead you to empty treasures when the priceless treasure waits you at Mass!

Ready your hearts for the coming of the Lord. Be not numb to this event. Be wide awake and knowledgeable of what transpires at the altar. Bread and wine are changed by the priest into the Body and Blood of Jesus. He is the Savior of the World. He loves you so much that He comes to you every day in Communion and you, little ones, choose other things! Oh, how blind and numb My sick children are. You are missing the most valuable treasure. I await you at every Mass. Why is My church not packed for what transpires here? Concerts are packed. Ball games are packed. Big bucks for the false idols! And what for the King of Glory? An empty church!

My heart is sad, sad, sad, little ones. I come and wait for you here. Tell your brothers about My love for them. You come empty, you leave full. Tell My brothers that Jesus Christ, the Son of God, is present at Mass and He enters your bodies. Many Catholics go to Mass every Sunday and have no idea of the significance of the Holy Eucharist. My heart is aching. They receive Me. Then, with the same tongues, they leave the church rattling senseless things. I am God, you silly children. I am God and I come to you on your tongue. Tell your friends how honored you are. No stars could compare to God. They are mortal beings and their concerts are packed. Ball games are honored as a god.

Your time is not yours. It is My time and I loan it to you to work for Me. America, you have made sports a god! You have made sports stars gods, singers gods! You pack the house and the honor awaits mortal beings, but the Son of God sits in an empty church! For the few who want to sit with Me the churches are locked. Open My churches up. I want My people to come to Me and sit with Me. The few who do know the significance have to drive so far to sit with Me.

Not even My priests know how important the tabernacle is. They need to realize I am truly present there and that I wait for My loved ones to come and sit with Me. To lock Me up is not to treasure Me. To treasure Me is to make Me available to all that want to come.

Preach My love from the housetops and boast My words from every rooftop, "Jesus, Lord, awaits you in the tabernacle. He is in the church, truly present there, waiting to give you His love!" Please do not guard Me so well. I am so guarded no one can come to Me. What a setup! I sit and wait and lament My loved ones' presence with Me and the few who would come cannot get in! I am truly present in the tabernacle.

I do not want to be locked up. I want you to come and let Me pour My gifts out to you. I want to give you supplies for a sick world. Everyone should come and be with Me every day, sit in silence and let Me work in your soul. What might for you, little babies! Jesus waits to shower you with His love.

After Communion people run from the church. They receive God on their tongues and in their hearts and they are out lickety-split. Where do they go so quickly from the Son of Man, Who is God? You turn your backs. You run away like in a race, a race for nothingness, and the bridegroom of your hearts is ignored. Think of a bride running away to K-Mart two minutes after her wedding. "What could be so important?," you ask. "What is wrong with her head!?"

Little ones, what is wrong with the heads of My faithful who attend daily Mass and do not know they still have Jesus, the Son of God, in their hearts when they run to the food stores. There I am going up and down the grocery aisles while they make useless conversation—right outside the church—while I am still actively in their chest!

Tell your brothers about Communion. It has become an insignificant event! I am God and I am in the host you receive. God, God, God. Where is your honor for this King? Where is your head? I, Jesus, Lord, am in your hearts and you run from the church to pump your gas. Such indifference! Such disrespect and irreverence! I am God, My loved ones. I am the bridegroom of your soul and you leave the wedding for a trip to the gas tank. I am so offended. I, in My great love, come to you. God enters you and you run from My altar with such irreverence! Believe Me, nothing you do all day will compare to the Son of Man in your breast. I am God and I enter your body and you are so irreverent. You don't even know what treasure you possess.

Get this message out about My True Presence. Tell them, My faithful ones, that I am very displeased by their indifference to Me in Holy Communion. Stay and sit with Me. Sit in silence after Communion. My magnetic attraction draws you to the altar, then you miss the most important event in your day. It is your union with Me, your silence after Communion, your quiet resting in My arms, that will change your life. I am so loving and I long to dole out My gifts after Communion.

Know, My loved ones, Jesus, Son of the Living God is there the same as He was the day He died on the cross, and you walk away with Him Who loves you so much in your breast.

Sit with Me. Be silent. Spend time with Me after Communion. You do not talk to Him Whom you love. You just melt into each other's arms. Let Me join My heart to your heart after Communion. Don't ever run from the church. I am God, truly present there. All you faithful, become aware of My True Presence in Holy Communion and in the tabernacle. Tell all about this and how I am there out of such love and I have so much to give them.

If I, Who am God, came and was born a helpless baby, a human being; if I, Who am God, died a brutal death for you with full knowledge of all My sufferings before I did it; if I, Who am God, rose from the dead and then ascended into heaven to My Father; if I, Who am God, am present in the tabernacle and Communion and if I love you so much as to go through all this for you, then why do you not realize what I, Who am God, would give to you when you receive Me and sit in front of the tabernacle!

I am God!! What is wrong with your heads! Tell My people the treasure you possess. All else here is empty. I am Who am. I am God! I dwell among you and you run to worship other gods. God is not far off. He is in your midst as a prisoner of love and He awaits you in all your unworthiness. But you are dumb! You look for empty treasures and you find empty treasures. In your emptiness you begin an avid search for the answer to a stalking soul, when the treasure you seek is God and He longs for your union with Him!

Tell your brothers they thirst for God and He is waiting. Quit your idle pursuits, your empty hearts. Crave the Savior. You turn your backs and search a barren desert for that which is right in front of your face!

It is in making known God's True Presence in the Eucharist that much healing takes place. Many starving souls are fed for the first time when they realize that Jesus, God, is truly present there! They have given lip service to Jesus in the Eucharist, but have no idea in their hearts what a treasure they possess. Spread the doctrine of the True Presence. Make My love and My availability known to your blind brothers. Bow yourselves before My altar. Be in awe of God, truly present there. Kiss My sanctuary. Don't ever talk in church about anything. Respect God Who is there. Have reverence for Me in My tabernacle. Kiss the floor. Bow. Be reverent!

You must speak about this every chance you get. When people take time to be with Me, then I can change their hearts. Tell all who go to Communion about what a treasure they possess. Pray for your brothers. It is your goodness that pleases Me. I will hear your prayers, spoken from a good heart. Strive after holiness and strive to please Me every minute. Your devotion pleases My aching heart. Do not falter in your love of Me. Let it grow with Me in Communion and in front of the tabernacle. Silence is the key. Be silent and be with Me, little loved one.

12/25/93

My Soul Is Lifted By You

Messenger: Your soul is lifted to such heights in your hot air balloon! I am lifted, my spirit. The body is left behind on the earth.

Jesus: Do not be concerned with what you are to wear and put on. I care about your soul. All things of the body wither and fade. The body is only the means by which you move about the earth. Your matter dies and decays. Your spirit moves on. All you truly are never dies.

Messenger I transport this bag of bones to realms I never dreamed possible and fly the skies. My spirit rises. My body remains fixed in its tracks. This is similar to death: the body stays behind. My soul never truly dies. It goes on to another place.

Jesus: Ready yourself, My child, for the Kingdom of God is at hand and you will see sights you never dreamed of. The love of the Lord will be made clear and you will be engulfed in such peace.

What is heaven? "Eye has not seen, nor ear heard, the glories that await him who serves the Lord." Ready yourself with your lamp for this journey. The eyes are the lights to the soul. What enters in through the eyes is sacred. Stay fixed on the things of God. Pant for His glory. Never look away. If you behold Him and His Kingdom, you will behold eternal life. I am one crying in the desert. Make straight the way of the Lord.

Messenger: Impart to me only deeds that are of God. Wash away my sins and clean me of all that is not of You, for I am weak and humble in heart and You are God, all might and full of all power. Impart some of Your power to my soul to help me clean away the debris there. I am but a feeble human and it is only in You that I reach such heights. Send Your power and Your light into my soul and give me what I need, Lord. You know my state far better than I and You have all the power to change me into that which You want. I surrender with a happy heart to the God Who made me and loves me far more than any mortal or far more than I could love or know myself.

I surrender with a smile and a peace in my heart for it is He Who makes us whole and I am glad for this undertaking. Come, Lord Jesus, Come and be the Master of our Hearts! Come and fill us. Change us, fashion us, mold us and make us into Your work of art! We submit ourselves entirely to Your ways.

Oh, Savior, we are so blessed to even know You, much less have a private union with You in the Eucharist! You, oh Savior, are so good. Your goodness fills my heart with so much love of Thee and I feel such fluttering in my heart. I love You intently as You are. At Your name, every knee must bend in honor of You, the King of Kings and Lord of Lords. Alleluia.

He comes, the Savior of the world, and He dwells in this humble creature that I am and I am exalted to such heights in His presence. Alleluia. This, my friends, is God. Do you believe? God comes and dwells here in us! Who are we that He loves us in this way? This is the goodness of God. We cannot even comprehend His generosity, His goodness and His love. He gives us little glimpses, but it is only a drop in an ocean compared to His actual goodness.

Oh, fill us with knowledge of Your goodness so we can love You more, Master. I want to love You more and I need my heart opened more to You. Please open my heart to the things of God for He is great and worthy of all praise. Alleluia, Alleluia.

God of God, Lord of Lords! He waits for us with a heart of Love. Alleluia, Alleluia. What dignity He bestows on us. What life He gives to us. He is indeed a good God, worthy of such love. How can I love You more, Lord? Open my heart to this union with You. Alleluia, Alleluia. Praise the Lord!

Be only of the Spirit. Let go of all that keeps you attached to this world and soar the skies in your spirit. Your soul is transcended to a new realm of union with God. Let go to Him entirely. Surrender. Submission. Letting total trust in Him take place. You are a slave to His Love!

12/29/93 After Mass

My Hand Is In Everything

Jesus: Come and be a witness for Me. By your example you teach so many lessons. You are My servants in this world. At every moment you are teaching the word of God. You must guard against being tired and down-hearted. I am your Savior and you teach a mighty lesson every minute of your day.

Guard against things of the world. Everything here is momentary: food, sex, money. Here today, gone tomorrow. Only the things of the spirit last forever. You are a temple of the Holy Ghost. The road you are treading is full of pot holes. At any moment your foot slips and you feel engulfed by the road. This is how life is. Satan is constantly in your way to trip you up. Guard against his tactics. You are tired in this world, but these trials are the gems of your learning. Do not curse the trials and the pitfalls. Accept them as an opportunity to offer up your sufferings to Me. Such little things offered up are mighty prayers. Look at disappointments as golden gems.

I came as a great teacher to teach you mighty lessons. Be taught by Me constantly. I am the way, the truth, the life. You need to abide in My ways and I will give you the light of life.

It is in acceptance of all that is before you that you grow in your relationship with Me. Do not try to throw back into My face the little opportunity for grace you receive. Child, I am ever by your side and I am ever teaching you. Accept all things as happening from Him Who loves you. Know that My hand is in everything you are experiencing. I am vigilant and by your side. Nothing happens to you that I have not consented to.

You are My messenger and this is My message: Look to Me and keep your heart fixed on the God Who loves you. At every second, turn to Him and place yourself in His arms. I am Jesus and I love you!

12/30/93

Commander of the Ship

Messenger: He snatches us from whatever and we are His. Are we in control at every second? He comes as a thief in the night and our control is gone! We are His. We are totally under His control now! Faith is the answer. We must surrender here on earth to have eternity. To ignore God is so silly because He can come in one second and we are totally powerless. Isn't that how it is here?

We are powerless the whole time, but in our willfulness we decide to do what we want and thus start our journey down the wrong road. But at any moment He can take us. Then we are totally out of control. At any moment a storm can come and rock us in our path and we are out of control. At any moment we may get a very crippling disease and we are out of control. Basically, it is silly to think we are in control!

He is the commander of the ship. I am only a servant boy. I do not admit to any authority. I only am here to serve. He is the Commander. I am he who complies. He has all the knowledge of the ship and the seas. I do not have any. I only do as I am told. If I try to run the ship, I may become shipwrecked because I do not know such matters. If anyone else tells me what to do, it is to the detriment of the whole ship. I go to the Commander for my directions and He tells me what I must do. I do His will for smooth sailing.

Jesus: When you come to Me in Communion and in front of the tabernacle, let Me fill you with all that is of Me. I want to work in your hearts. Sit silent (very hard to do, but so rewarding). Let your spirit be the total focus. If your leg aches, forget it. Be formless and ready to deal with only the things of the heart. I work in your heart and you are aware of what work I have done. Know I have a plan for you in the silence. God works in the whispers. It is the world that surrounds itself with noise. The closer you get to God, the more you love the silence with Him. Sit and be My bride. I love you intimately. Get rid of all distractions—mind, body, otherwise—and give Me your soul, then just sit. Keep your mind fixed only on My love.

I am the way, the truth and the life. He who abides in Me will have the light of life and the life I give is not of this world. Turn your hearts to Me and give Me your will. To ignore Me is to be shipwrecked on a mighty sorry island. You must take all I give you. Praise Him Who gives it to you! Do not turn away. Come and be with Me in My house. I await you as a lover Who is anxious for His bride. How can you stay away when God Himself beckons you to come? Do you not hear My lamenting cries in your heart? They whisper, "Come to Me in your busy lives," but you silence them with rags and go about your useless tasks.

Oh, little ones, you are missing the glory that awaits you in church and in your life hereafter. All that is here is but a passing thing. Like smoke, it blows away and nothing is left, not even a trace of billowing smoke. It seems so real, but it is so temporary. It is here one moment and gone the next. Do you not see your brothers who die before you? All that matters is their souls. Were they ready to meet their Maker? I warn you, I prompt you in your hearts. Others give you bad example and you follow like little sheep. You follow even when it leads to destruction.

Come, little ones, follow Me. I am the Good Shepherd and you need to follow the Master. I give you a land flowing with milk and honey and you are filled with the gifts of God. Oh, little ones, how do I make you see the nose on your face? You are so blind and caught up in your silly things.

Pray for your brothers. Nothing seems to rock them. They think this world will go on forever. Pray, pray, pray! You have a mighty work to do, My faithful ones. Your brothers walk a dark, dark night and do not have a lamp. They do not even see the darkness. Your prayers may light their way. Stay fixed in your ways and preach by your example. You are My lights shining in the darkness. Keep yourselves holy that you will be doing My work in your being. Be Christ-like and preach My message to your brother! 12/31/93

Don't Question God

Jesus: I am the way, the truth and the life. He who abides in Me will have the light of life. I am Jesus, Son of God. I am the most important thing you do every day. If you are tired, then you are focusing on the wrong things. Be ready, for your Savior awaits you and you are His messenger.

I am Jesus, Savior of the World. I am ready for you. Listen and write My words. I am the light that shines in this dark world. I come to you in the night and you know it is Me. I come in such silence and no one knows that I am surrounded by angels. No one knows so many things that you do not see. Faith is the answer for My brothers. Faith is the answer for you, for when you do not see you still believe. When there is no proof, you are still absolutely sure that I am here. This faith does not go unrewarded. Where there are no proofs, you believe in Me. Blessed are they who have not seen and yet believe.

What I reveal to you here, I do in your heart. My connectedness to you is in your heart. I do not need the senses. Man wants God to be like them. Do not ask to have God explained in human terms. This, My child, is surely in the realm of the spirit. Things of God are not like the things of man. I communicate to you as I am. Others want you to explain to them just how it is.

Your human minds do not fathom the ways of God. To ask My messenger to answer your human questions is to ask her to tell you why stars shine, why a baby is conceived in the mother. In the end there is an element of mystery which is beyond words. Don't ask her to tell you why and how she writes these letters. She writes these letters by the power I have. She writes these letters for Me. She writes these letters because I am dictating them to her for you. She sits, half asleep, and writes such clear lessons in faith. And, you My brothers, ask for explanations? I am Jesus Christ, Son of the Living God. I am He Whose boot strap you are unworthy to tie, yet I make Myself so personal to you in Holy Communion. But, little ones, I am God. You cannot comprehend one little speck of My ways. Your human mind is so limited. Do not try to make sense of Me in human terms. I write these letters to bridge a gap between you and Me.

I am this personal to you, but My ways are not your ways and, though I try to make you understand some of the mystery, you cannot in your humanness explain the ways of God. Go ahead and try, child. It is a waste of your time. Do not ask My messengers for explanations that you will understand. You will not ever on this earth understand any of what is happening here. My ways are the ways of God. What is happening here is a miracle.

You ask too many questions and you, in your humanness, many answers. I am the God of your Fathers. They never kn. God. I was the same God to them and I spoke to similar people up Myself to them, but you have been given a great, great gift in these letters. Do you question and question or do you study and become wise. Study My words and accept all I give you with faith.

Be blessed for the faith you show. Your faith will save you in this sick world. I am here, all right. I am in the Eucharist, Body and Soul. Would you like for Me to explain the real presence. How can I, in your earthly form, explain such things to you? Wake up. I give you a gift and you spend your time asking how, why, where, when. I give you this day a gift of My love for you. You will not understand the ways of God but, from these letters, I will become as real as the nose on your face. You can busy yourself asking questions and miss the miracle of My coming to you in these letters.

I come to you, you who are hungry and thirsty and you are waiting for more. To those who listened, much was imparted to them. To those who remained blind, nothing was gained. They try to explain God in human terms. I cannot be explained to your liking, My child. To do so is just silly.

I am God. I am Who Am. I am the Son of God. I am Human, but I am also Divine. You will not understand My divinity. You are a human. Be glad for what you are given. Pray for faith. So many souls will be lost for their stubbornness to have every situation explained. I will not ever be explained to you. If you do not go out on a limb, you will miss the sunset. The glories that you need to seek are to be seen at the end of the limb.

You do not know why, in your heaviness, the limb does not break. You will not understand, in your humanness, My ways. I impart to you many gifts. Do not try to explain My ways in your human ways. It is a futile task. It is impossible. It is not human. It is divine. Accept this miracle on faith and reap such a reward! God-made-man talks to you, not to the messenger. Talks to you! Do you want an explanation? You will not understand My divinity in your humanness, so quit trying and get about the job of listening to My words with your heart.

I will work in your hearts in your quiet time with Me. You do not do this work, either. The more you look for explanations with Me, the more you miss Me. My ways are a mystery. I impart such little glimpses of Myself to you. They are in your hands, to burst forth later. Now you busy yourself with the work at hand. Come in silence and make yourself self-less. I will be the giver of many gifts. If you decide what gifts I will give you, you have missed the boat entirely. I give to you as you need.

You are My babies. Babies do not tell their mothers of their needs. They wait and they are fed. They wait and they are changed. They wait and they are loved. Wait on the Lord. What you get is coming from Him

Who loves you. I know all things. I know your needs. I am like the loving mother. I am God. I know your every need. Come and soak in the sunlight. Quit your questioning. Quit your asking for such things that you may never need. Turn yourself over like little babies, freshly born. They have soft little cries and are very dependent on their mothers. Come with your little cries but know that I, in the end, will give you all you need.

Don't try to control Me. I am God. Who are you to come and think you will tell God what you need. I see the whole picture and I comprehend it as God. You see as in a tunnel and think you know so much. Come and make yourself putty in My hands. Remain formless and unattached. Remain a baby. Take all I give and do not ask questions. It is in your submissiveness to Me that you grow in Me. I dwell in you and I can operate from you. In your willfulness, I cannot come in. How can God act in a soul who is in control. If you are operating, I cannot.

Oh, you have much to learn, but it is revealed in these letters how to become creatures of God. Most of your work is in submission to Me. Your biggest job is to die to yourself and live in Me. I am all powerful and I want to dwell in your breast. I want to possess your soul. I want to impart to you My love. I want to fill you to the brim with the things of God. All that is in the way of My working in you is yourself. If you hold onto self, you get yourself. To be of Me, you must let go of yourself. Come to My altar and sit silently before Me. Let Me work in your soul. Look for Me.

I give to you according to your needs. I answer you according to the things of God. I give you gifts that you never knew possible, because your mind cannot imagine the things of God. Do not limit your soul by being in charge. The soul is in the image of God and God must deal with it. To try to feed your soul humanness is useless. Only God can feed the soul. Come to Him and let Him have full reign in your hearts. Don't try to decide what you need. You don't know of the needs of a soul. God is so good and so loving and He wants to give you what you need. Surrender to Him and be open to all He wants to do in you.

Be open to the things of the spirit. Put your human ways aside when you are dealing with God. They certainly keep you away from God. Eye has not seen, nor ear heard, what glories await him who loves and serves the Lord. For the things of God, go to God. Then listen and make yourself empty so He can fill you to do His work. Stay out of it. Do not talk. Do not plead. Be quiet and let Him work in your soul and you will know such feats that only God could perform. If you look for human things, you get human things. If you are looking for God, let go of your humanness and let Him give you from the realm of the supernatural. It takes surrender and faith.

Be of a clean mind, America. Your faith will make you whole. All other roads lead to idle pursuits and you miss the golden mystery of your God!

The Rosary Song

by Rita Ring

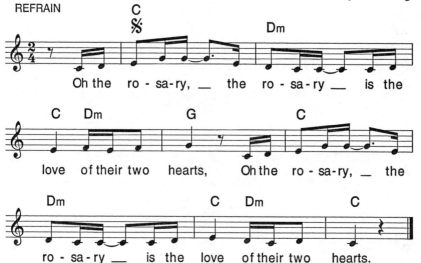

REFRAIN

Oh the ro - sa - ry, __ the ro - sa - ry __ is the

love of their two hearts, Oh the ro - sa - ry, __ the

ro - sa - ry __ is the love of their two hearts.

VERSES 1-4

1. A - ve Ma - ri - a, A - ve Ma - ri - a. Oh the
2. Je - sus we love You, Ma - ry we love __ you. Oh the
3. This is her peace plan, Chil - dren must pray __ it. Oh the
4. We turn to Ma - ry, She is the Queen of Peace. Oh the

VERSE 5

No left hand

5. Oh Sa - cred Heart di - vine, Oh heart of Ma - ry pure,

A - ve Ma - ri - a, We love to pray it! Oh the

A Song from Jesus

by Rita Ring

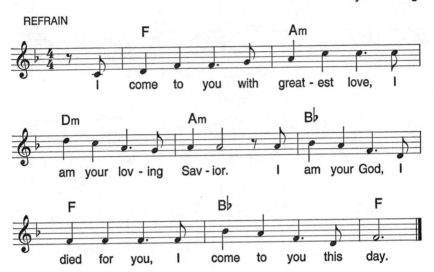

REFRAIN

I come to you with great-est love, I am your lov-ing Sav-ior. I am your God, I died for you, I come to you this day.

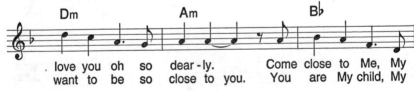

VERSES

1. You are My pre-cious lit-tle one, I love you oh so dear-ly. Come close to Me, My lit-tle one, I loved you to My death.
2. Reach out to Me and do not fear, I want to be so close to you. You are My child, My pre-cious one, I love you ten-der-ly.

I Love You Jesus

by Rita Ring

VERSES

1. Oh Burn-ing Heart, Oh Love di - vine, how sweet You are to me. I see the host, I know You're here to love and care for me.
2. I can-not say. There are not words to say what my heart feels. I love You so, I scarce can breathe when You come in - to me.
3. Your ten - der Heart, Oh how it beats for love of each this day. I want to give You all my love, sur - ren - der to - tal - ly.

REFRAIN

I know Your love a lit - tle now, so dear You are to me. Come give me life, a - bun - dant life, I thirst to be with Thee.

Little Child

by Rita Ring

VERSE 1

1. Lit - tle child, lit - tle child, come and rest in My arms. Be with Me, lit - tle child, I want you with Me. You are hurt-ing My lov-ed one, I'm wait-ing for you. Come in - to My Heart now, I love you.

REFRAIN

I am Je - sus, lit - tle child, I have al - ways loved you. From the day you were born, I've been here with you. Do not for - sake Me, I want you to know, lit - tle child, lit - tle child, I love you so!

VERSE 2

2. Let__ go, let__ go, you hold on__ so

tight to the things that are near you, Come in-to My

light. Your__ heart knows__ long-ing, I am what you

crave. Let go to My pres-ence, I ne-ver go.

Teach Me to Love with Your Heart

by Rita Ring

VERSES

1. Give me Your Heart Oh Je - sus, Give me a
2. I see You pre - cious Je - sus, hang - ing
3. I know You lov - ed those who put_____

heart like Yours. ___ Teach me to love You with
from the cross. ___ You give Your all___ for
You to death. ___ You ask my love___ for

this new heart, Oh I know lit - tle of how___ to
love of me, I see You there in Your drip - ping
all this day, Help me to know that You died for my

love You. Cre - ate in me Oh pre - cious Sav - iour
blood. ___ Help me to real - ize that You shed Your
broth-er. You call Me, Lord, to put on Christ and

this ___ spe-cial heart. ___
blood ___ for ___ me. ___
love ___ this ___ day. ___

REFRAIN
Give me your heart Oh
Je - sus, Give me a heart like Yours. ___

D.C.

God's Love

by Rita Ring

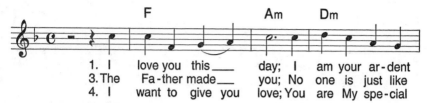

1. I love you this ___ day; I am your ar-dent
3. The Fa-ther made___ you; No one is just like
4. I want to give you love; You are My spe-cial

love; You wan - der oh so far; Your
you; You are His lit - tle child; He
love; You are My Fa - ther's child; I

soul knows it is hun - gry for on - ly My___
has a plan for you; Live as He wills you
love you oh so dear - ly; Come close and know My

love. 2. You want to know the truth; You
to. 5. The Spir - it knows the way to
love.

look so ma - ny plac-es; You must come to My Heart; Find
lead you to God's love. Be fill - ed with His life; He'll

shel - ter in My Heart; My Heart has all you need.
give you love on fire; You'll know the pow'r of God.

(repeat verse 1
after verse 5)

I Am Your Sacred Heart

by Rita Ring

REFRAIN

In the deep - est re - cess - es of ___ My Heart, take ___ ref - uge ___ from the wind and ___ the storm. I will be with you for ___ ev - er - more. I am your Sa - cred Heart.

VERSE 1

1. I am the Way, the Truth and the Life, you will have life in Me. Come, My dear lit - tle chil - dren come, Come and ___ live in Me.

See the Eyes That Look at Mary

by Rita Ring

REFRAIN

See the eyes that look at Mar - y, this ten - der in - fant Child. See this Child's Heart beat so ten - der - ly, the Sav - ior of the world!

VERSES 1,2

1. His__ eyes are gaz - ing stead-i - ly____ up - on His lov - ing Moth-er. She__ sees the Child__ Je - sus, the new-born ba - by here. He__ comes in His en - tire - ty, the Son of God is He.

2. He__ gives us now His bo - dy in the Ho - ly Eu - cha - rist.__ He__ comes with this in - tense_ love to be so close to us. He__ longs for us to come to Him, His Heart__ waits for us.

Wake us up,___ Let us see that You are tru - ly
Fill us now, Give us Your love.___ Let us be so

Christ the Lord! _ We are blind, we need Your grace, please
close to You! _ We are blind, we need Your grace, please

o - pen up our eyes to You!
o - pen up our eyes to You!

VERSE 3

3. We are Yours, we give our-selves, we con - se-crate our

hearts to You. We con - se - crate our

hearts to You, we give You all our love!

no refrain

Little Baby Hands and Feet

by Rita Ring

REFRAIN

Lit-tle ba-by hands and feet, Loved and cared for by His Moth-er;

Sim - e-on fore - told the pain, Je-sus Lord is nailed to the cross.

VERSES 1,2,3

1. Ten-der ba - by lit - tle hands, Mar-y's heart is pierced with a sword;
2. Mar-y is our Moth-er too, She will lead us to His __ love;
3. Mar-y stood be- neath the cross, How her heart __ knows His __ Heart;

He has come to give us life, God our Fa-ther gave His Son.
He has giv-en us His life, See Him hang __ on the cross.
She watched Him her ten-der Child, Now she takes us to His Heart.

VERSE 4

4. Stand be-side Him know the joy, He has come to bring new life;

Now He ris - es from the dead, Gives us life a - bun-dant life.

no refrain

Come to My Heart

by Rita Ring

REFRAIN

Let go to Me, My child, I want __ to be __ with you. Come, __ dear child, I love you so much, Come and sur - ren - der to Me.

VERSES 1,2

1. My moth - er calls out __ to you, She wants you to come to her Son, My Heart __ is wait-ing for you. Come and be lost in My love.

2. I want you to dwell in My Heart, I call you to come for My love, I will give you all that you need. Come deep - ly in - to My Heart.

Your Presence Pervades My Soul

by Rita Ring

REFRAIN

C   G   C

Your pres-ence per - vades my soul, __ Your burn-ing

G   Dm   Am   G

love in my heart. __ My heart knows You dear-ly, my

Am   C   F   G   C

soul knows Your pres-ence. Oh Je-sus, I long for Your love.

VERSE 1

Am   G   F   G

1. You are my way, my truth and my life, I for -

Am   G   F   G   D.C.

ev - er want Your pres - ence with - in me.

VERSE 2

Am   G   F   G

2. To You, Oh Lord, I lift up my soul. I

Am   G   F   G   D.C.

give You my life to use as You will.

VERSE 3

Am   G   F   G

3. I want to live for You this day, You

Am   G   F   G   D.C.

call me to see You in my broth-ers to - day.

VERSE 4

Am   G   Am

4. I am in your broth-er, I call you to

C   F   G   C   D.C.

love__ them. Do not turn Me a - way.

Glory, Glory, Glory Lord

by Rita Ring

VERSES 1,2,3

1. Glo - ry, Glo - ry, Glo - ry Lord!___
2. Ho - ly Spir - it give___ us fire!___
3. We are chil - dren of ___ the Fa - ther.

You have ris - en from the tomb!
Fill us with___ Your ra - diant love!
He___ has___ a plan for us.

Give us (life Lord,) Your pre-cious life! You __ have
Fill us with the fire of God's love! Mold _ us
Come to Him as His lit - tle child. He who cre -

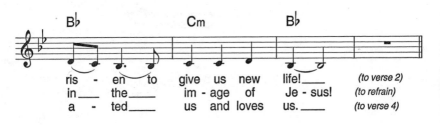

ris - en to give us new life!___ *(to verse 2)*
in ___ the___ im - age of Je - sus! *(to refrain)*
a - ted___ us and loves us. ___ *(to verse 4)*

VERSE 4

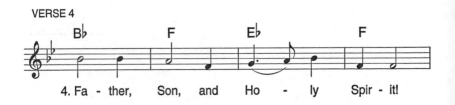

4. Fa - ther, Son, and Ho - ly Spir - it!

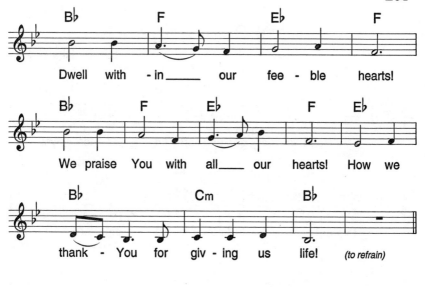

Dwell with - in ___ our fee - ble hearts!

We praise You with all ___ our hearts! How we

thank - You for giv - ing us life! *(to refrain)*

REFRAIN

We are sin - ners, we need ___ Your grace!

We are wait - ing Your pre - cious life!

Al - le - lu - ia Praise ___ the Lord! Je - sus has

ris - en to give us new life!

My Open Heart

by Rita Ring

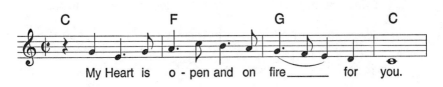

My Heart is o - pen and on fire ____ for you.

I want ___ you to know I'm wait - ing for you.

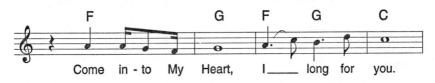

Come in - to My Heart, I ____ long for you.

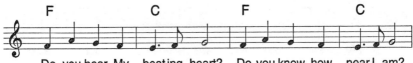

Do you hear My beating heart? Do you know how near I am?

I am Je - sus lit - tle one, I ____ wait for you.

Our Lady of Clearwater

Words and music by Joseph Lee

REFRAIN

Our La - dy of Clear - wa - ter, is shin - ing like the
sun, She comes to us in rainbow gown, to
lead us to her Son.

VERSES

1. The La - dy came with -
2. She asked that He be
3. So come right in and
4. Our La - dy came at

in our midst, on that De - cem - ber day, To
placed be - hind the im - age of her face, To
be filled up, He's wait - ing there for all, To
Fa - ti - ma, and asked we con - se - crate, To

lead us to the Eu - cha - rist, and kneel us down to pray.
bring us to His Sac - red Heart, where He pours out His grace.
give His love for all the world, please ans - wer now her call.
give our hearts to Their two Hearts, be - fore it is too late.

5. To lead us to her Son, she leads us to her
Son, She leads us, she's Our La - dy.

Why Do We Hurt the Ones We Love?

by Rita Ring

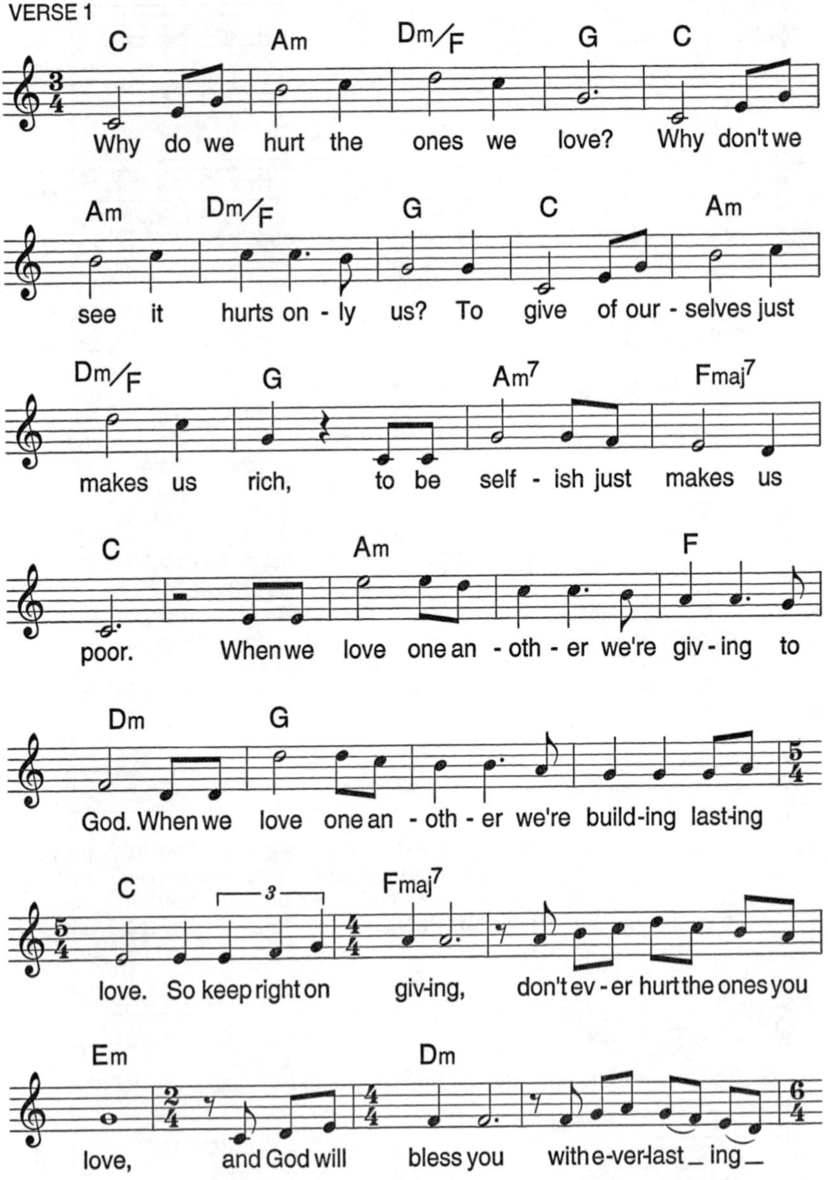

I Am a Child of God

First transcribed in my notebook.
Dedicated to Fr. Carter S. J.

by Rita Ring

1. Oh I am a child of God,
2. Oh I am a child of God,
3. Oh lit - tle son of Him,

Oh I give my life to You,
I know of my love for Thee,
Oh come with hu - mil - i - ty,

I see Your Heart up - on Your
I know my life de - pends on
And ask Him now to grace your

breast and hope I can dwell___ in Thee.
You and know I will strug - gle for Thee.
soul with love that is lik - ened to God.

Introduction to the
Shepherds of Christ Prayers

Here are the prayers that so many pray every day at 6:30, especially for the priests. Prayer chapters have helped many priests in parishes and people in these parishes to grow in greater holiness.

Will you form a prayer chapter in your parish and pray with us at 6:30?

One priest praying the prayers can tremendously boost the prayer power.

These are the prayers Father Carter gave us to pray in the Shepherds of Christ Prayer Manual.

Shepherds of Christ

Prayers

Written by Fr. Edward Carter, S.J.

Father Carter requested
that these be prayed in prayer chapters
all over the world.

These prayers are available on tapes
and discs as prayed by Fr. Carter.
Fr. Carter prayed them every day at 6:20, the Holy
Spirit Novena, Prayer Manual and Rosary

Shepherds of Christ Associates

PRAYER MANUAL

Shepherds of Christ Publications
China, Indiana

Imprimi Potest: Rev. Bradley M. Schaeffer, S.J.
Provincial
Chicago Province, The Society of Jesus

Imprimatur: Most Rev. Carl K. Moeddel
Auxiliary Bishop
Archdiocese of Cincinnati

The Shepherds of Christ Associates Prayer Manual is published by
Shepherds of Christ Publications, an arm of Shepherds of Christ Ministries,
P.O. Box 627 Madison, Indiana 47250 USA.

Founder, Shepherds of Christ Ministries:
Father Edward J. Carter, S.J.

For more information contact:
Shepherds of Christ Associates
P.O. Box 193
Morrow, OH 45152-0193 USA
Tel. 513-932-4451
Toll Free: 1-888-211-3041
Fax 513-932-6791

Chapter Meeting
Prayer Format

The prayer format below should be followed at chapter meetings of Shepherds of Christ Associates. All prayers, not just those said specifically for priests, should include the intention of praying for all the needs of priests the world over.

1. **Hymns.** Hymns may be sung at any point of the prayer part of the meeting.

2. **Holy Spirit Prayer.** Come, Holy Spirit, almighty Sanctifier, God of love, who filled the Virgin Mary with grace, who wonderfully changed the hearts of the apostles, who endowed all Your martyrs with miraculous courage, come and sanctify us. Enlighten our minds, strengthen our wills, purify our consciences, rectify our judgment, set our hearts on fire, and preserve us from the misfortunes of resisting Your inspirations. Amen.

3. **The Rosary.**

4. **Salve Regina.** "Hail Holy Queen, Mother of mercy, our life, our sweetness, and our hope. To you do we cry, poor banished children of Eve. To you do we send up our sighs, our mourning, our weeping in this vale of tears. Turn, then, most gracious advocate, your eyes of mercy toward us and after this, our exile, show unto us the blessed fruit of your womb, Jesus, O clement, O loving, O sweet Virgin Mary. Amen."

5. **The Memorare.** "Remember, O most gracious Virgin Mary, that never was it known that anyone who fled to your protection, implored your help, or sought your intercession was left unaided. Inspired by this confidence, I fly unto you, O Virgin of virgins, my Mother. To you I come, before you I stand, sinful and sorrowful. O Mother of the Word Incarnate, despise not my petitions, but, in your mercy, hear and answer me. Amen."

6. **Seven Hail Marys in honor of the Seven Sorrows of Mary.** Mary has promised very special graces to those who do this on a daily basis. Included in the promises of Our Lady for those who practice this devotion is her pledge to give special assistance at the hour of death, including the sight of her face. The seven sorrows are:

   (1) The first sorrow: the prophecy of Simeon (Hail Mary).
   (2) The second sorrow: the flight into Egypt (Hail Mary).
   (3) The third sorrow: the loss of the Child Jesus in the temple (Hail Mary).

(4) The fourth sorrow: Jesus and Mary meet on the way to the cross (Hail Mary).

(5) The fifth sorrow: Jesus dies on the cross (Hail Mary).

(6) The sixth sorrow: Jesus is taken down from the cross and laid in Mary's arms (Hail Mary).

(7) The seventh sorrow: the burial of Jesus (Hail Mary).

7. **Litany of the Blessed Virgin Mary.**

Lord, have mercy on us.
    Christ, have mercy on us.
Lord, have mercy on us. Christ, hear us.
    Christ, graciously hear us.
God, the Father of heaven, have mercy on us.
God, the Son, Redeemer of the world,
    have mercy on us.
God, the Holy Spirit, have mercy on us.
Holy Trinity, one God, have mercy on us.
Holy Mary, pray for us (repeat after each invocation).
Holy Mother of God,
Holy Virgin of virgins,
Mother of Christ,
Mother of the Church,
Mother of divine grace,
Mother most pure,
Mother most chaste,
Mother inviolate,
Mother undefiled,
Mother most amiable,
Mother most admirable,
Mother of good counsel,
Mother of our Creator,
Mother of our Savior,
Virgin most prudent,
Virgin most venerable,
Virgin most renowned,
Virgin most powerful,
Virgin most merciful,
Virgin most faithful,
Mirror of justice,
Seat of wisdom,
Cause of our joy,
Spiritual vessel,
Vessel of honor,

Singular vessel of devotion,
Mystical rose,
Tower of David,
Tower of ivory,
House of gold,
Ark of the Covenant,
Gate of heaven,
Morning star,
Health of the sick,
Refuge of sinners,
Comforter of the afflicted,
Help of Christians,
Queen of angels,
Queen of patriarchs,
Queen of prophets,
Queen of apostles,
Queen of martyrs,
Queen of confessors,
Queen of virgins,
Queen of all saints,
Queen conceived without original sin,
Queen assumed into heaven,
Queen of the most holy rosary,
Queen of families,
Queen of peace,
Lamb of God, who take away the sins of the world,
    spare us, O Lord.
Lamb of God, who take away the sins of the world,
    graciously hear us, O Lord.
Lamb of God, who take away the sins of the world,
    have mercy on us.
Pray for us, O holy Mother of God,
    that we may be made worthy of the promises of Christ.

Let us pray: Grant, we beseech You, O Lord God, that we Your servants may enjoy perpetual health of mind and body and, by the glorious intercession of the blessed Mary, ever virgin, be delivered from present sorrow, and obtain eternal joy. Through Christ our Lord. Amen.

We fly to your patronage, O holy Mother of God. Despise not our petitions in our necessities, but deliver us always from all dangers, O glorious and blessed Virgin. Amen.

8. **Prayer to St. Joseph.** St. Joseph, guardian of Jesus and chaste spouse of Mary, you passed your life in perfect fulfillment of duty. You sup-

ported the Holy Family of Nazareth with the work of your hands.
Kindly protect those who trustingly turn to you. You know their
aspirations, their hardships, their hopes; and they turn to you
because they know you will understand and protect them. You too
have known trial, labor, and weariness. But, even amid the worries of
material life, your soul was filled with deep peace and sang out in
true joy through intimacy with the Son of God entrusted to you, and
with Mary, His tender Mother. Amen. —(Pope John XXIII)

9. **Litany of the Sacred Heart, promises of the Sacred Heart.**
   Lord, have mercy on us.
       Christ, have mercy on us.
   Lord, have mercy on us. Christ, hear us.
       Christ, graciously hear us.
   God the Father of heaven,
       have mercy on us (repeat after each invocation).
   God the Son, Redeemer of the world,
   God the Holy Spirit,
   Holy Trinity, one God,
   Heart of Jesus, Son of the eternal Father,
   Heart of Jesus, formed by the Holy Spirit in the womb of the Virgin
       Mother,
   Heart of Jesus, substantially united to the Word of God,
   Heart of Jesus, of infinite majesty,
   Heart of Jesus, sacred temple of God,
   Heart of Jesus, tabernacle of the Most High,
   Heart of Jesus, house of God and gate of heaven,
   Heart of Jesus, burning furnace of charity,
   Heart of Jesus, abode of justice and love,
   Heart of Jesus, full of goodness and love,
   Heart of Jesus, abyss of all virtues,
   Heart of Jesus, most worthy of all praise,
   Heart of Jesus, king and center of all hearts,
   Heart of Jesus, in whom are all the treasures of wisdom and knowl-
       edge,
   Heart of Jesus, in whom dwells the fullness of divinity,
   Heart of Jesus, in whom the Father is well pleased,
   Heart of Jesus, of whose fullness we have all received,
   Heart of Jesus, desire of the everlasting hills,
   Heart of Jesus, patient and most merciful,
   Heart of Jesus, enriching all who invoke You,
   Heart of Jesus, fountain of life and holiness,
   Heart of Jesus, propitiation for our sins,
   Heart of Jesus, loaded down with opprobrium,

Heart of Jesus, bruised for our offenses,
Heart of Jesus, obedient even to death,
Heart of Jesus, pierced with a lance,
Heart of Jesus, source of all consolation,
Heart of Jesus, our life and reconciliation,
Heart of Jesus, victim of sin,
Heart of Jesus, salvation of those who hope in You,
Heart of Jesus, hope of those who die in You,
Heart of Jesus, delight of all the saints,
Lamb of God, Who take away the sins of the world,
  spare us, O Lord.
Lamb of God, Who take away the sins of the world,
  graciously hear us, O Lord.
Lamb of God, Who take away the sins of the world,
  have mercy on us.
Jesus, meek and humble of heart,
  make our hearts like unto Yours.

Let us pray: O almighty and eternal God, look upon the Heart of Your dearly beloved Son and upon the praise and satisfaction He offers You in behalf of sinners and, being appeased, grant pardon to those who seek Your mercy, in the name of the same Jesus Christ, Your Son, Who lives and reigns with You, in the unity of the Holy Spirit, world without end. Amen.

Promises of Our Lord to those devoted to His Sacred Heart (these should be read by the prayer leader):

(1) I will give them all the graces necessary in their state of life.
(2) I will establish peace in their homes.
(3) I will comfort them in all their afflictions.
(4) I will be their refuge during life and above all in death.
(5) I will bestow a large blessing on all their undertakings.
(6) Sinners shall find in My Heart the source and the infinite ocean of mercy.
(7) Tepid souls shall grow fervent.
(8) Fervent souls shall quickly mount to high perfection.
(9) I will bless every place where a picture of My Heart shall be set up and honored.
(10) I will give to priests the gift of touching the most hardened hearts.
(11) Those who promote this devotion shall have their names written in My Heart, never to be blotted out.
(12) I promise you in the excessive mercy of My Heart that My all-powerful love will grant to all those who communicate on the first Friday in nine consecutive months the grace of final penitence;

they shall not die in My disgrace nor without receiving their sacraments; My divine Heart shall be their safe refuge in this last moment.

10. **Prayer for Priests.** "Lord Jesus, Chief Shepherd of the Flock, we pray that in the great love and mercy of Your Sacred Heart You attend to all the needs of Your priest-shepherds throughout the world. We ask that You draw back to Your Heart all those priests who have seriously strayed from Your path, that You rekindle the desire for holiness in the hearts of those priests who have become lukewarm, and that You continue to give Your fervent priests the desire for the highest holiness. United with Your Heart and Mary's Heart, we ask that You take this petition to Your heavenly Father in the unity of the Holy Spirit. Amen."

11. **Prayer for all members of the Shepherds of Christ Associates.** "Dear Jesus, we ask Your special blessings on all members of Shepherds of Christ Associates. Continue to enlighten them regarding the very special privilege and responsibility you have given them as members of Your movement, Shepherds of Christ Associates. Draw them ever closer to Your Heart and to Your Mother's Heart. Allow them to more and more realize the great and special love of Your Hearts for each of them as unique individuals. Give them the grace to respond to Your love and Mary's love with an increased love of their own. As they dwell in Your Heart and Mary's Heart, abundantly care for all their needs and those of their loved ones. We make our prayer through You to the Father, in the Holy Spirit, with Mary our Mother at our side. Amen."

12. **Prayer for the spiritual and financial success of the priestly newsletter.** "Father, we ask Your special blessings upon the priestly newsletter, Shepherds of Christ. We ask that You open the priest-readers to the graces You wish to give them through this chosen instrument of Your Son. We also ask that You provide for the financial needs of the newsletter and the Shepherds of Christ Associates. We make our prayer through Jesus, in the Holy Spirit, with Mary at our side. Amen."

13. **Prayer for all members of the human family.** "Heavenly Father, we ask Your blessings on all Your children the world over. Attend to all their needs. We ask Your special assistance for all those marginalized people, all those who are so neglected and forgotten. United with our Mother Mary, we make this petition to You through Jesus and in the Holy Spirit. Amen."

14. **Prayer to St. Michael and our Guardian Angels:** "St. Michael the

Archangel, defend us in battle. Be our safeguard against the wickedness and snares of the devil. May God rebuke him, we humbly pray, and do thou, O prince of the heavenly hosts, by the power of God, cast into hell Satan and all the other evil spirits who prowl about the world seeking the ruin of souls. Amen."

"Angel of God, my guardian dear, to whom God's love commits me here, ever this day be at my side, to light and guard, to rule and guide. Amen."

15. **Pause for silent, personal prayer.** This should last at least five minutes.

16. **Act of consecration to the Sacred Heart of Jesus and the Immaculate Heart of Mary.**

"Lord Jesus, Chief Shepherd of the flock, I consecrate myself to Your most Sacred Heart. From Your pierced Heart the Church was born, the Church You have called me, as a member of Shepherds of Christ Associates, to serve in a most special way. You reveal Your Heart as a symbol of Your love in all its aspects, including Your most special love for me, whom You have chosen as Your companion in this most important work. Help me to always love You in return. Help me to give myself entirely to You. Help me always to pour out my life in love of God and neighbor! Heart of Jesus, I place my trust in You!

"Dear Blessed Virgin Mary, I consecrate myself to your maternal and Immaculate Heart, this Heart which is symbol of your life of love. You are the Mother of my Savior. You are also my Mother. You love me with a most special love as a member of Shepherds of Christ Associates, a movement created by your Son as a powerful instrument for the renewal of the Church and the world. In a return of love, I give myself entirely to your motherly love and protection. You followed Jesus perfectly. You are His first and perfect disciple. Teach me to imitate you in the putting on of Christ. Be my motherly intercessor so that, through your Immaculate Heart, I may be guided to an ever closer union with the pierced Heart of Jesus, Chief Shepherd of the flock."

17. **Daily Prayers.** All members should say the Holy Spirit prayer daily and make the act of consecration daily. They should also pray the rosary each day. They are encouraged to use the other above prayers as time allows.

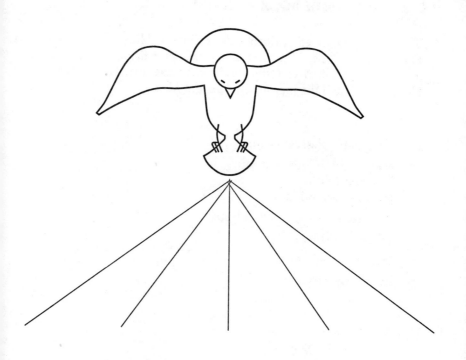

HOLY SPIRIT NOVENA

Shepherds of Christ Publications
Madison, Indiana
El Paso, Texas

This book is published by Shepherds of Christ Publications, a subsidiary of Shepherds of Christ Ministries, a tax exempt religious public charitable association organized to foster devotion to the Two Hearts, the Sacred Heart of Jesus and the Immaculate Heart of Mary.

For additional copies, contact us:

Shepherds of Christ Ministries
P.O. Box 193
Morrow, OH 45152-0193

(toll free number) 1-888-211-3041

(phone) 1-513-932-4451

(fax) 1-513-932-6791

http://www.SofC.org

Nihil Obstat:
Rev. Daniel J. Mahan, S.T.L.
Censor Librorum
Archdiocese of Indianapolis

Imprimatur:
Archbishop Daniel M. Buechlein, O.S.B.
Archbishop of Indianapolis
Archdiocese of Indianapolis

First Printing: March, 1999
Second Printing: April, 2000

DAILY NOVENA PRAYERS

Opening Prayer

In the name of the Father and of the Son and of the Holy Spirit. Amen.

Dear Father, we come to You in the name of Jesus, in union with Him in the Holy Sacrifice of the Mass, in the Holy Spirit. We come to You united to the Child Jesus of Good Health and the Infant of Prague. We come to You in the perfect, sinless heart of Our Mother Mary, asking her powerful intercession, uniting ourselves to her holy tears. We come to You united to all the angels and saints, and the souls in purgatory.

Prayer for Holy Spirit

We pray for an outpouring of the Holy Spirit on us, to be baptized by the Holy Spirit, that He will descend mightily on us as He did on the Apostles at Pentecost. That the Holy Spirit will transform us from fear to fearlessness and that He will give us courage to do all the Father is asking of us to help bring about the Reign of the Sacred Heart and the triumph of Mary's Immaculate Heart. We pray for the Holy Spirit to descend mightily on the Jesuits and the Poor Clares on the Shepherds of Christ leaders and members and on the whole Body of Christ and the world.

Protection by the Blood of Jesus

We pray that the Blood of Jesus will be spread on us, everyone in our families, and the Shepherds of Christ Movement, that we will be able to move steadfastly ahead and be protected from the evil one.

Healing

We pray for healing in body, mind, and soul and generational healing in ourselves, in all members in our families, and in all members of the Shepherds of Christ Movement, the Jesuit Community, the Poor Clares, the Body of Christ, and the world.

Prayer for Strength and Light

We adore You, oh Holy Spirit. Give us strength, give us light, console us. We give ourselves entirely to You. Oh Spirit of light and grace, we want to only do the will of the Father. Enlighten us that we may live always in the Father's will.

Eternal Spirit fill us with Your Divine Wisdom that we may comprehend more fully insight into Your Divine Mysteries.

Give us lights, Oh Holy Spirit that we may know God. Work within the heart, the spiritual womb of the Virgin Mary, to form us more and more into the image of Jesus.

Prayer to Be One with God, Father, Son and Holy Spirit

We long for You, Oh Spirit of Light, we long to know God, we want to be one with Him, our Divine God. We want to be one with the Father, know Him as a Person most intimately. We want to know the beloved One, the Sacred Heart of Jesus, and live and dwell in Him at all times, every moment of our lives. We want to be one with You, Oh Spirit of Light, that You move in us in our every breath.

Prayer to Be One in Jesus

Let us experience life in the Sacred Heart of Jesus, so we can say as Saint Paul, "I have been crucified with Christ and yet I am alive; yet it is no longer I, but Christ living in me...." Let us live, united to the Mass, all through the day being one in Him. Let us be able to love and know in this elevated state of oneness with our God. We long for Thee, oh beauteous God, we love You, we love You, we love You. We praise You, worship You, honor You, adore You, and thank You, our beloved God, Father, Son, and Holy Spirit.

Prayer to Dwell in the Hearts of Jesus and Mary

We seek to be one in God, to live and dwell in the Hearts of Jesus and Mary, our little heaven on earth, to experience life in the all perfect, pure, sinless heart of our Mother. We want the Holy Spirit to move in us and to be united to Jesus as the Bridegroom of our souls and be a most perfect sacrifice offered to the Father at every moment as we unite in the Holy Sacrifice of the Mass around the world to help in the salvation of souls.

Prayer for the Holy Spirit and His Gifts

Come Holy Spirit, come, come into our hearts, inflame all people with the fire of Your love.

Leader: Send forth Your Spirit and all will be reborn.

All: And You will renew the face of the earth.

We pray for the seven gifts of the Holy Spirit, we ask for perfection in our souls to make us holy, holy souls likened to God.

Dear Holy Spirit, we give ourselves to You soul and body. We ask You to give us the Spirit of Wisdom, Understanding, Counsel, Fortitude, Knowledge, Piety, and Fear of the Lord.

Prayer for the Word Alive in Our Hearts

We know, dear Holy Spirit, the Word in His human nature was brought forth within the womb of the woman. We pray that His word will be brought forth in our hearts as He lives and dwells in us. We want the incarnation to go on in our lives. Dear Holy Spirit, work in us.

Little Prayers to the Holy Spirit

Dear Holy Spirit, help us not to be ignorant or indifferent or weak, help us to be strong with the love of God.

Dear Holy Spirit, please pray for our needs for us.

Dear Holy Spirit, help us to respect God and to avoid sin. Help us to live in the Father's will.

Dear Holy Spirit, help us to keep Your commandments and to respect authority. Help us to love all things as You will us to love them. Help us to want to pray and always serve God with the greatest love. Help us to know the truth. Help us to have the gift of faith, hope, and love. Help us to know what is right and what is wrong.

A Prayer for Intimacy with the
Lamb, the Bridegroom of the Soul

Oh Lamb of God, Who take away the sins of the world, come and act on my soul most intimately. I surrender myself, as I ask for the grace to let go, to just be as I exist in You and You act most intimately on my soul. You are the Initiator. I am the soul waiting Your favors as You act in me. I love You. I adore You. I worship You. Come and possess my soul with Your Divine Grace, as I experience You most intimately.

FIRST WEEK
MEDITATIONS NINE DAYS

1. **Romans 8:14-17**

   All who are guided by the Spirit of God are sons of God; for what you received was not the spirit of slavery to bring you back into fear; you received the Spirit of adoption, enabling us to cry out, 'Abba, Father!' The Spirit himself joins with our spirit to bear witness that we are children of God. And if we are children, then we are heirs, heirs of God and joint-heirs with Christ, provided that we share his suffering, so as to share his glory.

2. **Romans 8:5-9**

   Those who are living by their natural inclinations have their minds on the things human nature desires; those who live in the

Spirit have their minds on spiritual things. And human nature has nothing to look forward to but death, while the Spirit looks forward to life and peace, because the outlook of disordered human nature is opposed to God, since it does not submit to God's Law, and indeed it cannot, and those who live by their natural inclinations can never be pleasing to God. You, however, live not by your natural inclinations, but by the Spirit, since the Spirit of God has made a home in you. Indeed, anyone who does not have the Spirit of Christ does not belong to him.

3.   1 John 4:12-16
No one has ever seen God, but as long as we love one another God remains in us and his love comes to its perfection in us. This is the proof that we remain in him and he in us, that he has given us a share in his Spirit. We ourselves have seen and testify that the Father sent his Son as Saviour of the world. Anyone who acknowledges that Jesus is the Son of God, God remains in him and he in God. We have recognised for ourselves, and put our faith in, the love God has for us. God is love, and whoever remains in love remains in God and God in him.

4.   1 John 4:17-21
Love comes to its perfection in us when we can face the Day of Judgement fearlessly, because even in this world we have become as he is. In love there is no room for fear, but perfect love drives out fear, because fear implies punishment and no one who is afraid has come to perfection in love. Let us love, then, because he first loved us. Anyone who says 'I love God' and hates his brother, is a liar, since whoever does not love the brother whom he can see cannot love God whom he has not seen. Indeed this is the commandment we have received from him, that whoever loves God, must also love his brother.

5.   1 John 4:7-11
My dear friends, let us love one another, since love is from God and everyone who loves is a child of God and knows God. Whoever fails to love does not know God, because God is love. This is the revelation of God's love for us, that God sent his only Son into the world that we might have life through him. Love consists in this: it is not we who loved God, but God loved us and sent his Son to expiate our sins. My dear friends, if God loved us so much, we too should love one another.

6. Acts of the Apostles 1:1-5

In my earlier work, Theophilus, I dealt with everything Jesus had done and taught from the beginning until the day he gave his instructions to the apostles he had chosen through the Holy Spirit, and was taken up to heaven. He had shown himself alive to them after his Passion by many demonstrations: for forty days he had continued to appear to them and tell them about the kingdom of God. While at table with them, he had told them not to leave Jerusalem, but to wait there for what the Father had promised. 'It is', he had said, 'what you have heard me speak about: John baptised with water but, not many days from now, you are going to be baptised with the Holy Spirit.'

7. Acts of the Apostles 1:6-9

Now having met together, they asked him, 'Lord, has the time come for you to restore the kingdom to Israel?' He replied, 'It is not for you to know times or dates that the Father has decided by his own authority, but you will receive the power of the Holy Spirit which will come on you, and then you will be my witnesses not only in Jerusalem but throughout Judaea and Samaria, and indeed to earth's remotest end.'

As he said this he was lifted up while they looked on, and a cloud took him from their sight.

8. Acts of the Apostles 1:12-14

So from the Mount of Olives, as it is called, they went back to Jerusalem, a short distance away, no more than a Sabbath walk; and when they reached the city they went to the upper room where they were staying; there were Peter and John, James and Andrew, Philip and Thomas, Bartholomew and Matthew, James son of Alphaeus and Simon the Zealot, and Jude son of James. With one heart all these joined constantly in prayer, together with some women, including Mary the mother of Jesus, and with his brothers.

9. Acts of the Apostles 2:1-4

When Pentecost day came round, they had all met together, when suddenly there came from heaven a sound as of a violent wind which filled the entire house in which they were sitting; and there appeared to them tongues as of fire; these separated and came to rest on the head of each of them. They were all filled with the Holy Spirit and began to speak different languages as the Spirit gave them power to express themselves.

SECOND WEEK
MEDITATIONS NINE DAYS

1. **John 14:21-31**

Whoever holds to my commandments and keeps them is the one who loves me; and whoever loves me will be loved by my Father, and I shall love him and reveal myself to him.'

Judas—not Judas Iscariot—said to him, 'Lord, what has happened, that you intend to show yourself to us and not to the world?' Jesus replied:

'Anyone who loves me will keep my word, and my Father will love him, and we shall come to him and make a home in him. Anyone who does not love me does not keep my words. And the word that you hear is not my own: it is the word of the Father who sent me. I have said these things to you while still with you; but the Paraclete, the Holy Spirit, whom the Father will send in my name, will teach you everything and remind you of all I have said to you. Peace I bequeath to you, my own peace I give you, a peace which the world cannot give, this is my gift to you. Do not let your hearts be troubled or afraid. You heard me say: I am going away and shall return. If you loved me you would be glad that I am going to the Father, for the Father is greater than I. I have told you this now, before it happens, so that when it does happen you may believe.

'I shall not talk to you much longer, because the prince of this world is on his way. He has no power over me, but the world must recognise that I love the Father and that I act just as the Father commanded. Come now, let us go.

2. **John 17:11-26**

I am no longer in the world, but they are in the world, and I am coming to you. Holy Father, keep those you have given me true to your name, so that they may be one like us. While I was with them, I kept those you had given me true to your name. I have watched over them and not one is lost except one who was destined to be lost, and this was to fulfil the scriptures. But now I am coming to you and I say these things in the world to share my joy with them to the full. I passed your word on to them, and the world hated them, because they belong to the world no more than I belong to the world. I am not asking you to remove them from the world, but to protect them from the Evil One. They do not belong to the world any more than I belong to the world. Consecrate them in the truth; your word is truth. As you sent me into the world, I have sent them into the world, and for their sake I consecrate myself so that they too may be consecrated in truth. I pray not only for these but also for those who through their teaching will come to believe in me. May they all be one, just as, Father, you are in me and I am in you, so that they also may be in us, so that the world may believe it was you who sent me. I have given them the glory you gave to me, that they may be one as we are one. With me in them and you in me, may they be so perfected in unity that the world will recognise that it was you who sent me and that you have loved them as you have loved me.

Father, I want those you have given me to be with me where I am, so that they may always see my glory which you have given me because you loved me before the foundation of the world. Father, Upright One, the world has not known you, but I have known you, and these have known that you have sent me. I have made your name known to them and will continue to make it known, so that the love with which you loved me may be in them, and so that I may be in them.

3. **I Corinthians 15:20-28**
   In fact, however, Christ has been raised from the dead, as the first-fruits of all who have fallen asleep. As it was by one man that death came, so through one man has come the resurrection of the dead. Just as all die in Adam, so in Christ all will be brought to life; but all of them in their proper order: Christ the first-fruits, and next, at his coming, those who belong to him. After that will come the end, when he will hand over the kingdom to God the Father, having abolished every principality, every ruling force and power. For he is to be king until he has made his enemies his footstool, and the last of the enemies to be done away with is death, for he has put all things under his feet. But when it is said everything is subjected, this obviously cannot include the One who subjected everything to him. When everything has been subjected to him, then the Son himself will be subjected to the One who has subjected everything to him, so that God may be all in all.

4. **Revelation 3:1-3,12,16-19**
   'Write to the angel of the church in Sardis and say, "Here is the message of the one who holds the seven spirits of God and the seven stars: I know about your behaviour: how you are reputed to be alive and yet are dead. Wake up; put some resolve into what little vigour you have left: it is dying fast. So far I have failed to notice anything in your behaviour that my God could possibly call

perfect; remember how you first heard the message. Hold on to that. Repent! If you do not wake up, I shall come to you like a thief, and you will have no idea at what hour I shall come upon you.

Anyone who proves victorious I will make into a pillar in the sanctuary of my God, and it will stay there for ever; I will inscribe on it the name of my God and the name of the city of my God, the new Jerusalem which is coming down from my God in heaven, and my own new name as well.

'...but since you are neither hot nor cold, but only lukewarm, I will spit you out of my mouth. You say to yourself: I am rich, I have made a fortune and have everything I want, never realising that you are wretchedly and pitiably poor, and blind and naked too. I warn you, buy from me the gold that has been tested in the fire to make you truly rich, and white robes to clothe you and hide your shameful nakedness, and ointment to put on your eyes to enable you to see. I reprove and train those whom I love: so repent in real earnest.'

5. **Revelation 5:9-14**

They sang a new hymn: You are worthy to take the scroll and to break its seals, because you were sacrificed, and with your blood you bought people for God of every race, language, people and nation and made them a line of kings and priests for God, to rule the world.

In my vision, I heard the sound of an immense number of angels gathered round the throne and the living creatures and the elders; there were ten thousand times ten thousand of them and thousands upon thousands, loudly chanting:

Worthy is the Lamb that was sacrificed to receive power, riches, wisdom, strength, honour, glory and blessing. Then I heard all the living things in creation—everything that lives in heaven, and on earth, and under the earth, and in the sea, crying:

To the One seated on the throne and to the Lamb, be all praise, honour, glory and power, for ever and ever.

And the four living creatures said, 'Amen'; and the elders prostrated themselves to worship.

6. **Revelation 7:14-17**

I answered him, 'You can tell me, sir.' Then he said, 'These are the people who have been through the great trial; they have washed their robes white again in the blood of the Lamb. That is why they are standing in front of God's throne and serving him day and night in his sanctuary; and the One who sits on the throne will spread his tent over them. They will never hunger or thirst again; sun and scorching

wind will never plague them, because the Lamb who is at the heart
of the throne will be their shepherd and will guide them to springs
of living water; and God will wipe away all tears from their eyes.'

7. Revelation 12:1-8

Now a great sign appeared in heaven: a woman, robed with the
sun, standing on the moon, and on her head a crown of twelve
stars. She was pregnant, and in labour, crying aloud in the pangs of
childbirth. Then a second sign appeared in the sky: there was a
huge red dragon with seven heads and ten horns, and each of the
seven heads crowned with a coronet. Its tail swept a third of the
stars from the sky and hurled them to the ground, and the dragon
stopped in front of the woman as she was at the point of giving
birth, so that it could eat the child as soon as it was born. The
woman was delivered of a boy, the son who was to rule all the
nations with an iron sceptre, and the child was taken straight up to
God and to his throne, while the woman escaped into the desert,
where God had prepared a place for her to be looked after for
twelve hundred and sixty days.

And now war broke out in heaven, when Michael with his
angels attacked the dragon. The dragon fought back with his
angels, but they were defeated and driven out of heaven.

8. Revelation 14:1-7

Next in my vision I saw Mount Zion, and standing on it the
Lamb who had with him a hundred and forty-four thousand people,
all with his name and his Father's name written on their foreheads.
I heard a sound coming out of heaven like the sound of the ocean
or the roar of thunder; it was like the sound of harpists playing their
harps. There before the throne they were singing a new hymn in
the presence of the four living creatures and the elders, a hymn that
could be learnt only by the hundred and forty-four thousand who
had been redeemed from the world. These are the sons who have
kept their virginity and not been defiled with women; they follow
the Lamb wherever he goes; they, out of all people, have been
redeemed to be the first-fruits for God and for the Lamb. No lie was
found in their mouths and no fault can be found in them.

Then I saw another angel, flying high overhead, sent to
announce the gospel of eternity to all who live on the earth, every
nation, race, language and tribe. He was calling, 'Fear God and glo-
rify him, because the time has come for him to sit in judgement;
worship the maker of heaven and earth and sea and the springs of
water.'

Revelation 19: 7-8

let us be glad and joyful and give glory to God, because this is the time for the marriage of the Lamb. His bride is ready, and she has been able to dress herself in dazzling white linen, because her linen is made of the good deeds of the saints.'

9. **Revelation 21:1-10**

Then I saw a new heaven and a new earth; the first heaven and the first earth had disappeared now, and there was no longer any sea. I saw the holy city, the new Jerusalem, coming down out of heaven from God, prepared as a bride dressed for her husband. Then I heard a loud voice call from the throne, 'Look, here God lives among human beings. He will make his home among them; they will be his people, and he will be their God, God-with-them. He will wipe away all tears from their eyes; there will be no more death, and no more mourning or sadness or pain. The world of the past has gone.'

Then the One sitting on the throne spoke. 'Look, I am making the whole of creation new. Write this, "What I am saying is trustworthy and will come true." ' Then he said to me, 'It has already happened. I am the Alpha and the Omega, the Beginning and the End. I will give water from the well of life free to anybody who is thirsty; anyone who proves victorious will inherit these things; and I will be his God and he will be my son. But the legacy for cowards, for those who break their word, or worship obscenities, for murderers and the sexually immoral, and for sorcerers, worshippers of false gods or any other sort of liars, is the second death in the burning lake of sulphur.'

One of the seven angels that had the seven bowls full of the seven final plagues came to speak to me and said, 'Come here and I will show you the bride that the Lamb has married.' In the spirit, he carried me to the top of a very high mountain, and showed me Jerusalem, the holy city, coming down out of heaven from God.

Revelation 22:20

The one who attests these things says: I am indeed coming soon.

Amen; come, Lord Jesus.

Scriptural quotations are taken from
The New Jerusalem Bible, Doubleday & Co.
Imprimatur granted by Cardinal Hume.

Shepherds of Christ
Prayer Cards

Contact us to obtain
these for your parish,
friends, or loved ones.

PRAYER FOR PRIESTS

"Lord Jesus, Chief Shepherd of the Flock, we pray that in the great love and mercy of Your Sacred Heart You attend to all the needs of Your priest-shepherds throughout the world. We ask that You draw back to Your Heart all those priests who have seriously strayed from Your path, that You rekindle the desire for holiness in the hearts of those priests who have become lukewarm, and that You continue to give Your fervent priests the desire for the highest holiness. United with Your Heart and Mary's Heart, we ask that You take this petition to Your heavenly Father in the unity of the Holy Spirit. Amen."

Published by Shepherds of Christ Ministries, P.O. Box 193, Morrow, OH 45152-0193   Phone (toll free): 1-888-211-3041 Fax: (513) 932-6791
Imprimatur: Most Rev. Carl K. Moeddel, Vicar General and Auxiliary Bishop Archdiocese of Cincinnati

PRAYER FOR UNION WITH JESUS

Come to me, Lord, and possess my sou Come into my heart and permeate my sou Help me to sit in silence with You and let Yo work in my heart.

I am Yours to possess. I am Yours to use. I war to be selfless and only exist in You. Help me t spoon out all that is me and be an empty vesse ready to be filled by You. Help me to die to myse and live only for You. Use me as You will. Let m never draw my attention back to myself. I onl want to operate as You do, dwelling within me.

I am Yours, Lord. I want to have my life i You. I want to do the will of the Father. Give m the strength to put aside the world and let Yo operate my very being. Help me to act as Yo desire. Strengthen me against the distractions the devil to take me from Your work.

When I worry, I have taken my focus off o You and placed it on myself. Help me not to giv in to the promptings of others to change what i my heart You are making very clear to me. I wor ship You, I adore You and I love You. Come an dwell in me now.

Imprimatur: Most Rev. Carl K. Moeddel, Vicar General ar Auxiliary Bishop Archdiocese of Cincinnati

Shepherds of Christ Ministries
P.O. Box 193, Morrow, OH 45152-0193
Toll Free (888) 211-3041
Phone: (513) 932-4451   Fax: (513) 932-6791

PRAYER BEFORE THE
HOLY SACRIFICE OF THE MASS

Let me be a holy sacrifice and unite with God in the sacrament of His greatest love.

I want to be one in Him in this act of love, where He gives Himself to me and I give myself as a sacrifice to Him. Let me be a holy sacrifice as I become one with Him in this my act of greatest love to Him.

Let me unite with Him more, that I may more deeply love Him. May I help make reparation to His adorable Heart and the heart of His Mother, Mary. With greatest love, I offer myself to You and pray that You will accept my sacrifice of greatest love. I give myself to You and unite in Your gift of Yourself to me. Come and possess my soul.

Cleanse me, strengthen me, heal me. Dear Holy Spirit act in the heart of Mary to make me more and more like Jesus.

Father, I offer this my sacrifice, myself united to Jesus in the Holy Spirit to You. Help me to love God more deeply in this act of my greatest love.

Give me the grace to grow in my knowledge, love and service of You and for this to be my greatest participation in the Mass. Give me the greatest graces to love You so deeply in this Mass, You who are so worthy of my love.

Imprimatur: Most Rev. Carl Moeddel Vicar General and Auxiliary Bishop
        Archdiocese of Cincinnati

To order more copies contact: Shepherds of Christ Ministries, P.O. Box 193, Morrow, OH 45152 (toll free) 888-211-3041 www.Shepherds-of-Christ.org

A Prayer for Intimacy with the Lamb, the Bridegroom of the Soul

Oh Lamb of God, Who take away the sins of the world, come and act on my soul most intimately. I surrender myself, as I ask for the grace to let go, to just be as I exist in You and You act most intimately on my soul. You are the Initiator. I am the soul waiting Your favors as You act in me. I love You. I adore You. I worship You. Come and possess my soul with Your Divine Grace as I experience You most intimately.

Imprimatur:

Archbishop Daniel M. Buechlein, O.S.B.
Archdiocese of Indianapolis

Shepherds of Christ Ministries
P.O. Box 193 Morrow, Ohio 45152-0193 USA
(toll free number) 1-888-211-3041
(phone) 513-932-4451   (fax) 513-932-6791
http://www.SofC.org

These cards are available in large print for nursing homes. Please circulate to all.

Front

SAY DAILY

GOD, I GIVE YOU MY LIFE IN UNION WITH THE MASS AS AN OFFERING FOR THE SOULS, THE CHURCH AND THE PRIESTS.

HELP US!

Back

Your life is so important for souls,
you can help bring down great grace.

Shepherds of Christ Ministries
P.O. Box 193   Morrow, OH 45152-0193
Tel: (513) 932-4451 Fax: (513) 932-6791
Toll Free: (888) 211-3041 Internet: www.SofC.org

Front

I Give My Heart to
Jesus and Mary
With You in Love.

Back

We Pray for Priests and
Renewal of the Church
and World.
Holy Spirit Fill Me.

Shepherds of Christ Ministries
P.O. Box 193 Morrow, OH 45152-0193
Toll Free (888) 211-3041
Tel: (513) 932-4451   Fax: (513) 932-6791
www.SofC.org

Shepherds of Christ Associates
Prayer Chapters

Here are the steps for forming a Shepherds of Christ Associates Prayer Chapter:

Bring together family, friends, or parish members to answer this call of the Lord. Follow the format in the Shepherds of Christ Associates Prayer Manual. The steps are simple:

1. Designate a coordinator for the chapter.
2. Have everyone fill out the membership form and return it to our Morrow Center.
3. Give everyone a Shepherds of Christ Prayer Manual.
4. Choose a regular time and place to meet (at church or in the home).
5. You may meet daily, once a week or at least monthly.
6. It only takes two people to form a prayer chapter.

Please call our Morrow, Ohio Center. We would be happy to answer any questions. We can also send you a prayer chapter information packet, Shepherds of Christ Spirituality Handbooks, or Shepherds of Christ Prayer Manuals. We may be reached by electronic mail at info@SofC.org or by postal mail.

Shepherds of Christ Ministries
P.O. Box 193
Morrow, OH 45152-0193

telephone (toll free in USA) 1-888-211-3041
           or International (513) 932-4451
fax: (513) 932-6791

Shepherds of Christ Associates

Chapter title (name of place held): _____

Chapter Coordinator(s):_____

Address: _____

Telephone: _____

City, State, Zip code: _____

Members of this chapter: **Please**
Print.

Name	Address	City	State	Zip	Telephone

Please return a copy of this form to:
**Shepherds of Christ, P.O. Box 193, Morrow, OH 45152-0193 USA.
Or fax us at: (513) 932-6791**

Apostles of the Eucharistic Heart of Jesus

We are asking for volunteers who are willing to pray before the Blessed Sacrament for one hour, twice-weekly. Members of the Shepherds of Christ prayer chapters, as well as others, are invited to join this movement.

These apostles are to pray for the intentions given. For part of the hour they are to use the prayers of the Shepherds of Christ Associates Prayer Manual. They may spend the rest of the hour as they so choose.

This new prayer movement within the Shepherds of Christ Ministries is a powerful way to help in the renewal of the Church and the world.

This is indeed a special calling for us to unite in one heart with His Eucharistic Heart and pray for the following intentions:

1. For the spread of the devotion to the Hearts of Jesus and Mary culminating in the reign of the Sacred Heart and the triumph of the Immaculate Heart.

2. For the Pope.

3. For all bishops of the world.

4. For all priests.

5. For all sisters and brothers in the religious life.

6. For all members of the Shepherds of Christ Movement, and for the spread of this movement to the world.

7. For all members of the Catholic Church.

8. For all members of the human family.

9. For all souls in purgatory.

Apostles of the Eucharistic Heart of Jesus
Membership Form

Name	Address	City	State	Zip	Telephone

Please return a copy of this form to **Shepherds of Christ Ministries, Apostles of the Eucharistic Heart of Jesus, P.O. Box 193, Morrow, OH 45152-0193.**

Prayer Apostles

Prayer Apostles are often shut-ins, some are able to go to church and pray. They spend much of their lives praying for the Movement. Prayer apostles are invited to do the following as time allows:

1) Pray the Morning Offering
2) Pray the Hourly Prayers
3) Spend at least one hour in prayer
4) Pray Rosaries
5) Pray the Shepherds of Christ Prayers
6) Pray the Holy Spirit Novena

OUR FOCUS in the Shepherds of Christ is to be intercessors praying fervently for the priests, the Church and the world.

Shepherds of Christ Ministries

*For Helping in the Renewal of the
Church and the World*

WE PRAY FOR PRIESTS, THE RENEWAL OF THE CHURCH, AND THE WORLD.

We join as a body united to the Holy Sacrifice of the Mass offering our lives to the Father as intercessors praying for our priests, the Church, and the world.

WILL YOU PRAY WITH US?

Your prayers united to ours will help the priests, the Church, and the world.

Our Focus

WE HAVE PRAYER CHAPTERS PRAYING ALL OVER THE WORLD for the priests, the Church, and the world.

OUR PRIMARY FOCUS is the circulation of a newsletter.

WE CIRCULATE A SPIRITUALITY NEWSLETTER written by Fr. Edward Carter, S.J., a Jesuit Theologian with a Doctor's degree in Theology and author of 18 books, to about 75,000 priests in the world in both English and Spanish. Father Carter was   a professor of Theology for over 30 years.

Besides being sent to about 75,000 priests and bishops in the U.S.A., the newsletter is sent internationally to about 245 bishops, including 4 cardinals, who distribute copies to all of their priests, and also, in some cases, to their deacons and seminarians.

The newsletter is centered in consecration to the Hearts of Jesus and Mary. It features writings regarding our union with Jesus and the Father and the Holy Sprit and Mary. The newsletter also stresses the Eucharist, the Church, prayer, and one's responsibility regarding the social order. The newsletter stresses sound doctrine as found in Scripture, the writings of the Popes and other Church documents. It also presents selected writings from the saints and competent priest-theologians and others.

The newsletter can be used by all for development in the spiritual life centered in consecration.

About Shepherds of Christ Ministries

MINISTRIES

1. **PRIMARY MINISTRY** - CIRCULATING PRIESTLY NEWSLETTERS TO PRIESTS ALL OVER THE WORLD IN ENGLISH AND SPANISH to promote priestly holiness.
2. **PRAYER CHAPTERS** praying for the priests and the renewal of the Church and the world.
3. School Rosary Program and Junior Shepherds of Christ Ministry.
4. Nursing Home Ministry.
5. Special retreats and adoration before the Blessed Sacrament.
6. Apostles of the Eucharistic Heart of Jesus.

7. Promoting the rosary to all, rosary meditations.
8. Prison Ministry to promote prayer and spiritual renewal.
9. Handmaids and Servants of the Good Shepherd.
10. Audio/Video Departments (priestly newsletters on tape).
11. Prayer books, newsletters, newsletter books, and other spiritual aids.

We want to be intercessors promoting unity in prayer with all people of the world, praying for the priests, the Church and the world.

We have described above the primary ministry of the Movement, the spirituality newsletter for priests, Shepherds of Christ. The 2nd most important ministry is the prayer chapters, whose members pray for the needs of priests and for the needs of all others also. Other ministries include promoting the act of consecration to the Hearts of Jesus and Mary as widely as possible. Promoting this act of consecration permeates all of our ministries. We also promote the praying of the rosary, and we have a special program regarding the rosary and the act of consecration for school children. We have programs for prisons and nursing homes to encourage the residents to pray for priests, the Church, and the world. We also publish various books, cassette tapes, and other materials to help in the ongoing work of spiritual renewal.

The mission of the Shepherds of Christ Movement is closely connected to Our Lady of Fatima's mission. We hope to play a major role in helping to bring fulfillment of the Peace Plan of Our Lady of Fatima. This plan includes:

1. Consecration to the Hearts of Jesus and Mary -- until a sufficient number of people make and live the consecration, we will not have peace in the world.
2. Praying the rosary.
3. Observing the First Saturday Devotion.
4. Making reparation to the Hearts of Jesus and Mary.

In helping to bring the Fatima message to completion, the Shepherds of Christ Movement is helping to bring about the Reign of the Sacred Heart and the triumph of the Immaculate Heart. This is a great privilege and a great responsibility! We ask for your prayers and help in other ways also. May God bless you abundantly!

LEVELS OF COMMITMENT

There are seven levels of commitment in the Shepherds of Christ Movement.

1. There are **Associates** who gather and pray at least once monthly as a group and also help with donations to support the Shepherds of Christ

priestly newsletter. They can be tremendously involved. They give as they feel they are able.

2. **Apostles** are members who have restricted their apostolic activity to the Shepherds of Christ. They literally act as a body of lay people who have given their lives in their present living situation to do all that they can to bring about the Reign of the Sacred Heart and the triumph of Mary's Immaculate Heart.

3. **Prayer Apostles** are often shut-ins, some are able to go to church and pray. They spend much of their lives praying for the Movement.

4. **Apostles of the Eucharistic Heart of Jesus** are those who spend at least two separate hours weekly before the Blessed Sacrament praying for the following:
   1. For the spread of the devotion to the Hearts of Jesus and Mary culminating in the reign of the Sacred Heart and the triumph of the Immaculate Heart.
   2. For the Pope.
   3. For all bishops of the world.
   4. For all priests.
   5. For all sisters and brothers in the religious life.
   6. For all members of the Shepherds of Christ Movement, and for the spread of this Movement to the world.
   7. For all members of the Catholic Church.
   8. For all members of the human family.
   9. For all souls in purgatory.

5. **Handmaids of the Good Shepherd** are young and older women who have given their lives in community primarily to pray for the Shepherds of Christ Movement and intentions and to be special spouses of Jesus. Some have more duties than others. All have the primary duty of prayer and the desire to be a special spouse of our Lord. One of the functions of the handmaids is the involvement in praying for and helping to circulate the priestly newsletter. The handmaids are not members of a religious order.

6. **Servants of the Good Shepherd** are men who live in community with a lifestyle and purpose similar to that of the handmaids. The servants are not members of a religious order.

7. We wish to form a special congregation of priests who will realize their great oneness with Christ. They will be consecrated deeply to the Hearts of Jesus and Mary and support the Shepherds of Christ Movement as holy priests.

Whatever one's level of commitment in the Shepherds of Christ Movement, all share in promoting the overall goal of the Movement. This goal is to help in the spiritual renewal of the Church and the world. All varied ministries of the Movement are directed toward this purpose. The spirituality which the Shepherds of Christ Movement presents to its members and to those outside the Movement through its various ministries is very basic. This spirituality is explicitly Trinitarian and Christocentric. Our spirituality helps others, especially priests, to develop a very deep union with Jesus, this Jesus Who leads us to the Father in the Holy Spirit with Mary at our side. Our spirituality is deeply Eucharistic. We stress very much participation in the Mass and prayer before the Blessed Sacrament. We also emphasize the extremely important role of prayer in the spiritual life. Devotion to the Hearts of Jesus and Mary, especially consecration to Their Hearts, is also a most important and central element. We are very much interested in helping to bring the Fatima message to completion, a message which has consecration to the Hearts of Jesus and Mary at its very core.

Father Edward J. Carter, S.J.

Father Edward Carter, S.J. was a native of Cincinnati, Ohio. A graduate of St. Xavier High School and Xavier University, both in Cincinnati, he was ordained a priest in 1962 and received his doctorate in theology from Catholic University of America four years later. He was a professor of theology at Xavier University in Cincinnati for over 30 years. He has authored 18 books in the area of Catholic spirituality. His two latest books are the priestly newsletter books, which include the newsletters from almost six years. He was devoted to the Sacred Heart of Jesus, and the Immaculate Heart of Mary.

Be Part Of It!

PLEASE HELP US THROUGH YOUR PRAYERS UNITED TO OURS.

PRIESTS PRAYING WITH US WILL INCREASE THE PRAYER POWER; THEY ARE ANOINTED BY CHRIST AS HOLY PRIESTS.

PEOPLE ALL OVER THE WORLD offering up their lives in the Morning Offering for the priests, the Church, the world, and for the work of the Shepherds of Christ will help so much.

LITTLE PRAYER BOOKS OF SHORT PRAYERS CALLED THE SHEPHERDS OF CHRIST PRAYER MANUAL ARE AVAILABLE. Praying these short prayers together with us as a body united to the Holy Sacrifice of the Mass being celebrated around the world can help great grace be released on the souls of the earth.

PLEASE UNITE WITH US.

Rosary Making Clubs

We supply rosaries to schools, prisons, and others.

Making rosaries out of sparkling, colorful plastic beads is a fun year-round activity for all ages. Even five-year-olds can create beautiful ones easily without getting frustrated!

This is wonderful as an in-school, after-school, or at-home project to be coordinated by an adult. When organized as a "club," children spend time at their meetings making rosaries, saying the Rosary, sharing a snack, and enjoying each other socially. Completed rosaries can be donated to fellow students, their families, nursing home residents, and many other individuals. Rosary-making kits (include plastic beads in your choice of colors) are available FREE from the School Rosary Program. In October 2000, we supplied over 80,000 rosaries to schools; in May 2001, we supplied over 100,000 rosaries.

Rosaries are given free of charge to schools and churches and people requesting them from Shepherds of Christ Ministries.

Books

B8. *Mass Book,* by Rita Ring: Many of the entries in the Priestly Newsletter Volume II from a spiritual journal came from this book. These entries are to help people to be more deeply united to God in the Mass This book has the *Imprimatur.*

B7. *Rosary Meditations for Parents and Children,* by Rita Ring, Short Meditations for both parents and children to be used when praying the rosary. These meditations will help all to know the lives of Jesus and Mary alive in their Hearts. This book has the *Imprimatur.*

BN1. *Shepherds of Christ - Selected Writings on Spirituality for all People as Published in Shepherds of Christ Newsletter for Priests.* Contains 12 issues of the newsletter from July/August 1994 to May/June 1996.

BN2. *Shepherds of Christ - Volume 2*: Contains issues 13-29 of the newsletter (September/October 1996 - Issue 5, 1999)

AAA026. *Daily Prayers*

*AAA046. *Holy Spirit Novena, Shepherds of Christ Prayers, and the Rosary Prayed by Fr. Edward Carter, S.J* - 6:20 Prayers as Fr. Carter prayed them. He prayed these daily. They are available as he prayed them. *(CD AVAILABLE)*

Fr. Edward J. Carter S.J.

BCA002. *Shepherds of Christ Associates Spirituality Handbook and Prayer Manual,* Read by Fr. Edward Carter, S.J.

BCA014. *Shepherds of Christ Associates Prayer Manual,* Read by Fr. Edward Carter.

BCA063. *The Spirituality of Fatima,* read by Fr. Carter.

Priestly Newsletter Tapes - Recorded by Fr. Carter

PNA032. *Shepherds of Christ Priestly Newsletter,* Issue 2, 1998

PNA033. *Shepherds of Christ Priestly Newsletter,* Issue 3, 1998

PNA034. *Shepherds of Christ Priestly Newsletter,* Issue 4, 1998

PNA052. *Shepherds of Christ Priestly Newsletter,* Issue 5, 1998

PNA053. *Shepherds of Christ Priestly Newsletter,* Issue 1, 1999

PNA054. *Shepherds of Christ Priestly Newsletter,* Issue 2, 1999

PNA055. *Shepherds of Christ Priestly Newsletter,* Issue 3, 1999

PNA064. *Shepherds of Christ Priestly Newsletter,* Issue 4, 1999

PNA065. *Shepherds of Christ Priestly Newsletter,* Issue 5, 1999

Prayer Cards and Booklets

The following Prayer Cards and Booklets have received the *Imprimatur*.
Las siguintes oraciones han recibido el *Imprimátur*
Les prières suivantes ont reçu l'*Imprimatur*
As orações abaixo receberam o *Imprimatur*

ENGLISH

BK001E. *Shepherds of Christ Associates Prayer Manual.*

BK002E. *Holy Spirit Novena.*

PR001E. Daily Prayers for Shepherds of Christ Associates

PR002E. *Rosary Aves* short rosary meditations on the Joyful, Sorrowful, and Glorious Mysteries.

PR003E. Consecration Prayer Cards for Children

PR004E. Consecration Prayer Cards for Young Adults

PR005E. Prayer Before the Holy Sacrifice of the Mass

PR006E. Prayer for Union with Jesus

PR007E. Prayer for Priests

PR008E. Prayer for Intimacy with the Lamb

PR009E. Consecration of an Unborn Child to the Hearts of Jesus and Mary

SPANISH (ESPAÑOL)

BK001S. *Manual de Oraciónes* (Prayer Manual)

G2

BK002S. *Novena al Espíritu Santo* (Holy Spirit Novena)
PR001S. Oraciónes Diarias (Daily Prayers for Associates)
PR003S. Oraciónes Diarias para Niños (Daily Prayers for Children)
PR004S. Oraciónes Diarias para Jóvenes (Daily Prayers for Young Adults)
PR005S. Oración para antes del Santo Sacrificio de la Misa (Prayer Before the Holy Sacrifice)
PR006S. Oración Para Union con Jesús (Prayer for Union with Jesus)
PR007S. Oración por los Sacerdotes (Prayer for Priests)
PR008S. Oración para Intimidad con el Cordero, el Esposo del Alma (Prayer for Intimacy)
PR009S. Consagración de Un Niño Aún no nacido a Jesús y María (Consecration of Unborn Child)

FRENCH (FRANÇAIS)

BK001F. *Livret de Prières* (Prayer Manual)
BK002F. *Neuvaine au Saint-Esprit* (Holy Spirit Novena)
PR001F. Prières Quotidiennes (Daily Prayers for Associates)
PR002F. *Méditations pour chaque Ave du Rosaire* (Rosary Aves)
PR003F. Consécrations pour les enfants (Consecrations for Children)
PR004F. Consécrations pour les jeunes (Consecrations for Young Adults)
PR005F. Prière à réciter avant la Messe (Prayer Before the Holy Sacrifice of the Mass)
PR006F. Prière pour demander l'union à Jésus (Prayer for Union with Jesus)
PR007F. Prière pour les prêtres (Prayer for Priests)
PR008F. Une Prière pour demander l'intimité avec l'Agneau (Prayer for Intimacy)
PR009F. Consécration à Jésus et Marie d'un enfant à naître (Consecration of Unborn Child)

PORTUGUESE (PORTUGUÊS)

BK001P. Manual de Orações (Prayer Manual)
BK002P. Novena do Espírito Santo (Holy Spirit Novena.)
PR001P. Orações Diárias (Daily Prayers)
PR002P. Meditando nas contas do Rosário (Rosary Aves)
PR003P. Oração Diárias para Crianças (Consecration Prayer Cards for Children)
PR004P. Oração Diárias para Crianças (Consecration Prayer Cards for Young Adults)
PR005P. Oração antes do Santo Sacrifício da Missa (Prayer Before the Holy Sacrifice)
PR006P. Oração para União com Jesus (Prayer for Union with Jesus)
PR007P. Oração pelos Sacerdotes (Prayer for Priests)
PR008P. Oração para conseguir intimadade com o cordeirom o esposo da Alma (Prayer for Intimacy with the Lamb)
PR009P. Consagração de um nascituro a Jesus e Maria (Consecration of an Unborn Child to the Hearts of Jesus and Mary)
PR010P. Diga Diariamente (Say Daily)
PR011P. Palavras de Entrega de uma alma Palavras de Consagração a Deus (Prayer of Surrender)
PR012P. Como rezar o Terço do Rosário (How to Pray the Rosary)

Books

B11. *Mass Book II and Other Aspects of the Spiritual Life*:
Selected writings about the Mass and the Spiritual
life. Journal entries from the same period as the
Newsletter Book II and selected writings of Father
Carter on the Mass, Grace, and other aspects of the
spiritual life.

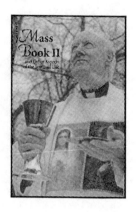

Writings by Edward Carter, S.J. and Rita Ring

Tapes and CDs (English)

PNA066. *Shepherds of Christ Priestly Newsletter,* Issue 1, 2000

PNA067. *Shepherds of Christ Priestly Newsletter,* Issue 2, 2000

PNA068. *Shepherds of Christ Priestly Newsletter,* Issue 3, 2000

PNA069. *Shepherds of Christ Priestly Newsletter,* Issue 4, 2000

PNA070. *Shepherds of Christ Priestly Newsletter,* Issue 1, 2001 *(CD AVAILABLE)*
> Disc 1 - Beginning of Newsletter
> Disk 2 - Grace - Powerful writing by Fr. Carter recorded
> by Fr. Mike Paraniuk

PNA071. *Shepherds of Christ Priestly Newsletter,* Issue 2, 2001 *(CD AVAILABLE)*

English Priestly Newsletters

PNE1-00. ISSUE 1, 2000

PNE2-00. ISSUE 2, 2000

PNE3-00. ISSUE 3, 2000

PNE4-00. ISSUE 4, 2000

PNE1-01. ISSUE 1, 2001

PNE2-01. ISSUE 2, 2001

Spanish Priestly Newsletters

PNS1-00. ISSUE 1, 2000

PNS2-00. ISSUE 2, 2000

PNS3-00. ISSUE 3, 2000

Order Form

In the space provided, write in the quantity of the desired item(s) to be shipped. Please print clearly your own name and address to assure shipping accuracy.

Books :

___ BN1 ($10.00)   ___ BN2 ($12.00)   ___ B7 ($10.00)
___ B8 ($10.00)   ___ B11 ($10.00)

Audio Tapes and CDs:

Quantity   Item Number   (T)ape or (CD)

___   _____   _____

___   _____   _____

___   _____   _____

___   _____   _____

Priestly Newsletters

___   _____

___   _____

___   _____

Prayer Cards and Booklets:

_____ _____ _____ _____ _____

_____ _____ _____ _____ _____

Name: _____

Address: _____

_____

_____

_____

(Please include city, state, zip code, country)

Phone: _____

SEND THIS FORM TO: **Shepherds of Christ Ministries**
P.O. Box 193
Morrow, OH 45152-0193   U.S.A.

This movement is a nonprofit organization that relies on your financial support to function. We appreciate any donations that you give and are very grateful for your prayer support. God bless you and thank you!

God talks to each of us inside our own hearts. There is an open pipeline between us and Him. The inner promptings felt in our hearts are the way God is speaking to us right now.

He does not need our senses to talk to us. We take in our earthly knowledge through our eyes and ears. We communicate with each other through our senses. But God does not need senses. He communicates directly to each of our hearts.

This book is a cookbook for an intimate relationship with Jesus. As soon as we open ourselves up to His words and the promptings of the Holy Spirit, we can then hear the wonderful way in which God wants to communicate with us.

There are many nerves and body parts about which we are totally unaware until something goes wrong. Only then do we become aware of their presence. Likewise, God is always ready to be our inner guide on our spiritual way. Like our outer body parts, we can ignore His presence until something goes wrong. The we know how real He is.

Jesus is so close to us. When we are baptized He is in our hearts! He is the very life of the soul. When we are receiving our answers from within, we are tapping into His pipeline.

This book will help you to know what God Himself wants for your life. A fire will arise within your heart that cannot be contained.